4

The Athenian Agora

NEW ASPECTS OF ANTIQUITY

General Editor: COLIN RENFREW

Consulting Editor for the Americas: JEREMY A. SABLOFF

JOHN M. CAMP

The Athenian Agora

Excavations in the Heart of Classical Athens

with 200 illustrations, 11 in color

THAMES AND HUDSON

*To Edith S. C. Camp and the
memory of Gregory Nott Camp*

Frontispiece: Cavalry on the surviving fragment of a victory monument found in the Agora in 1970, just behind the Royal Stoa.

© 1986 Thames and Hudson Ltd, London

First published in the United States in 1986 by
Thames and Hudson Inc., 500 Fifth Avenue,
New York, New York 10110

Library of Congress Catalog Card Number 85-51469

Printed in Spain by Artes Graficas Toledo S.A.
D.L.: TO-218-1986

Contents

General Editor's foreword   7

Preface   9

1   Introduction   14

2   Before the Agora   19

THE PREHISTORIC BACKGROUND 19 THE AGORA AREA IN THE
NEOLITHIC PERIOD 24 THE BRONZE AGE 25 THE DARK AGES AND
THE GEOMETRIC PERIOD 27

3   The Archaic Agora   35

ATHENS IN THE 6TH CENTURY 35 SOLON 38 THE ATHENIAN
TYRANTS: PEISISTRATOS AND HIS SONS 39 THE CONSTITUTIONAL
REFORMS OF KLEISTHENES 48 MARATHON AND OSTRACISM 57
THE PERSIAN SACK OF 480 BC 59

4   The Classical Agora   61

HISTORICAL BACKGROUND 61 KIMONIAN ATHENS 66
PERIKLEAN ATHENS AND THE REBUILDING OF SANCTUARIES 77
THE PELOPONNESIAN WAR AND ITS AFTERMATH 87
PUBLIC BUILDINGS OF THE ATHENIAN DEMOCRACY 90
PRIVATE INDUSTRY AND COMMERCE 135 PRIVATE HOUSES 148
RECOVERY AFTER 400 BC 150

5   Macedon and the Hellenistic period   153

MACEDONIAN RULE: DEMETRIOS POLIORCETES 162
THE 3RD CENTURY BC: CIVIL WARS 166 THE 2ND CENTURY BC:
RECOVERY 168

6   The Roman period   181

THE HERULIAN SACK OF ATHENS IN AD 267 197   THE 4TH CENTURY AD:
ALARIC AND THE VISIGOTHS 198   THE SLAVIC INVASION 212

Epilogue   215

Chronological table   218

Ancient passages cited or translated   220

Bibliography   221

List of illustrations   224

Index   227

General Editor's foreword

Athens is the original home of Western civilization. For it is back to Greece that we trace not only the origins of the modern world – the development of coinage, the market economy, the politics of democratic government – but our idea of just what it means to be human. So to Greece also we turn for the philosophy of Sokrates and of Plato, the origins of the theatre, of Classical sculpture and the arts.

If Athens was the heart of Greece (as she made herself by force as much as by eminence in achievement), the Agora was the effective focal centre of Athens. It was here that much of the political business of the great city was conducted, and here too that much of its commerce was transacted.

The excavations in the Agora of Athens have been one of the great triumphs of urban archaeology of recent years, bringing to life in a remarkable way many aspects of the world of Classical Athens, which had hitherto been glimpsed only in the often slight and scanty passing references preserved in the writings of the Classical authors. But whereas the great imperial forum at Rome had never been lost to view – since the ruins of its principal buildings were still standing throughout the Middle Ages – the Agora of Athens had disappeared completely, so that even its location was uncertain.

Since 1931 the American School of Classical Studies at Athens has undertaken the formidable task of excavating this public centre and principal market and meeting place of the ancient city. John Camp has been closely associated with this work for twenty years, since 1973 as Assistant Director, and here he gives an authoritative and first-hand account of what has been achieved. The Acropolis of Athens, with its temples, notably the Parthenon itself, has always been the shining symbol of the City of Athena, but it was at its feet in the Agora that the life of the city was at its most intense. Here, as Camp describes, were such important buildings as the Senate House (the Bouleuterion) and the Headquarters of the General Staff (the Strategeion), the Mint, the Bureau of Standards, as well as the lawcourts and many of the great monuments. The finds illustrate and document in a very graphic way the development of the great city from its earliest beginnings in the prehistoric period, through its heyday in the 5th century BC, its decline during the period of Macedonian rule, its revival under the Roman emperor Hadrian and its final demise under the onslaughts of Visigoths and Slavs.

Sometimes when one visits a great museum or a major excavation, there comes a moment of intense, almost personal contact with the past. For me, such a moment came twenty years ago, when I first visited the display in the Agora in the rebuilt Stoa of Attalos and looked at an exhibit of sherds of pottery, each with a name scratched upon it. I could make out, in the rather scrappy Greek letters, the names of some of the great leaders of Athens in the 5th century BC – Alkibiades, Themistokles the statesman, Perikles himself. These potsherds had been discarded on different occasions, after the political procedure of 'ostracism'. As Camp describes, the entire body of citizens of Athens would gather on an appointed day, when it was found that a public figure was becoming too powerful or too arrogant for the good of the state, and each had the right to scratch upon a sherd of pottery (an *ostrakon*) – the equivalent of a modern ballot paper – the name of a public figure whom he thought should be banished. In 417 BC Hyperbolos was ostracized and banished in this way, the rival leaders Nicias and Alkibiades narrowly escaping the same fate. And here, after 2500 years, are the very sherds, or some of them, with these great names upon them, just as they were scratched by a group of Athenian citizens in the Agora one fine day in 417 BC. The history of the Agora reflects, in a complex and fascinating way, the whole life of Athens during the years of her rise, her greatness and her decline.

There are just a few places and times when the records of written history and the materials unearthed by archaeology come together to offer a surprisingly full and graphic picture of a vanished era. The Agora of Athens in its Classical heyday is outstanding among them.

Colin Renfrew

Preface

At first glance, it may seem peculiar to find in a series entitled 'New Aspects of Antiquity' a site that has been under excavation for more than fifty years. But there are several good reasons why the results of the Agora excavations should be presented in this form. Much of the research on the site lies buried in scholarly journals readily available only to specialists, and yet the results are of sufficient importance and interest to merit a wider audience. Therefore, while I hope it will be of some use to colleagues and students, the material for this volume has been assembled and is presented specifically for the interested non-specialist. Furthermore, the last comprehensive study of the Agora as civic centre is now thirteen years old, whereas the excavations have continued up until recent times. Though all the monuments are discussed in this account, there is, accordingly, some emphasis on the new discoveries. In addition, research on the old buildings has gone forward, modifying some of the old views, and this is an appropriate time to offer an up-to-date survey of the most recent results of such scholarship. *The Agora of Athens* (1972) by Homer Thompson and R. E. Wycherley presented the monuments thematically, and the site guide *The Athenian Agora* (1976) describes the ruins topographically, as they lie on the site. The present work follows a chronological order, presenting the monuments in their historical context in an attempt to show how the civic centre of Athens developed over the centuries. As it is written from this point of view, for a wider audience, and presenting new material and theories, there is ample justification for telling again, in this series, the story of the Agora excavations.

The excavations have been a huge undertaking, involving decades, millions of dollars, and hundreds of people. The full bibliography of the site runs to forty books and four hundred articles, written by some 110 different people. Given this amount of scholarship it is hard to speak of an *opinio communis* on all aspects of the site; the evidence for a given building can often be interpreted in a variety of ways. In this account I am presenting my views, although I have tried to indicate areas where other positions have been taken, without subjecting the reader to overly detailed arguments. In such a large project the views of dozens of specialists have been called into play, and it is appropriate to acknowledge the contributions that many have made directly or indirectly to this volume. First, I would thank the two successive field directors with whom I have worked on the site for twenty years: Homer A. Thompson and T.

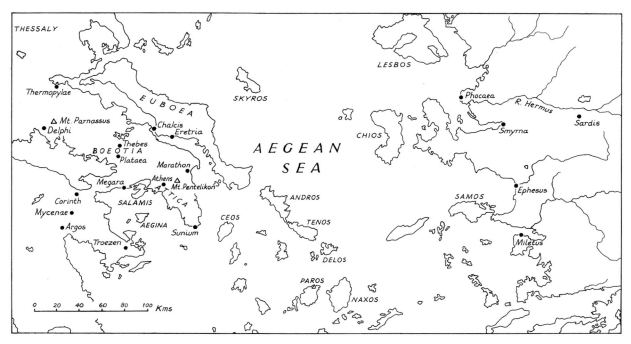

1 Athens and the southern Aegean.

L. Shear, Jr. Both men have been unstintingly generous to me with their time and knowledge, and the success of the excavations rests on their dedication and high standards of scholarship. My friend W. B. Dinsmoor, Jr., the architect (draughtsman) of the excavations, has also guided me and contributed in many ways, not least in the dozens of new drawings which so enliven and clarify the text. Other scholars have provided specific information on their special fields of interest; their knowledge has been incorporated from their published work, from consultations on the site, or from casual conversations around the Agora tea table. I am indebted to all the following: Alison Adams, Larry Angel, Judith Binder, Alan Boegehold, Fred Cooper, Sterling Dow, Alison Frantz, Virginia Grace, Evelyn Harrison, Caroline Houser, Leslie Ike, Sara Immerwahr, David Jordan, John Kroll, Mabel Lang, Margaret M. Miles, Stephen Miller, Susan Rotroff, Ione Shear, Evelyn Smithson, Ronald Stroud, Dorothy Thompson, John Travlos, Eugene Vanderpool, Alan Walker, and Malcolm Wallace. In addition to the above, I have relied heavily on the work of R. E. Wycherley, whose volume on the ancient testimonia of the Agora has been essential. Most of the references quoted here have been taken directly from his work. Other translations are generally those of the Loeb Classical Library.

2, 3 *The area of the Agora in 1931* (above) *before excavations had begun and in 1959* (below) *after the reconstruction of the Stoa of Attalos – both views from the west. In each photograph the Hephaisteion ('Theseion') is visible at the far left and the Acropolis far right.*

On the practical side, the secretary of the excavations Margot C. Camp has been invaluable in every way, not least in keeping the records in order and accessible, as well as in serving as liaison with the darkroom. I must thank also the Agora photographer Craig Mauzy for many of the photographs, particularly those in colour, and his assistant K. Moustaki for continuing to print photographs during difficult times. Credit for many of the record photographs should go also to previous staff photographers: Alison Frantz, James Heyle, Eugene Vanderpool, Jr., and R. K. Vincent, Jr. The balloon photographs are the work of J. Whittlesey, and Will and Ellie Myers. For much help with the typescript I am indebted to Patricia Felch-Niterou.

The excavations have gone forward only with the financial support of many individuals. The contributions of the late John D. Rockefeller, Jr., whose help was instrumental in so many ways, must be cited first. In addition, it is appropriate to record here and acknowledge the support at different times of the Ford Foundation, the Rockefeller Brothers Fund, the Andrew W. Mellon Foundation, the S. H. Kress Foundation, and the National Endowment for the Humanities. Most recently the work has been generously funded largely by the David and Lucile Packard Foundation.

The excavations that have brought the Athenian Agora to light are still continuing. Funded by these private contributions and foundation grants, they are the work of the American School of Classical Studies at Athens, which first undertook the task in 1931. Until that time the exact location of the Agora was unknown. As late as the 1890s W. Dörpfeld was able to propose that several buildings he excavated west of the Areopagos should be identified with known monuments of the Agora, and a plan of the ancient city published by W. Judeich in 1931 placed many of the civic buildings far to the south of their true location. Despite some work in the right area, nothing could be recognized as 3, 4 identifying the Agora. The 'Theseion' was always visible on the hill to the west, and the Stoa of Attalos to the east was cleared by the Greek Archaeological Society in 1859–62. Later work by the society and the German Archaeological Institute cleared the giants of the façade of the Odeion as well as parts of the Metroon and temple of Apollo Patroos. The certain identification of the Agora was possible only in 1934, when the American excavators uncovered the distinctive round form of the Tholos and the Altar of the Twelve Gods, followed in 1938 by the discovery of a boundary stone still in place. Thus, unlike most of the great sites of Classical antiquity, the Agora was recognized only in relatively recent times. While the modern city above has often resulted in a horrendous state of preservation below, the ancient buildings have at least been spared the attentions of enthusiastic but unscientific investigators of the sort which many long-known sites have suffered. Stored in the Stoa of Attalos are hundreds of notebooks and thousands of drawings which record in detail the process of excavation, from the demolition of the modern houses to the clearing of bedrock. Precise recording of the stratigraphy and the material found in each layer has allowed

4 Model of the Agora with the Acropolis behind as they would have appeared in about AD *150. The Hephaisteion can be seen at the lower right, and the Stoa of Attalos at the left.*

a detailed unravelling of the complicated architectural history of the Agora.

The main area, which comprises three sides of the square as well as residential areas to south and southwest, was cleared in the 1930s, with supplementary work carried out on a smaller scale after the Second World War. The Stoa of Attalos was reconstructed in the 1950s to serve as the museum; it houses the full collection of some 180,000 objects recovered, as well as the records and workrooms of the excavations. In 1969 work was extended northward beyond the modern (1891) railway line and eastward I
towards the Roman Agora. The excavations were further extended in 1980 in order to expose fully the buildings which ran along the northern side of the square. In all, close to four hundred modern houses have been removed since the beginning of the work, to be replaced by a fully landscaped (1950s) II, III
archaeological park. The following chapters will not be limited to the Agora proper but will cover the full area exposed in the excavations, in order to include those discoveries from the adjacent residential areas which further enliven our view of ancient Athens.

1 Introduction

If Classical archaeology can be defined as the study of ancient history and culture through physical remains, then the discovery of the agora of a Greek city should be one of the primary goals of the excavator, for there he will learn most about the history, social institutions, commerce, art, technology, and cults of a site. In its simplest form the agora was a large open square reserved for public functions. Here large numbers of citizens could congregate for a variety of activities: assemblies, elections, festivals, athletic contests, parades, markets, and the like. Inevitably the principal public buildings of the city came to be built around the space where the people so frequently met together, and the agora became the centre of the *polis*. As such, the Greek agora is the predecessor of the fora of imperial Rome and the great piazzas and squares of the capitals of Europe. Administrative, legislative, judicial, commercial, social, and religious activities all took place in and around the area and made the agora the heart of an ancient city.

The Agora of Athens is no exception, accommodating as it did all these aspects of ancient life. The five hundred legislators of the Athenian senate (Boule) met daily in the Bouleuterion along the west side of the square. Other buildings, such as the Royal Stoa and South Stoa I, sheltered those responsible for the day-to-day administration of the city, while the Metroon housed the central archives. Lawcourts at the northeast and southwest corners of the square remind us of the close connection between the Agora and the judiciary. Commercial activity took place every day in the area, in large market buildings, in small private shops, and in the streets and square itself. Long stoas – large open colonnades which protected the visitor from the elements in summer or winter while providing ample light and air – lined the square. Here the citizens congregated to discuss business, politics, or philosophy, and the stoas fulfilled an important social function in the life of the city. Furthermore, the Agora served also as a major religious centre; in addition to the Hephaisteion, the temple which crowned the hill to the west, the square was dotted with numerous altars and small sanctuaries, many dedicated to demigods known as heroes. These shrines, set right in the midst of daily life, often received far more regular and popular attention than did the great cult buildings erected by the state on the Acropolis. As Pindar wrote in the 5th century BC, 'Come hither to the dance and send us your glorious favour, Olympian gods, who in holy Athens approach the navel of the city, fragrant with incense, and the famous richly adorned Agora, to receive garlands of violets and songs gathered in the spring.'[1] Finally, the open square was used also for theatrical performances, religious processions, and athletic contests and displays.

Though in all ways a typical agora as the focal point of the public life of its city, the Agora of Athens has a much broader significance as well, and several aspects set it apart from the other great civic centres explored thus far in Greece. This is due largely to the pre-eminence of Athens herself. Most of the preserved history and literature of Greece is in fact Athenian in origin, and the Agora of Athens thus served as the background and setting for many of the significant events of Greek history. Of the figures associated with the greatest accomplishments of Classical Greek civilization, many were native Athenians, and others were drawn from all over the Mediterranean to contribute to a remarkable period of intellectual and artistic achievement. Statesmen and playwrights, historians and artists, philosophers and orators, such as Thucydides, Aeschylus, Sokrates, Pheidias, Demosthenes, and Praxiteles, flourished here in the 5th and 4th centuries BC, when Athens was the most powerful city-state in Greece; collectively they were responsible for sowing the seeds of Western civilization. All will have frequented the Agora. Here, too, the political institution of democracy first took root under the guidance of Solon, Kleisthenes, and Perikles. Even when her political, economic, and military significance waned, Athens remained an influential cultural and educational centre for centuries, drawing teachers and students of philosophy, logic, and rhetoric until the 6th century AD. Nowhere is this remarkable history more richly illustrated than in the Agora. Within the great open square monuments were set up to commemorate her triumphs, along its edges were the civic buildings for the administration of her democracy, while beyond its borders crowded the houses and workshops of those who made Athens the foremost city of Greece. The archaeological exploration of the Agora of Athens has thus led to a greater understanding not just of a single site but of all aspects of Classical Greek civilization.

Conversely, the extensive literary tradition we have for Athens and Athens alone sheds unique light on the Agora and its buildings. Structures so poorly preserved that their remains barely rise above the surface of the ground are brought to life by written sources describing a meeting or trial held there, a philosopher's performance, or the paintings which once decorated the walls. In all, close to seven hundred references in the ancient authors specifically mention the Agora and its monuments; for nowhere else in Greece do the sources so enliven our understanding of the remains. In this volume many of these descriptions will be presented in translation so that the reader may appreciate for him- or herself the richness of the written accounts and their value in helping the mind's eye reconstruct life in ancient times in the Athenian Agora. Specific passages are numbered consecutively and their sources listed at the back of the volume.

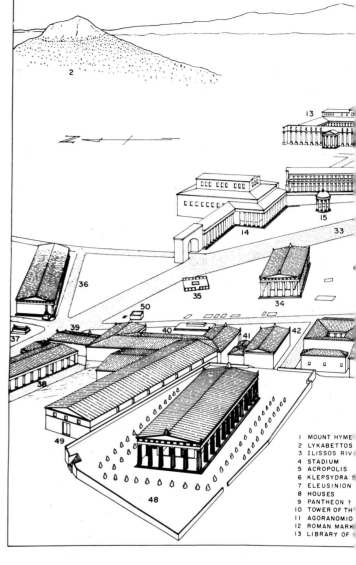

5 Reconstructed view of the Agora from the west in about AD 150, with the Acropolis at upper right.

1 MOUNT HYME
2 LYKABETTOS
3 ILISSOS RIV
4 STADIUM
5 ACROPOLIS
6 KLEPSYDRA S
7 ELEUSINION
8 HOUSES
9 PANTHEON ?
10 TOWER OF TH
11 AGORANOMIO
12 ROMAN MARK
13 LIBRARY OF

In this context it is worth noting our single most important source, Pausanias. Of all the written works preserved by chance from antiquity, one of the most curious and most useful for the archaeologist is Pausanias' *Description of Greece*. Written as a guide book between *c.* AD 150 and 175 and full of rambling digressions and maddening omissions, the book describes in detail the towns and monuments of Greece as they stood in the 2nd century AD. His account of the Agora, running to some twenty pages, is our principal aid in identifying many of the buildings, and we shall have occasion to refer to his work repeatedly.

ATHENIAN

AGORA

A.D. 150

14 ROMAN BASILICA	27 TRIANGULAR SHRINE	40 STOA OF ZEUS ELEUTHERIOS
15 MONOPTEROS	28 CIVIC OFFICES	41 TEMPLE OF ZEUS PHRATRIOS
16 STOA OF ATTALOS	29 SOUTHWEST TEMPLE	AND ATHENA PHRATRIA
17 LIBRARY OF PANTAINOS	30 EPONYMOUS HEROES	42 TEMPLE OF APOLLO PATROOS
18 SOUTHEAST STOA	31 ALTAR OF ZEUS AGORAIOS ?	43 METROON
19 SOUTHEAST TEMPLE	32 ODEION	44 BOULEUTERION
20 NYMPHAION	33 PANATHENAIC WAY	45 PROPYLON TO BOULEUTERION
21 SOUTHEAST FOUNTAIN HOUSE	34 TEMPLE OF ARES	46 THOLOS
22 MIDDLE STOA	35 ALTAR OF THE 12 GODS	47 STRATEGEION ?
23 EAST BUILDING	36 POIKILE STOA	48 HEPHAISTEION
24 SOUTH STOA II	37 ALTAR	49 ARSENAL ?
25 HELIAIA ?	38 ROMAN STOAS	50 CROSS-ROAD SANCTUARY
26 SOUTHWEST FOUNTAIN HOUSE	39 ROYAL STOA	

W. B. DINSMOOR, JR.
1980

Related to the literary sources are the inscriptions. The Athenian democracy required extensive and permanent record-keeping, and Athens more than any other city wrote her history in stone. In all some 7,500 inscriptions have been found in the Agora: laws, treaties, honorary decrees, dedications, building accounts, temple inventories, boundary stones, and statue bases. These, along with the literary record, enhance our understanding of buildings which the passing centuries have often left in a pitiable state of disrepair. The texts of many of these documents will be provided here since inscriptions, whether laws on marble stelai or simple shopping lists scratched on potsherds, put us in direct contact with the ancient Athenians, bridging in a unique fashion the centuries between us.

A typical inscription is very precise in its chronology, beginning with a heading that gives the day, month, and year in which the document was passed. The year is given as the name of the chief magistrate of the city, the eponymous archon. Plato tells us that every schoolboy knew in order the names of the previous two hundred archons, so anyone reading a decree which began, for instance, with the heading 'In the year in which Diotimos was archon' would know which year was meant. In modern reckoning Diotimos served in 354/3 BC; the date is given as part of two years since the Athenian year began near midsummer. Thus Diotimos' year ran from roughly July 354 BC until June 353.

When inscriptions and written sources are lacking, the chronology of the development of the Agora and its buildings is based on stylistic analysis. Almost all elements – pottery, sculpture, architecture, and coins – changed with the passage of time. Just as at a movie one can tell at a glance the era being represented by the clothing, style of architecture, form of automobiles, and the like, so the practised eye can date a scrap of pottery or a fold of marble drapery. By far the most useful and reliable indicator is pottery. Made in great abundance and virtually indestructible, fragmentary pottery is found in every level excavated, and the shape, glaze, and decoration allow one to date the pieces and hence the layer with a fair degree of precision. Indeed, the excavations of the Agora have produced such an abundance of datable material that the basic chronology of Greek and Roman pottery and lamps used by archaeologists all over the eastern Mediterranean follows the classification developed in Athens.

Thus for these various reasons the excavations of the Agora have contributed substantially not only to our knowledge of Athens but also to almost all aspects of Greece in antiquity, from Neolithic times until the medieval period. In looking for the origins of Western culture, art, and political thought, one is led inevitably back to Classical Athens, the heart and soul of which was the Agora.

2 Before the Agora

The prehistoric background

Human habitation in Greece is now well attested far back into the Palaeolithic period, a time when men were nomadic hunters and gatherers, moving with the seasons and following the herds of wild animals, especially red deer. The great innovations for early man developed far to the east, where domestication of animals and the cultivation of grains changed forever the course of human affairs. These developments permitted a settled life, leading to a growth in population and the beginnings of villages, towns, and cities; with settlements came specialized crafts and a stratified society, the principal elements of civilization. Domestication and cultivation reached Greece in the years around 6000 BC, starting what is referred to as the Neolithic period. Athens, and particularly the Acropolis, offered much that appealed to Neolithic man. The steep slopes of the citadel were dotted with caves and overhangs of the sort favoured in the years around 3000 BC, with the Klepsydra spring immediately below to provide water. Beyond lay a large fertile plain, crossed by two rivers, with ready access to the sea.

Shortly after 3000, the old Neolithic population of Greece was eclipsed by a more advanced civilization which flourished especially in the Cycladic islands. Among the great innovations of this period was the development of metallurgy, particularly the manufacture of bronze, made of copper and tin, which allowed for tools and weapons far more effective than their stone predecessors. Other advances probably to be dated to this early phase of the Bronze Age (3000–2000 BC) are the domesticated olive and vine, destined to become mainstays of Greek agriculture and economy. Seafaring, known in the Aegean since about 8000 BC, also improved with the introduction of the longship, propelled by oars. Indeed, this maritime civilization of islanders changed the pattern of settlement on the mainland of Greece, where most of the favoured sites were now headlands and peninsulas along the coast. This is true of Attica, where the area of the Acropolis was largely abandoned for coastal sites such as Aghios Kosmos, Askitario, and Marathon.

Around 2000 BC another group of people arrived in Greece, this time from the north and by land, apparently. They are the first Greeks as we know them in later times, and several new elements set them apart from their predecessors. They brought with them an improved technology for the manufacture of pottery, the first to be made on the potter's wheel. Other innovations included a new style of architecture, with apsidal or curved back walls rather than rectilinear plans, new burial customs involving individual rather than multiple burial, the horse, and the Greek language. To judge from the material remains, this Middle Bronze Age culture (2000–1600) was at first less advanced than its predecessor, with less evidence of foreign contacts and accumulated wealth.

Further changes took place around 1600 BC, perhaps involving more people arriving from the north but also attributable to new contacts with the advanced civilization of Minoan Crete. Burial customs shifted back to a preference for multiple graves, and the shaft graves of Mycenae have grave goods indicating unprecedented accumulated wealth and foreign contacts. This last phase of the Bronze Age is often referred to as the Mycenaean period, taking its name from the rich site where this remarkable civilization was first brought to light in the 1870s by Heinrich Schliemann. Large palaces surrounded by massive fortification walls were constructed at several places in the Peloponnese, in Boeotia, and in Athens. Palace walls were decorated with gaily coloured frescoes, and royal families were buried in large tombs with lavish grave goods. The complex administration of the palace economy required sophisticated records and led to the introduction of Linear B, a cumbersome way of writing Greek with symbols representing syllables. Extensive trade in raw materials brought foreign luxury imports flooding into Greece: amber from the Balkans, silver from Anatolia, ivory from Syria, lapis lazuli from Afghanistan, faience from Egypt, and ostrich eggs from Nubia.

Following these three phases of the Bronze Age, all of Greece entered a period aptly known as the Dark Ages (1100–750 BC), when the splendours of the palaces were replaced by the lowest form of material culture. Various reasons have been given to explain the fall of this prosperous civilization: foreign invasion by land from the north, invasion by sea, drought, earthquake, or internal revolution. In historical times most of the Peloponnese was occupied by Dorians from central Greece, and Classical tradition attributed the downfall of the Mycenaeans to their arrival. The result was the destruction of the palaces, usually by fire, and the total collapse of the social system which supported them. For three centuries there were few signs of material wealth or monumental art. The palaces and fortifications were replaced by hovels, the brightly decorated pottery by sombre dark-glazed pieces, and almost all trace of foreign contacts and trade disappeared. Even the ability to write was lost and forgotten as the Greek world reverted to a bare subsistence economy. To judge from the archaeological remains, life was bleak and hard. Little is known of the political developments in this period, but when Greece emerged from these silent centuries it was transformed. The basic political unit that replaced the old palaces was now the *polis*, or independent city-state, which occupied an area of land defined and limited by natural boundaries, usually mountains and the sea. Generally there was room for only one polis in each plain or valley; thus the Argolid, which supported several major centres in the Mycenaean period, was occupied in later times solely by Argos, which

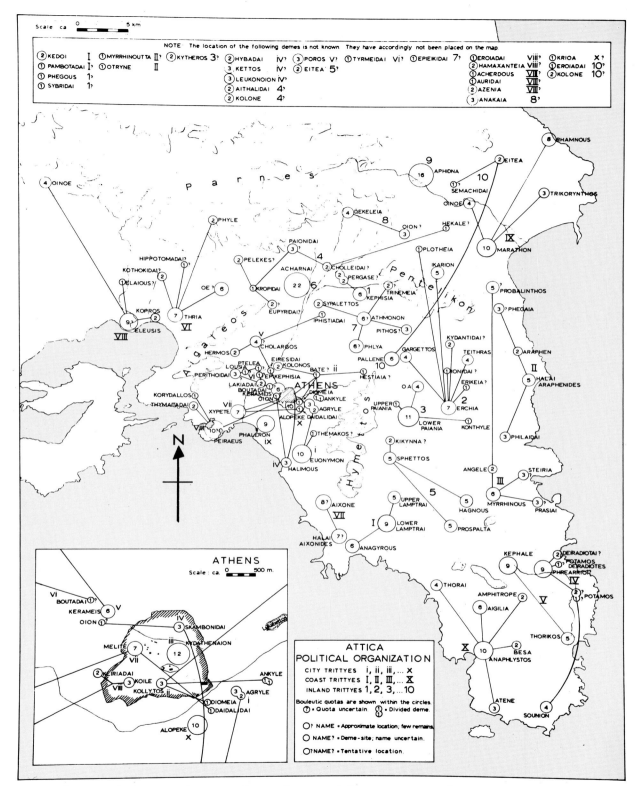

6 Map of Attica – the territory of ancient Athens – showing tribal representation in the Athenian senate. The figures within each circle indicate the number of representatives sent from that township or deme; lines between circles indicate tribal affiliations of the demes.

eliminated her rivals Asine, Nauplion, Tiryns, and Mycenae one by one. The polis of Athens occupied a large peninsula known as Attica, extending as far south as Cape Sounion, east to the plain of Marathon, and west as far as Megara, once Eleusis had been annexed. All who lived in this area were citizens of Athens, which grew up around the Acropolis. The territory of Attica included several natural resources which in later times contributed much to her economic prosperity and artistic leadership. Foremost among these were the rich deposits of silver and lead from Laureion on the southeast coast. Important for her architecture were two marble mountains, Penteli, which produced an excellent white marble, and Hymettos, which produced a very hard bluish marble. In addition, extensive clay beds north of the city helped her to become one of the foremost centres for the production of pottery. Fine natural harbours on the Peiraieus peninsula encouraged trade and the development of a powerful navy. Thus when Athens emerged as a polis she controlled a very large area of land encompassing resources which put her at a considerable advantage.

In part the eventual recovery from the Dark Ages in the 8th century was due to renewed foreign contacts, particularly with the Levant. The alphabet and writing were probably introduced from Phoenicia at this time, beginning the historical era. The evidence suggests regular trade both with the East and Italy, and this was soon followed by a wave of colonization from mainland Greece. From 750 to about 600 BC the poleis of central Greece and the islands established dozens of new settlements which spread Greek culture all over the Mediterranean. Athens, for reasons not fully understood, failed to take part in this first colonizing movement; Athenian interest in colonization began much later, around 600 BC. Athens was late also in another political development characteristic of the 7th century: tyranny. A common progression in the government of many city-states led from monarchy to aristocracy to a tyranny, the tyrant often seizing power with popular support. Athens eventually had a tyrant in Peisistratos, but he appeared only in the 6th century, a generation or more after the tyrants of many other poleis. This Athenian quiescence is reflected also in the history of Athenian trade and ceramics as preserved in the archaeological record. From 1000 to 300 BC Athenian pottery was widely exported and imitated. The only period when Athenian ceramics were not dominant was the first half of the 7th century, when Corinthian pottery was found all over the Mediterranean and even imported into Athens.

The written record is slight, and few historical facts are known for Athens in the 7th century. The constitution continued to develop. We learn, for instance, that in 683/2 BC the chief magistracy was changed from a tenure of ten years to one year. In 632 BC an Olympic victor, Kylon, tried to establish a tyranny with the help of his father-in-law, Theagenes of Megara, but failed through a lack of popular support. And in 621/0 BC a new constitution was drawn up by Drako,[2] whose laws on homicide remained in force at least until the end of the 5th century BC.

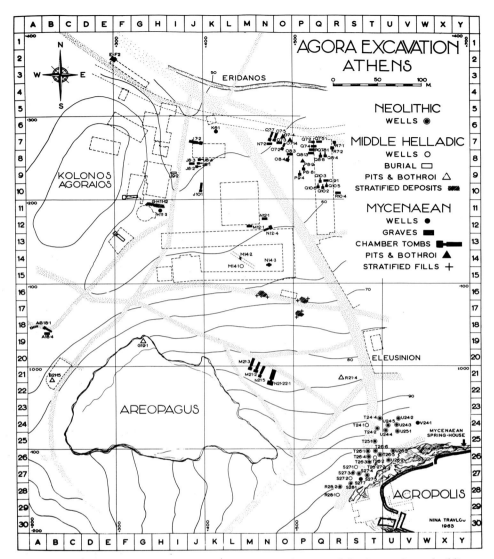

7 The distribution of prehistoric wells and graves in the area of the Agora. Later buildings are shown in dotted outline.

This sketchy picture of early Athens is reflected in the archaeological record as well. On the Acropolis, some of the Mycenaean fortifications survive, and but a scrap of the palace. For the later periods there are some roof tiles which perhaps date to the 7th century along with the battered remnants of two limestone column bases that presumably indicate the presence of an early temple. Later building has obscured or destroyed almost all other traces of the early Acropolis.

7   When one turns to the area of the Agora, however, the picture of early Athens comes into somewhat clearer focus. The area was used as a cemetery from the Bronze Age through the end of the 7th century, and many of the graves survived intact, set into bedrock. Similarly, the wells which reflect the positions of early houses were dug deep into bedrock and give some idea of the density of habitation when the area was being used as a residential district from about 1000 to 600 BC. In beginning to tell the history of the Agora, then, we start with the graves and wells which reflect the use of the area long before the establishment of the civic centre. In so doing we shed light not only on the Agora, but on all of Athens in prehistoric times.

The Agora area in the Neolithic period (6000–3000 BC)

On the slopes above the Agora, to the south, some twenty shallow wells were sunk into the soft grey-green bedrock to collect water from the Klepsydra spring. Pottery recovered from these wells, which includes a handsome red

8   burnished ware, dates to the end of the Neolithic period, close to 3000 BC. This represents our earliest evidence of habitation in Athens. No trace has been found of the settlement which must have used these wells, though presumably it was close by, perhaps in and around the shallow caves immediately above. Within the area of the Agora itself the Neolithic period is represented by a single well and single burial, that of an adult male in his early thirties. An examination of the skeleton reveals that our earliest known Athenian stood just under 1.65 m tall, may have suffered from arthritis, and lost one tooth during his lifetime.

8 Red-burnished Neolithic pots, c. 2800 BC, from a well south of the Agora.

9 A Middle Helladic cup, c. 1800 BC. Ceramics of this period were the first to be made on the potter's wheel in Greece.

The Bronze Age (3000–1100 BC)

During the Early Bronze Age, Athens, despite its defensible Acropolis and reliable water supply, was apparently too far (8 km) from the sea for the maritime civilization of the times, and except for scattered sherds there is little evidence of activity or habitation during the millennium from 3000 to 2000 BC.

In the Middle Bronze Age (2000–1600 BC) five more wells were sunk in the area of the Klepsydra spring, after a thousand years of apparent abandonment. In the area of the Agora proper, the lowest levels of the streets include characteristic 'Minyan ware' pottery of Middle Helladic type. Made of a smooth grey clay in shapes with sharply angled profiles, it was the first Greek pottery to be made on the fast wheel. Its distribution indicates general occupation or use of the area, though no architectural remains or graves survive.

9

The Late Bronze Age (1600–1100 BC) not only saw the flourishing of the great Mycenaean palaces but also was the era of most of Greek mythology. The *Iliad*, the *Odyssey*, the 'Voyage of the Argo', the 'Labours of Herakles', the trials of Oedipus, and many more stories were believed by the Classical Greeks to have occurred at this time, the Heroic Age. Whether these events occurred at all and, if so, when, are subjects still debated amongst scholars. Archaeology seems the best and perhaps only way to test the historical basis of the old myths.

On the subject of early Athens, Thucydides wrote that prior to King Theseus 'what is now the Acropolis was the city, together with the region at the foot of the Acropolis toward the south.'[3] Other literary sources also indicate that the Acropolis was the site of one of these early palaces,[4] and although later construction has eliminated all traces of the building itself, massive fortification walls, a secret fountain, and terrace walls all indicate its position on the citadel. Other excavations have revealed numerous scattered deposits of wells and bothroi (storage pits) found south of the Acropolis suggesting extensive habitation in that quarter of the city. Four wells in the area of the Agora point to only limited habitation north of the Acropolis. What in later times was to become the centre of the city was used in the

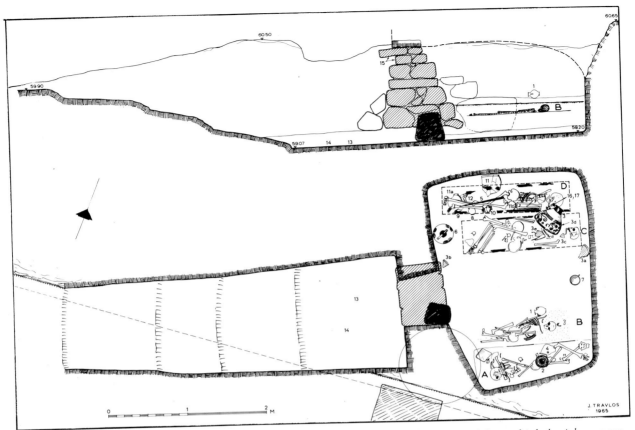

10 A typical Mycenaean chamber tomb from the Agora, used for multiple burials, c. 1400 −1375 BC.

7   Mycenaean era as a burial ground, and Thucydides' account of the extent of early Athens seems to be correct.

The Late Bronze Age cemetery under the Agora is large. Some forty-seven tombs have been found and doubtless many others were disturbed in later building activities; in at least one instance later grave gifts were added, apparently to appease the dead whose tomb was inadvertently dug into. Twelve of these tombs are cist or pit graves, each containing a single burial.

10, 12   Twenty-two are the common Mycenaean chamber tombs, hollowed out of bedrock and approached by an entrance passage (dromos), used for successive multiple burials. No example of the best-known and richest type of Mycenaean grave, the built beehive-shaped tholos tomb, has been found in Athens, though perhaps they simply failed to survive. Examples of such royal tombs have been found scattered throughout Attica, at Menidhi, Marathon,

6   and Thorikos, and their distribution perhaps lends credence to the accounts by both Thucydides[5] and Plutarch of the early city and its unification by Theseus,

a process known as synoecism. According to the story, Attica had previously been divided into numerous separate and independent towns and that Theseus 'after doing away with the town-halls and council chambers and magistracies in the scattered communities, and after building a common town-hall and council chamber in the present upper city, named the city Athens and instituted a Panathenaic festival.'[6]

Despite the lack of a royal tholos tomb, several of the chamber tombs contain rich grave goods indicating that Athens was a thriving Mycenaean state. One tomb in particular is of interest, apparently that of a rich Athenian lady. One says 'apparently' because the occupant and some of the finest grave goods were removed in antiquity. Left behind were some handsomely painted pots, a bronze lamp and mirror, gold ornaments, and a large ivory pyxis (cosmetics box) decorated with winged griffins attacking a deer. Other V individuals were not so wealthy but tried to keep up appearances; one grave contained eleven clay cups and goblets covered with tin foil, apparently in imitation of silver vessels of similar shapes. The same grave also had two bronze swords, and other finds of swords and spearheads remind us of a fondness for war and hunting in Mycenaean times. In general the Bronze Age cemetery of the Agora gives the impression of a rich, powerful Mycenaean centre, though with the exception of a few luxury goods and a single Canaanite jar there is little evidence of foreign contacts or trade beyond the Greek mainland.

Theseus was revered not only for his synoecism but also for his conquest of the bull-headed Minotaur of Crete. A gold signet ring from one of the chamber tombs, the only such ring from Athens, perhaps contains some reflection of VI this story. Dated about 1400–1375 BC, it shows the unique scene of a bull-headed human or a man in a bull mask leading two captive females by a rope or a chain. Thus those with the inclination to believe that a reflection of historical truth should be sought in Greek mythology will find some fertile ground in Mycenaean Athens in the orientation of the early city towards the south, the unification of Athens under Theseus, and perhaps even in the story of the Minotaur, with its suggestion of Cretan influence on the mainland.

The Dark Ages and the Geometric period (1100–700 BC)

In the century between 1200 and 1100 BC the Mycenaean world came to a violent end, presumably, as noted, at the hands of invading Dorians. The Classical Athenians had a tradition of being autochthonous, having always lived in Attica. They claimed that when the Dorians moved south they ignored Athens and turned aside into the Peloponnese; and in the historical period the Athenians were in fact of Ionian rather than Dorian Greek stock. Nonetheless, Mycenaean Athens apparently came to an end at about the same time the other palaces did. It may be that a single palace could not survive when all those in the Peloponnese and central Greece had fallen and when the economic system

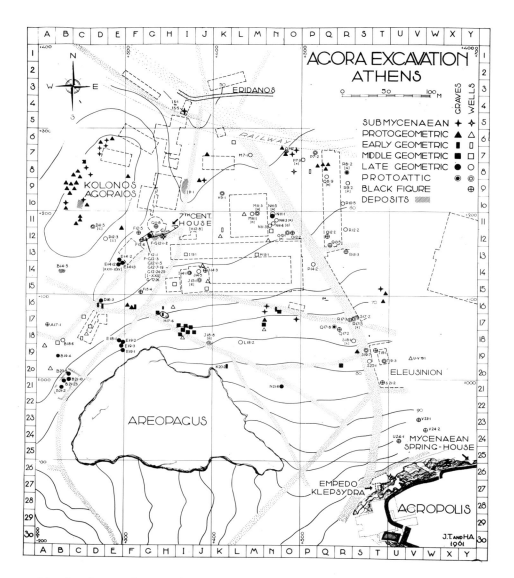

11 The distribution of Iron Age wells and graves in the area of the Agora. Later buildings are shown in dotted outline.

which maintained them dissolved. Whatever the means of dissolution, Athens too entered the Dark Ages, though now more often than not as a leader or innovator in the slow revival.

11   The area of the later Agora continued to be used at first as a burial ground, and in all some eighty graves of this period have been found. As one might expect, these have far fewer and poorer grave goods than the Mycenaean graves. In addition, distinct changes in burial customs can be noted. The

practice of cremation rather than inhumation was introduced and became *14, 17*
standard for adults for the period 1000–800 BC; after that both procedures
were employed about equally. In addition, the common Mycenaean use of a
multiple tomb was given up in favour of individual graves. Another innovation
characteristic of the Dark Ages that is reflected in the tombs is the presence of
iron, a harder and more durable material for tools and weapons; the transition
from Mycenaean to Dark Ages represents the change from the Bronze Age to
the Iron Age. The technology appears first in Greece at Athens, and was
apparently imported from the East. The pottery also changed with the
introduction of new shapes, and the floral motifs and curvilinear abstract
designs of Mycenaean times were replaced by rigid bands of Geometric design *12, 13*
on an otherwise black-glazed pot. The use of triangles, circles, swastikas, and
meanders, first confined to the necks, shoulders, and bellies of the pots,
expands gradually until by the 8th century the designs cover the whole surface *15, 18*
of the vase. This style of decoration of the pottery lends its name to the later
phases of this era, the Geometric period (900–700 BC).

12, 13 (Above) Mycenaean
pottery from the chamber
tomb illustrated in ill. 10,
c. 1400–1375 BC. (Below) A
selection of Protogeometric
pottery, c. 1000 BC, showing
the new Geometric designs
which replaced the abstract
curvilinear decoration of the
Mycenaean pieces.

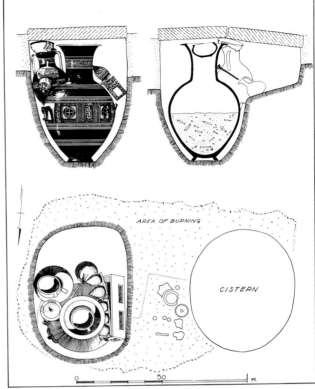

14, 15 *Geometric pottery from a cremation burial of a rich lady, c. 850 BC. The bones and ashes were found in the large pot, along with gold jewelry and a faience necklace. The other vessels were placed around it as grave offerings.*

16 *A ceramic jewelry box, or pyxis, from the Geometric cremation burial (ills. 14, 15), with representations of five granaries on the lid.*

Social organization

With the collapse of the Mycenaean palaces the entire political structure of Greece changed, and it is in the Dark Ages that we must seek the origins of the independent city-state, or polis, which became the basic political unit of the Classical Greek world. It is reasonable then to examine the archaeological record carefully for possible indications of the origins of Athenian social structure in this period. Among the graves there is an unusually rich cremation 14, 15 burial of an Athenian lady dating to about 850 BC. Her ashes were buried in a large amphora with more than fifty pots placed around it. Luxury items found with her included a faience and glass bead necklace, ivory seals, several gold rings, and a set of spectacularly ornate gold earrings with representations of pomegranates, with intricate filigree and granulation. Yet the most interesting object of all was apparently made for the burial. It is an elongated chest of baked clay, presumably for cosmetics, covered with Geometric designs. On its lid are set five beehive-shaped objects, with small openings near their tops, which have been plausibly identified as granaries. It is tempting to read some symbolic significance into this enigmatic object, particularly since the highest property classification of 6th-century Athens in the time of Solon was the pentekosiomedimnoi, those whose land produced at least 500 medimnoi (*c.* 730 bushels) of grain a year. According to Aristotle, Solon 'arranged the constitution the following way: he divided the people by assessing into four classes, as they had been divided before: 500-medimnos men, horsemen, teamsters, and labourers'.[7] Aristotle refers to the property classification as being earlier than Solon, and elsewhere he says that as early as the time of Drako (*c.* 621 BC) highest offices were held in accordance with birth and wealth.[8] Perhaps we are to suppose that such a property classification in fact goes back to the 9th century BC and that the five model granaries are meant to indicate that this aristocratic Athenian lady was a member of the pentekosiomedimnoi.

In a similar vein we turn now to a second cremation burial, also of the 9th century BC, though somewhat earlier (*c.* 900 BC) and this time of a warrior. Wrapped around the burial urn in such a way as to preclude anyone else ever

VI

16

17

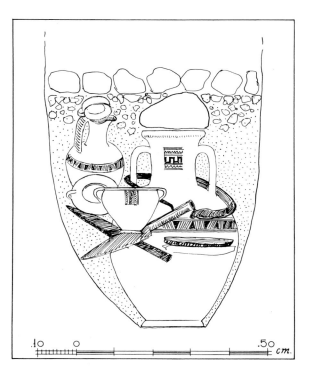

17 (left) *A cremation burial of the Geometric period, c. 900 BC: a warrior buried with his iron sword and spear-heads, and the bridle-bits of his horse.*

18 (above) *A Geometric pottery jewelry box of the 8th century BC, with three horses forming the handle on the lid.*

using it was the dead man's sword. Also found were two spearheads, two knives, and an axe. Most interesting, however, are two iron bridle bits. Do these corroded scraps of metal indicate that we have here the earliest-known member of the cavalry, the hippeis, who, as we have seen, are of the second rank in Solon's property classification in the 6th century? This possibility *18* would seem to be supported by several 9th- and 8th-century lidded pyxides found in other Agora graves, all of which have small terracotta figures of horses serving as handles.

Art and ceramics
By the late 8th century Athens and the other poleis were enjoying the fruits of a great renaissance that lifted Greece out of the Dark Ages. With the reintroduction of the alphabet, probably from Phoenicia, the great oral epics such as the *Iliad* and the *Odyssey* were first written down. Not long thereafter, apparently, Greek artists began to use these myths as sources of inspiration. As early as about 775, representations of human figures began to appear on Geometric vases, usually as mourners in a funerary scene that decorated the burial urn. At some point the Athenian artist broke away from these formulaic scenes of ritual and began to use the figures in a narrative way, to tell a story. One of the earliest certain instances of Greek narrative art is to be found on an *19* 8th-century pitcher recovered from another Agora grave. Here we see a battle scene of a sort not uncommon in this period. What tells us that here we have the story of a specific event, however, are the two figures fighting behind a single great shield. These surely are the Molione, the Siamese twins of the *Iliad* who of necessity had to fight together.⁹ With this piece we stand at the beginning of the long tradition of Greek painted pottery illustrating myth. Shortly thereafter pictorial art came to dominate Athenian vase painting, and the Geometric style lost favour rapidly. Much of the impetus and inspiration of the new style, called Orientalizing, came from the Near East, transmitted through the great trading city of Corinth. Pottery from the Agora in the 7th

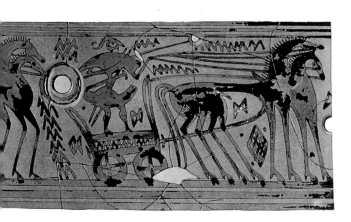

19 Roll-out watercolour of a Geometric wine pitcher of the 8th century BC. The scene depicts the Siamese twins (Molione) of the 'Iliad', fighting from behind a single square shield (centre). This is one of the earliest certain representations of a specific myth in Greek art.

20 Amphora of the 7th century BC, showing use of curvilinear designs and a representation of a bull's head at a large scale. Contrast this with the Geometric designs of the 9th and 8th centuries BC (ills. 14, 18).

century is wildly exuberant and experimental with a wide range of new styles, techniques, and scale being tried in reaction to the rigid canons of Geometric decoration.

20

Habitation and population

To the Dark Ages should be dated the beginnings of regular and extensive habitation in what was later to become the Agora. The evidence is indirect but clear that starting in the years around 1000 BC and continuing down to 600 BC the area was used for houses as well as burials. Later quarrying and levelling of the Agora have removed all trace of actual structures from these early periods, but the shafts of wells sunk into bedrock remain. The assumption is that each well stood in the courtyard of a private house and that they can be used to indicate the probable location and density of prehistoric houses now lost. Together with the burials they show a pattern of increasing population in this part of Athens from 1000 to 700 BC. Surprisingly, there is a sharp break at the end of the 8th century. All sixteen wells in the Agora dating from the last third of the century were filled up around 700 BC. The simultaneous abandonment of almost all the wells in use at one time would seem to indicate a period of

11

severe, prolonged drought in Athens. This notion is further borne out by the pattern of worship at the sanctuary of Zeus Ombrios (Showery), a rain god, on nearby Mount Hymettos. That this drought may have been accompanied by epidemic disease which affected the population is perhaps indicated by both the wells and graves. There are twenty-eight graves from the period 750–700 BC in the Agora and only four from 700–650. Similar figures prevail at other Attic cemeteries such as the Kerameikos, Eleusis, and Thorikos, and the ratio of late-8th-century graves to early-7th-century graves is somewhere between five and four to one. This suggests an unusually high mortality rate in the second half of the 8th century with a drop in population apparent in the 7th. The Agora wells would seem to corroborate this conclusion in that there were twenty-seven wells in use in the 8th century and fourteen in the 7th. If this theory of drought and epidemic is correct, it can perhaps be used to explain Athens' failure to colonize at this time, when numerous city-states in central Greece and the islands were founding new settlements all over the Mediterranean. Athens, suffering from epidemic, experienced a drop in population matching that of her neighbours who, their food supply affected by the drought, were sending out colonies in order to reduce their populations. Whatever the cause, Athens was uncharacteristically quiescent in the 7th century BC, recovering only in the 6th century when the Agora first developed as the centre of one of the foremost poleis of Greece.

3 The Archaic Agora

Athens in the 6th century

Following the decline in the 7th century, Athens recovered quickly. She became a major polis in the 6th century, a period of relative equality among the city-states, a time when no one of them – with the possible exception of Sparta – could claim to be appreciably more powerful or wealthy than the others. Athens, Corinth, Thebes, Argos, Corfu, Naxos, Samos, Paros, and many others flourished on just about an equal footing, each developing local styles of sculpture, architecture, and pottery and even using different letter forms in their alphabets. Indeed, this regional diversity is one of the most appealing aspects of the Archaic period.

Internally there was considerable strife in Athens as the aristocrats were gradually made to surrender much of their control. Early in the 6th century Solon was appointed archon to arbitrate the dispute, and he drew up a series of reforms that redistributed power and, by his own admission, satisfied no one. In the second quarter of the century the tyrant Peisistratos seized power, ruling until his death in 527 BC, when he was succeeded by his sons, Hippias and Hipparchos. Following the murder of Hipparchos in 514 and the expulsion of Hippias in 510, constitutional reforms were instituted by Kleisthenes in 508/7 that further eroded the power of the old aristocracy and set Athens on a course towards democratic rule. The new order was tested in 506 when Athens' traditional enemies, Boeotia and Chalkis, attacked simultaneously and were both defeated in a single day. Still greater victories enhanced Athens' reputation when, having supported the Ionian Greeks in their ill-fated revolt against Persia, she herself came under attack by the Persians. A force sent by Darius landed at the plain of Marathon in 490 BC and was met there and bested by the Athenians, helped by a small contingent from Plataia. This victory against the great Eastern empire resulted in a tremendous rise in her standing among the cities of Greece. Followed by further successes in 480/79 BC, particularly at the sea battle of Salamis, Athenian action in the Persian wars catapulted her into the front rank of city-states. By the early 5th century Athens and Sparta had laid claim to the hegemony of Greece, and most other poleis found themselves firmly in the sphere of influence of one or the other as the Archaic period came to an end and the Classical period opened.

The rapid rise of Athens to this position of prominence is fully reflected in the archaeological record. In contrast to the paucity of monuments in the 7th century, the Acropolis in the 6th century was transformed into a flourishing sanctuary richly adorned with temples and statuary. The old citadel, heavily fortified in earlier times, became the cult centre of Athena Polias, patron deity of the city, and the approach was now made easy by the addition of a monumental ramp. Two large limestone temples with marble trim were built, one dating to before the middle of the 6th century and the other sometime in the last quarter. Whether either is specifically a Peisistratid building is unclear, though tyrants generally and the Peisistratids specifically were often associated with temples and similar religious projects in the lower city. There is no specific ancient reference to Peisistratid work on the citadel, though one source records that in 566 BC Peisistratos reorganized the Panathenaia, the great festival in honour of Athena, which included a huge procession up to the Acropolis and the sacrifice there of dozens of animals. It is easy to believe that the ramp at least and perhaps some of the buildings were built during this reorganization. In addition to the two large temples, there was also a smaller shrine of Athena Nike, goddess of victory, which stood just outside the entrance to the Acropolis. On top of the citadel there were five or six small Doric buildings, decorated with lively scenes in sculpted relief, which served as treasuries, designed to hold both sacred and secular funds.

In addition to temples and treasuries, the 6th-century Acropolis was covered with free-standing dedications to Athena, usually statues of white island marble. Most common are the korai, heavily draped standing maidens, one hand holding a skirt, the other outstretched with an offering. Less common are horsemen, hounds, and young men (kouroi). In all, several dozen of these masterpieces have been recovered. Another common class of dedication were the perirrhanteria, broad open marble basins looking much like modern bird-baths, which were used for holy water. Specific historical events were commemorated as well. The victory over the Boeotians and Chalcidians in 506 BC occasioned the dedication of a bronze chariot, along with the fetters used to chain the prisoners. It also seems likely that a third temple was started after 490 to celebrate the great victory at Marathon. This new temple, a predecessor to the Parthenon and standing on the same spot, was to be of marble rather than limestone and much larger than the two 6th century temples. It was only partially finished when the Persians returned under Xerxes in 480 BC and deliberately burned the buildings on the Acropolis. Stone temples could and did burn, and there are several instances when they are known to have been set afire by accident. They were equipped with wooden furniture along with hangings and tapestries, the walls often carried paintings, and they were illuminated with oil lamps. Once this material was set ablaze, the woodwork of the ceiling and roof might catch fire. Huge amounts of wood were used in the roofing of temples, and if one or two beams burnt sufficiently the roof would fall in, leaving a roaring bonfire in the middle of the building, the heat of which would cause the stone walls to fracture and break apart. In the case of the unfinished older Parthenon there would have been sufficient scaffolding to

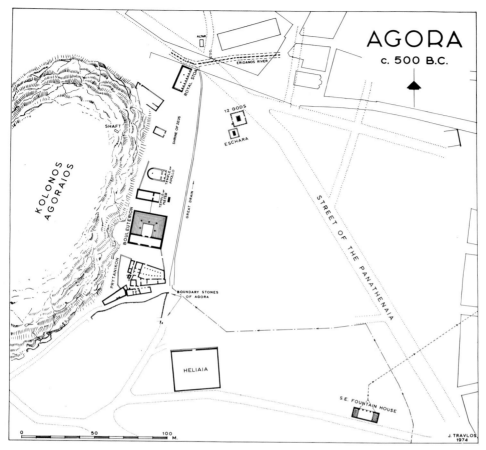

21 The Agora in the Archaic period, c. 500 BC.

assure a good fire. This sudden violent destruction of the Acropolis by the Persians actually did posterity a good turn. When the Athenians returned they were confronted with temples and treasuries in ruins and dozens of statues knocked off their bases and broken. Many of the pieces, all of which were sacred to Athena, were carefully gathered up and buried in pits all over the Acropolis where they remained until their discovery in the 19th century, in a condition so fresh that much of the original paint survives. When a site is abandoned much of the material is taken by those leaving. If a site stands too long the sculpture and architecture suffers from exposure, vandalism, and a host of other woes. Ironically, violent destruction often serves best to preserve archaeological material, and the Persian sack of Athens in 480 is a good example, comparable to the sudden ends of Pompeii and Thera as a result of volcanic activity.

Like the Acropolis, the Agora also reflects the history and development of 6th century Athens. The laying out of the great public square began around 21

600 BC, if we may judge from the cumulative evidence of wells and graves. Along the west side, where later the principal civic buildings were located, exiguous traces of the earliest public buildings date back to close to the time of Solon. Peisistratid interest in the area is most clearly indicated by the establishment of the Altar of the Twelve Gods within the square in 522/1 BC, the construction of an aqueduct and fountainhouse, and perhaps even a mansion where the ruling family lived and held court. The overthrow of the tyrants was commemorated with statues of Hipparchos' assassins, Harmodios and Aristogeiton. And at the end of the century the Agora became even more of a focal point of civic activity following the constitutional reforms of Kleisthenes. The square was formally delimited by a series of marble boundary stones, and several new buildings were needed to accommodate the new government, among them the Bouleuterion, Royal Stoa, and a lawcourt. In addition, small shrines to Zeus, Apollo, and the Mother of the Gods were built along the west side. As is the case with the Acropolis, the Persian attack of 480 left all these buildings in ruins, a clear end to the period which saw the Agora transformed from cemetery and residential district to the civic centre of the foremost city of Greece. With this as background, we turn now to a more detailed account of the monuments and their place in the history of Archaic Athens.

Solon

Confronted by intense factional strife between rich and poor early in the 6th century, the Athenians chose Solon as archon to serve as mediator and law-giver. Plutarch and Aristotle describe in some detail his constitution and the new laws handed down, following which Solon went into his voluntary exile in order not to be pressured into amending his legislation. The law code itself, along with some 7th-century laws on homicide attributed to Drako, was inscribed and displayed on objects known as *axones* and *kurbeis*. The appearance and material of these items has been a subject of considerable debate, though it seems clear that some of them at least were triangular in shape and that axones were of wood and kurbeis of bronze or stone. These early laws originally stood on the Acropolis and were later moved to the Agora according to Pollux: 'The kyrbeis and axones were of old deposited on the Acropolis; but afterwards, so that all might have access to them, they were transferred to the Prytaneion and the Agora.'[10] Harpokration recorded that some of the laws were set up in the Bouleuterion,[11] and Aristotle located them in the Royal Stoa.[12] This first concrete evidence concerning the Athenian constitution coincides with the beginnings of the laying-out of the Agora as the civic centre. The area chosen was the gently sloping land northwest of the Acropolis, bounded on the south by the Areopagos hill, on the north by the Eridanos river, and along the west by the low hill that came to be known as Kolonos Agoraios (Market Hill). Until the 6th century, as we have seen, this area had been given over to cemeteries and private houses, criss-crossed by

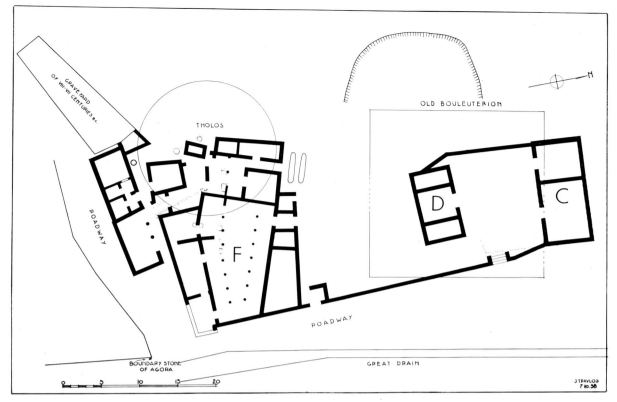

22 *The earliest civic buildings along the west side of the Agora, 6th century BC. Later buildings are shown in outline (cf. ill. 27).*

several age-old thoroughfares. Its conversion to the civic centre was apparently a gradual process, not one carried out as a single act. The earliest example of what seems to be a public building dates to the early 6th century, along the west side at the foot of Kolonos Agoraios, under the Bouleuterion of Classical times. Building C is rectangular in plan, measuring 6 by 14 m and divided into two rooms. It faced south, overlooking an open courtyard which was supported by a terrace wall on the east side and enlarged on the west by cutting back into the bedrock. Shortly after the middle of the 6th century a second rectangular building (D) was constructed to the south. The overall arrangement does not look domestic, and as this area was occupied in later times by buildings of known public function it seems reasonable to suppose that these too represent civic buildings, the earliest in the Agora. Though one might propose that the old Solonian council of 400 may have been accommodated hereabouts, we cannot be specific about the use of the buildings, given their exiguous state of preservation.

The Athenian tyrants: Peisistratos and his sons

Later in the 6th century, despite the Solonian reforms, factional strife erupted again and eventually led to the rise of Peisistratos as tyrant of the city. Like many other Greek tyrants, Peisistratos seized power unconstitutionally, but there is evidence that his reign was not unduly oppressive. Aristotle specifically states that for the most part he governed according to the existing constitution, though with his own men in the principal offices and magistracies.[13] He first seized power in the 560s and was ousted twice, finally establishing himself only in 545. Upon his death in 527 BC he was succeeded by his sons Hippias and Hipparchos. Tyrants at this time were often patrons of the arts, and they were usually responsible for great building programmes. Here that spirit of rivalry which is a characteristic feature of Greek society comes into play, as tyrants of different poleis competed with one another in huge construction projects, particularly temples and water supply systems. For the first time since the days of the Mycenaean palaces, Athens had the two elements necessary for monumental art: a strong centralized authority and accumulated wealth. Several large projects were started under the Peisistratids: work was done on the Acropolis, the temple of Dionysos was built just below, and the colossal temple of Olympian Zeus – the largest on the Greek mainland – was laid out. During their reign the Agora took on a more monumental form. To judge from the filling of wells and the demolition of houses, the public area of the Agora expanded gradually to the east and south during the second and third quarters of the 6th century. In addition, new buildings and monuments were erected, several of which can be directly associated with the Peisistratids, and others which from the archaeological evidence seem to have been built during their tenure.

The Altar of the Twelve Gods

23, 24   Within the open area of the Agora the corner of an enclosure was found in 1934, the rest of it lying underneath the Athens–Peiraieus railway, which was extended in 1891 and runs through the northern part of the Agora. Supplementary excavations were carried out in the railway bed in 1946, and it was determined that the enclosure in its final form was almost square in plan. The preserved foundation of squared blocks supports a low sill of limestone blocks. On its upper surface this still carries the marks of the stone fence it once supported, with a deep square cutting for a fence post at the corner and dowel holes *c*. 1.2 m apart for attaching other fence posts. We have here an enclosure set off by a low parapet wall. What stood within is now lost but known, thanks to the fortuitous preservation of an inscribed statue base still in place along the west side. The base once carried a bronze statue, as is clear from the cuttings for tenons on its top. The front face is lightly stippled except for a band cut smooth across the upper edge along which runs the inscription 'Leagros the son of Glaukon dedicated this to the 12 Gods', carved sometime between 490 and 470 BC. From this it seems clear that the adjacent enclosure wall must have surrounded the Altar of the Twelve Gods, perhaps but not certainly the twelve Olympians. This altar was famous in antiquity as a place of asylum and refuge. In 519 BC, for instance, ambassadors from the city of Plataia came as

23, 24 The Altar of the Twelve Gods: a reconstruction drawing and a view of the extant southwest corner, with the base for the statue dedicated by Leagros in the foreground. The Altar was the point from which all distances from Athens were measured.

suppliants to the altar to ask for Athenian help against Thebes.[14] The association of this altar with the Peisistratids is attested by Thucydides:

> The city itself enjoyed the laws before established, except that the tyrants took precaution that one of their own family should always be in office. Amongst others of them who held the annual archonship of Athens was Peisistratos, a son of the tyrant Hippias. He was named after his grandfather and when he was archon dedicated the altar of the twelve gods in the Agora and that of Apollo in the Pythian precinct. The people of Athens afterwards, in extending the length of the altar in the Agora, effaced the inscription.[15]

A fragmentary list of 6th century archons found in the excavations indicates that the younger Peisistratos was archon in 522/1 BC.[16] Here, then, is direct evidence of Peisistratid interest in the development of the Agora as the heart of Athens, particularly as we learn from two sources that distances from the city were measured from this altar. Herodotos wrote: 'The road up from the sea to Heliopolis is similar in length to the road from the altar of the twelve gods at Athens to the temple of Olympian Zeus at Pisa';[17] and on a rare example of a Greek milestone, dated *c.* 400 BC, we read: 'The city set me up, a truthful monument to show all mortals the measuring of their journeying; the distance to the altar of the twelve gods from the harbour is forty-five stades.'[18] The altar, placed near the middle of the Agora square, was clearly to be thought of as the actual centre of Athens.

The Southeast Fountainhouse

25 A second building with some claim to a Peisistratid origin is to be found at the southeast corner of the square. Here private houses remained in use into the third quarter of the 6th century, at which time they were demolished to make way for a rectangular building 6.8 by 18.2 m, consisting of a large central chamber with a smaller one at either end. Only a few blocks of hard Kara limestone set in a polygonal style remain in place above foundation levels. Pottery from beneath the floor as well as building material and techniques (polygonal masonry and the use of z-clamps) suggest that the structure should be dated to the years around 530–20 BC. Its identification as a fountainhouse is certain thanks to the discovery of the supply line which brought water to the building as well as overflow pipes leading out from the small chambers at
26 either end of the building. The pipes are carefully made of baked clay with heavy collared joints; removable lids aided installation. The chambers at either end would have been supplied by means of spouts set into the wall. Their foundations suggest that the western basin served as a tank or reservoir from which water could be drawn over a parapet, while the eastern chamber could be entered and a water jar filled by holding it directly under a spout.

The discovery of an Archaic fountainhouse in the Agora leads one to think immediately of the nine-spouted fountain, the Enneakrounos, built by the Peisistratids. Many tyrants took an active interest in the water supply of their

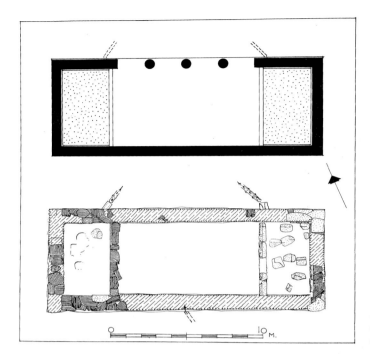

25 (left) *The Southeast Fountainhouse, actual state after excavation (below) and restored plan, c. 530–520 BC.*

26 (above) *Part of the terracotta pipeline which carried away overflow from the basins of the Southeast Fountainhouse, c. 530–520 BC.*

cities, and aqueducts and fountainhouses built by tyrants are known from Megara, Corinth, and Samos. The Enneakrounos was among the most famous of all Athenian buildings if we may judge from the unusually large number of references to it in the ancient literature. There is, however, a problem concerning the location of the fountainhouse. Pausanias, writing in the 2nd century AD, apparently saw this building as he made his way up the Panathenaic Way as it passed through the Agora.[19] Thucydides, however, places the Enneakrounos south of the Acropolis,[20] and other sources associate it with the Kallirrhoe springs in the bed of the Ilissos river, southeast of the citadel. On balance, it seems inconceivable that Thucydides, who lived in Athens in the 5th century BC, did not know the location of the Enneakrounos, whereas Pausanias, visiting some 700 years after the Peisistratids, may have been shown the last surviving Archaic fountainhouse of Athens, to which he or his guide gave the name Enneakrounos. Though not the famous fountain, the Southeast Fountainhouse is almost certainly a Peisistratid building, and its presence indicates the growing significance of the Agora square and the need of a ready supply of water for the many people congregating there.

Such fountains must have been a great source of pleasure; much easier to fill a jar with clean, fresh running water from a spout, rather than laboriously draw it 10 m out of a well constantly threatened by contamination or a drop in the water table. The local fountainhouse must have served also as something of a social centre for the women when they went to draw water, one of the few occasions when they could hope to get out of the house, for otherwise Athenian society and custom bound them firmly to the home. Scenes of young women collecting water at a fountain became very popular on black-figure hydrias (water jars) at just this period when the Peisistratids were building fountainhouses. In contrast to these stately ladies waiting their turn, Aristophanes describes a lively, bustling scene at a fountainhouse in the 5th century BC: 'Trouble it was before I could fill my hydria, in the dusk of the morning, at the fountain on the slopes; with the clatter of pitchers, the noise and press of the crowds, pushing with slaves, snatching it filled . . . '[21]

Building F

21, 27   Other buildings in the Agora do not have the same direct association with the tyrants but seem to date to their reign and thus may well have been built by them. One such structure, at the south end of the west side, is known simply as Building F, lacking as it does a formal identification. It is a large irregular structure, roughly trapezoidal in plan, measuring 27 m east–west by as much as 18.5 m north–south. There are many rooms, grouped around two sides of a colonnaded courtyard. On the west side two cooking pits were found. The general appearance of the building is that of a private house, although the scale is much larger than usual and its location alongside the Agora is noteworthy. The building was erected *c.* 550–525 BC, if we may judge from the pottery, and it was destroyed by the Persians in 480. Though originally the Peisistratids

27 Plan of Building F and the Old Bouleuterion, or Senate House, along the west side of the Agora, c. 500 BC.

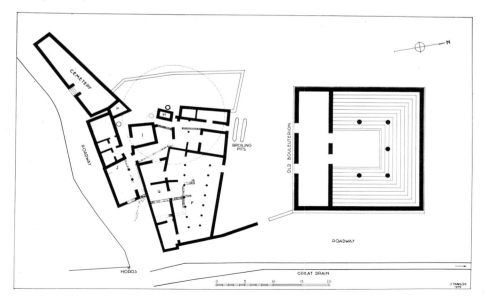

28 The Panathenaic Way just east of the Altar of the Twelve Gods, view from the north. In the foreground are postholes to support the wooden seats (ikria) set up for spectators at the games and festivals. In the background are five stone sockets which supported a starting device on the racecourse.

occupied the Acropolis, there is no clear evidence of where they lived; if they had some sort of palace, as we know the tyrants of other cities did, then Building F should be regarded as a likely candidate on the basis of its date, plan, scale, and location.

The Panathenaic Way

An important element in the topography of the Agora is the great street which passed diagonally through the square, as it ran from the Dipylon gate to the Acropolis. This street is referred to in the ancient sources as both the dromos and the Street of the Panathenaia. Though one of the main thoroughfares of the city, it is surprisingly modest in its construction; throughout its long history, its surface for most of its length was simply packed gravel which was renewed dozens of times over the centuries. Later, in Hellenistic times, the southwest side was lined with a stone gutter with settling basins. There was no such definition of the northeast side, and the street was apparently wide enough for the cavalry to train on. The line of the road must be very ancient, going back to prehistoric times when it led to the Iron Age cemetery at the Kerameikos. It was clearly incorporated into the design of the 6th century Agora, however. The Altar of the Twelve Gods takes its orientation from the street, and Peisistratos is specifically credited with reorganizing the Panathenaia,[22] the festival in honour of Athena, a highlight of which was the great parade which followed this road through the Agora on its way up to the Acropolis. This is the procession depicted on the sculptured frieze of the Parthenon, much of which is now in the British Museum. In the Agora, special wooden

28   grandstands, called *ikria*, were erected for spectators: 'When he was hipparch at the Panathenaia he set up an *ikrion* for Aristagora';[23] 'Grandstand-makers are those who construct the *ikria* around the Agora.'[24] Excavations along both sides of the Panathenaic Way have brought to light post-holes for the wooden posts which anchored these *ikria* in the 5th and 4th centuries BC. The roadway seems also to have been used for some athletic events as well, at least until the construction of the great stadium by the Ilissos river in 330 BC. The blocks for

66   the starting line of a race course in use in the 5th century were found in 1971 just east of the Altar of the Twelve Gods. In addition, the Panathenaic event known as the *apobates*, in which the contestant, wearing full armour, leapt on and off a racing chariot, was apparently held on the street.[25]

The Orchestra

During the 6th century the whole Agora – including the roadway – was used for a variety of theatrical events and displays: singing, dancing, and plays. A part of the square was referred to as the orchestra, and it too would be provided with ikria for the spectators. ('Ikria. The structures in the agora from which the people watched the Dionysiac contests before the theatre in the shrine of Dionysos was built';[26] 'The ikria were upright timbers with planks attached to them, like steps; on these planks the audience sat, before the theatre was built.'[27]) In the early 5th century BC after the ikria in the Agora collapsed during a performance, injuring many people,[28] most theatrical events were moved to the new theatre of Dionysos, south of the Acropolis.

Despite the transfer of most athletic and theatrical events from the Agora by the Classical period, the area was still regarded as a suitable location for the erection of monuments commemorating victories in the contests, and many have come to light in the excavations.

The lawcourt

21, 29   In the southwest corner of the Agora there is a large enclosure, almost square in plan, measuring 27 by 31 m; only a single course above the foundations is preserved. It was approached by five steps built all along the north side. Within, there were no rooms or internal divisions or roof in the original period. The building was erected in the 6th century BC, perhaps around the middle of the century, to judge from the ceramic evidence. There is no known ancient reference to the building, and for its identification we must rely on the remains alone. The usual function of a large walled temenos is to enclose a sacred area, but excavations carried down to bedrock within most of the building revealed no trace of an altar or shrine and no trace of votive offerings of the sort commonly found in sanctuaries. Its large size, early date, and prominent location by the Agora all suggest that it is a public building; a likely candidate would be one of the lawcourts of the city. We have a great deal of indirect evidence in the literary sources about lawcourts, though no certain examples. The basic requirement of a court is that it should be large enough to

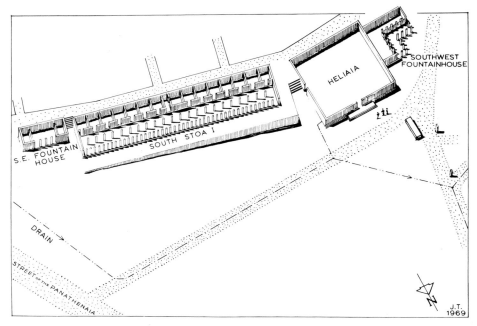

29 The south side of the Agora in a partially restored perspective looking south. The building labelled Heliaia may be the principal lawcourt of Athens. Two boundary stones (ill. 30) appear at the far right.

contain the hundreds of jurors who made up an Athenian court. The courts segregated the jurors, but outsiders could often overhear the proceedings; several courts were unroofed and open to the sky. All these elements apply to this structure, which should therefore in all likelihood be identified as one of the earliest courts of Athens. It has been further suggested that it is, in fact, the Heliaia, the largest court of Athens, which was regularly made up of as many as 1,500 members and on one occasion, at least, had 2,500. While not unlikely, the association rests on the same arguments of size, date, and location, and in assigning the building a specific name its identification becomes even more tentative.

Thus during the second half of the 6th century the Agora under the Peisistratids began to take its basic form, and several of its important monuments had already been built. Peisistratos himself was succeeded by two of his sons, Hippias and Hipparchos, as we have seen, but in 514 BC Hipparchos was killed by Harmodios and Aristogeiton while he was marshalling the Panathenaic procession. According to both Thucydides[29] and Aristotle[30] the murder took place at the Leokoreion, a shrine which stood in the Agora.[31] Dedicated to the three daughters of Leos who were sacrificed to save the city at the time of a plague or famine, the shrine has not been located, though it has been associated by some with a small crossroads sanctuary at the northwest corner of the square. Thucydides and Aristotle both regarded this assassination as a personal vendetta resulting from a lover's quarrel, but it soon came to be regarded as a political act. Hippias continued to reign, far more harshly, until he was turned out in 510 BC by a rival family, the Alkmaionidai, with the help of the Spartans under Kleomenes. Shortly thereafter statues of the tyrannicides were set up near the centre of the Agora where they served as a landmark for generations. They represent one of the earliest known instances of honorary statues of mortals being set up in Athens. In addition, the descendants of Harmodios and Aristogeiton were fed at public expense for life in the Prytaneion (Town Hall), an honour reserved for the greatest benefactors of the state.

The constitutional reforms of Kleisthenes

Following several years of political instability, a new constitution was introduced in 508/7 BC by Kleisthenes. These reforms, designed to break the family ties of the old landed aristocracy and the regional factions which resulted, gave power to more people and represent the foundations of the Athenian democracy. Henceforth all Athenian citizens belonged to one of ten newly-created tribes which shared equally in the administration of the state. About 140 demes (townships) of Attica and Athens were assigned to the tribes, and citizens were now referred to by name, patronymic, and demotic: Sokrates, son of Sophroniskos, of Alopeke.

6

During the period from the Kleisthenic reforms to the Persian sack of Athens in 480 BC, the Agora continued to develop gradually. The square itself was officially laid out, and several new buildings were needed as more people were drawn into the process of governing the city.

Boundary stones

In the years around 500 BC the Agora was formally defined by means of boundary stones (horoi). These were placed at the entrances, wherever a street led into the open square. Two remain *in situ* along the west side, and one more found in the excavations is now in the museum store-rooms. They consist of a simple vertical shaft of marble with an inscription on the face, running across the top and down one side. The text reads 'I am the boundary of the Agora'.[32] Among the three examples the letters and words run both left to right and right to left; apparently the Athenians of the late 6th century read so well or so badly that it did not matter to them which way the writing went. The need to define the limits of the Agora was twofold: religious and practical. There was a

29, 124

30

---

1 (*opposite*) *The area of the Agora excavations taken from a balloon at 500 m in 1975. The Hephaisteion can be seen at the far left and the reconstructed Stoa of Attalos far right. The modern railway cuts across the line of the Panathenaic Way.*

II

III

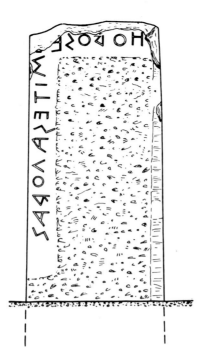

30 *Boundary stones of the Agora,*
both found still in situ (cf. ill. 29).
The text reads: 'I am the boundary
of the Agora.' Note that in this early
period (c. 500 BC) the writing could
go in either direction. The stones
stood about a metre high.

tendency in antiquity as in modern times to use the word 'agora' loosely to refer to the whole market area or civic centre. Strictly speaking, however, the agora was just the large open square, reserved for public functions such as elections, meetings, festivals, processions, and the like. As such, it was a quasi-religious area, the sacred character of which was reflected in the placement of perirrhanteria (basins for holy water) at the entrances to the square. As a religious centre, the Agora was off-limits to various groups of miscreants according to Aeschines: 'So the lawmaker keeps outside the perirrhanteria of the Agora the man who avoids military service, or plays the coward or deserts, and does not allow him to be crowned nor to enter public shrines.'[33] Others are listed by Demosthenes: 'Surely those who are traitors to the commonwealth, those who mistreat their parents, and those who do not have clean hands, do wrong by entering the Agora.'[34] To be banned from the Agora was to be denied a share in much of the public and social life of the city, and the limits accordingly had to be clearly defined.

The second, practical reason for the boundary stones was to prevent architectural encroachments on the open square. Public buildings and even private houses crowded in from all sides, and the boundaries of the Agora had

II *General view overlooking the Agora square from the west, showing the reconstructed Stoa of Attalos at the left, and the Acropolis with its temples at the right.*

III *The Agora excavations from the Areopagos hill, looking north, with modern Athens and Mt Parnes behind.*

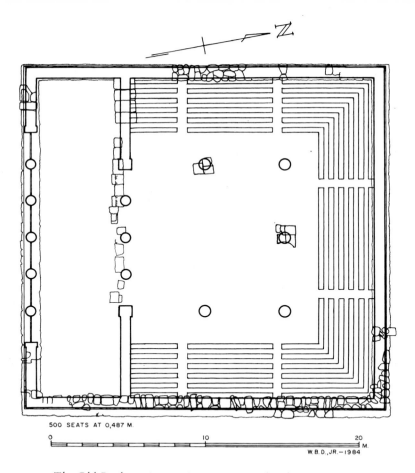

500 SEATS AT 0,487 M.

31 *The Old Bouleuterion, or Senate House, showing a restored plan superimposed over the extant remains, c. 500 BC. The building is known to have seated 500 senators.*

to be well defined lest the open area be infringed upon by unauthorized buildings. Such an occurrence is known from the deme of Sounion in the 4th century BC, when a certain Leukios donated two plethra of land for a new agora when the old one had become cluttered with buildings and monuments.[35]

The Old Bouleuterion

21, 27   In the area along the west side a large new building was erected to the north of
31   Building F and partially over Building D. It is almost square in plan, measuring just over 23 m on a side and facing south. There were probably five interior supports, but no trace of any other internal divisions has been found. From its plan, size, and location it has been identified as the Bouleuterion (Senate House), built to accommodate the members of the Boule (Senate), created at the time of the Kleisthenic reforms. Five hundred senators, fifty from each of the ten new tribes, replaced an earlier council of four hundred. The members

of this new senate were elected to serve for one year, during which time they met every day in the Bouleuterion, except on festival days, to propose and consider legislation. Archaeological evidence for the date of the building is slight; a date around 500 has been generally accepted although a later date has recently been proposed, and the newly-created council would surely have required appropriate housing in the area which can be shown in later periods to have been the seat of government.

The Royal Stoa

Another building apparently constructed in the 6th century BC is a stoa at the northwest corner of the Agora, first excavated in 1970. Eight columns of the severe Doric order ran across the front of the building, which faced east overlooking the open square and the Panathenaic Way. The central ridge of the roof was originally supported by two interior columns and later by four Doric columns. The steps of the stoa are of a hard tan stone, resting on a foundation of reused column shafts. The north wall stands three courses high, built of well-cut squared blocks of yellowish limestone. The upper parts of the building were also of limestone, except for the roof of terracotta (baked clay) tiles and ornamental sculpture (acroteria) also of terracotta. The building is very small for a stoa, only about 18 m long and 7.5 m wide.

The evidence for the date of the building is somewhat puzzling. The architectural elements which fit the foundations, fragments of columns and a Doric frieze, should be dated on stylistic grounds to the middle years of the 6th century BC. Pottery from under the floor, presumably thrown in when the building was constructed, dates to the years around 500 BC, however. While a 6th century date seems likely, this discrepancy is odd, and not easily explained. The reused material in the foundations has led to the suggestion that its construction should be dated after the Persian occupation of 480 BC, when such material was most readily available.

If the date of the building is somewhat ambiguous, its identification is not, thanks to Pausanias and two inscriptions. The traveller comes into the Agora along the Panathenaic Way which passes immediately to the north of our stoa and begins his account in good guide-book fashion: 'First on the right is the Royal Stoa, where sits the "king" when he holds the annual magistracy called "kingship". On the tiled roof of this stoa are images of terracotta, Theseus throwing Skiron into the sea, and Hemera carrying off Kephalos . . . '.[36] In addition, two inscribed bases still in place on the steps of the building carry dedications of king archons, those who were second in command of the Athenian government. The earlier base, dated to about 400 BC, reads: 'Onesippos, the son of Aitios, of the deme of Kephisia, the king, set this up'.[37] Just next to it is a similar one to be dated about a century later: 'Exekestides, the son of Nikokrates, of the deme Alopeke, having been the king, set this up'.[38] Thus with these two bases and the testimony of Pausanias, we may identify the building as the Royal Stoa, headquarters of the king archon. We

21

32

33, 36

34

35

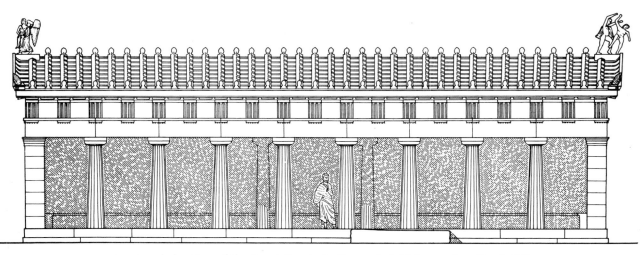

32 *A restored elevation of the Royal Stoa in its first period. This was the office building of the King Archon (second-in-command of the Athenian government).*

33 *Remains of the Royal Stoa viewed from the south.*

34 *Foundations of the exterior colonnade of the Royal Stoa, showing column shafts reused from an earlier building.*

35 *Inscribed base for a herm dedicated by the King Archon Onesippos, c. 400 BC. The inscription records also the winning poets and producers in comedy and tragedy in the theatrical contests of that year.*

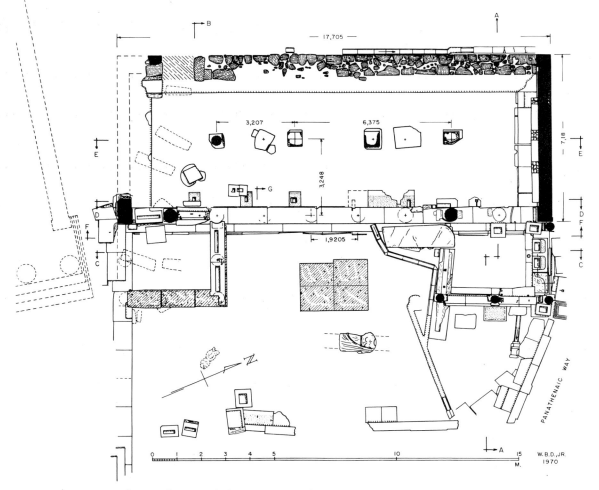

36 *The Royal Stoa and the courtyard in front of it, actual state plan.*

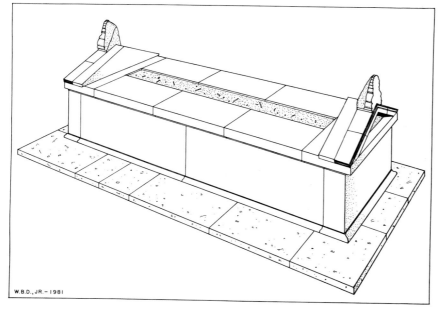

37, 38 *The Altar of Aphrodite Ourania, as found* (above), *viewed from the south, and* (left) *in a restoration drawing seen from the southwest.*

W.B.D., JR.-1981

shall have occasion to discuss the function and history of the building more fully in the next chapter; for the moment, it is enough to list it here among the monuments erected in the Agora during the 6th century.

The Altar of Aphrodite Ourania

At the northwest corner of the Agora, just across the Panathenaic Way from the Royal Stoa, a handsome marble altar was uncovered in 1981. The altar is one of the earliest and most beautiful to come to light in the excavations. The focal point of worship in a Greek sanctuary was such an altar, set outside where the actual sacrifice took place. The temple, if a sanctuary had one, was built to house the cult statue of the deity and any votive offerings but was rarely the site of the liturgy itself as is the case with churches, synagogues, and mosques today. Preserved here is a platform of hard purplish limestone which measures 5.1 by 2.4 m. On top stood the altar itself, although now only its southern half survives. The core of the altar was made up of soft, yellowish, porous limestone blocks set on edge *c.* 0.3 m apart, and around them were set orthostats of white marble from one of the Cycladic islands, probably Paros or Naxos. The orthostats are carved with a handsome moulding at the base. The crowning course is missing, though two pedimental end pieces decorated with floral motifs were found nearby and are probably from the altar. Pottery found up against and inside the base suggests that the altar should be dated to *c.* 500 BC, as does the use of marble from the islands rather than the local quarries on Mount Pentele, which first began to be exploited extensively around 490 BC.

37, 38

Its identification as an altar is certain from the form of the monument as well as from the ashes and bones of the sacrifices found inside the core, mostly pigs, sheep, and goats, with an occasional bird. The identification as an altar of Aphrodite seems likely. Pausanias describes a sanctuary of Aphrodite Ourania (Heavenly Aphrodite) at about this spot after he passes the Hephaisteion and makes his way to the Painted Stoa along the north side of the square: 'Nearby is a shrine of Aphrodite Ourania. . . . The statue still extant in my time is of Parian marble and is the work of Pheidias.'[39] Two fragments of a marble relief found in the area clearly depict Aphrodite and add their weight to the identification. At present we are uncertain as to the limits of the sanctuary. It may have been a simple open-air shrine with the altar standing alone, at least originally, though Pausanias' account of a statue done by the master sculptor Pheidias suggests a temple as well. If there were a temple, we would expect to find it west of the altar, beyond the limits of the excavated area and still buried under modern houses.

Marathon and ostracism

In 490 BC the Persians, eager to avenge the burning of Sardis in 498 BC, made an expedition against Athens. Landing at the broad plain of Marathon in eastern Attica, they were met and defeated there by the Athenians under Kallimachos and Miltiades, in a battle described by Herodotos.[40] This victory was never forgotten by the Athenians. Monuments and paintings commemorating the battle could be seen at Athens, Delphi, and Olympia hundreds of years after the event, and Athenian orators referred to it incessantly. Along with a contingent of Plataians, Athens had stood alone against a Persian army and prevailed, and the boost to her prestige in Greece and self-esteem at home is hard to overestimate.

Sailing with the Persian fleet and guiding it in the decision to land at Marathon was Hippias, by now a very old man, still hoping and expecting to be reinstated as tyrant of Athens once the Persians had won. The Athenians were undoubtedly alarmed at the presence of the old tyrant and fearful of a new attempt to set up a tyranny; in 488 BC they began to ostracize certain citizens.[41] Designed to thwart any attempt at a tyranny, the law had been passed earlier, presumably as part of the Kleisthenic reforms, but it was first used only after Marathon.

The procedure of ostracism was simple. Once a year the people would meet in the Agora and take a vote to determine if anyone was becoming too powerful and was in a position to establish a tyranny. If a simple majority voted yes, they met again in the Agora two months later. At this second meeting each carried with him an ostrakon (potsherd) on which he had scratched the name of the person he wished ostracized. If at least 6,000 votes were cast, the man with the most votes lost and was exiled for ten years. The procedure was used frequently in the 480s and less often thereafter. While an interesting idea, it did not really work, for a prominent man, if powerful enough, could use it to eliminate his chief rival. Such an occurrence is recorded in 443 BC, when Perikles was facing vociferous criticism of his policies, especially his building programme; an ostracism was held which resulted in the exile of his main opponent, Thucydides, the son of Milesias. The system degenerated still further in 417 BC, when Nikias and Alkibiades were rivals for power and an ostracism was held to break the deadlock between them.[42] In the days before public opinion polls, the outcome was uncertain; the two conspired together and a third man, Hyperbolos, was exiled instead. After such a distortion of the original intent of the law, ostracism in Athens was abandoned.

Useless immediately after the counting, the actual ostraka were simply discarded in the street or any convenient hole. Like most baked pottery, they are virtually indestructible; excavations of the Agora have produced over 1,000 examples, and those of the Kerameikos, several thousand. More than any literary text, the ostraka bring to life a sense of Athenian power politics as waged centuries ago. They preserve the names of all the well-known statesmen as well as several unknown aspirants to political power. One group found together to the southeast of the Agora is of special interest. It is made up of 190 ostraka, mostly the round feet of kylixes (goblets), all inscribed with the name of Themistokles, son of Neokles, of Phrearrhios, the far-sighted architect of

39

39 Inscribed pieces of pottery (ostraka) with the names of Aristeides, Themistokles, Kimon, and Perikles. Ostraka were used in voting to exile those who seemed to be aiming at establishing a tyranny. Of the four men here, only Perikles was not exiled.

Athenian naval power so crucial to Athens at the battle of Salamis (480 BC) and throughout the rest of the 5th century. The picture of party politics comes into sharper focus when one examines the handwriting carefully, for these 190 ostraka were written by only fourteen people. Clearly the enemies of Themistokles were equipped beforehand with ready-made ostraka for distribution to illiterate or undecided voters.

Most ostraka were written by the individual voters, however, and thereby provide useful information on literacy, the pronunciation of ancient Greek, and the development of the Athenian alphabet during the 5th century.

The Persian sack of 480 BC

Though thwarted at Marathon, the Persians remained intent on revenge and in 480 they were back, this time with a huge land army as well as the fleet. Realizing that they were no match for the Persians on land, the Athenians abandoned Athens, ferrying women and children to Salamis and Troezen, and met the Persians at sea near Artemision and Salamis. The Persian army thus took Athens in 480 BC against only token resistance and carried out an extensive campaign of destruction both on the Acropolis and in the lower city. Before withdrawing to Thebes in 479 BC the Persian general Mardonios 'first burnt Athens and utterly overthrew and demolished whatever wall or house or temple was left standing', according to Herodotos.[43] Thucydides describes the city in similar terms:

The Athenians when the Barbarians had departed from their territory, straightaway began to fetch back their wives and their children and the remnant of their household goods from where they had placed them for safety, and to rebuild the city and the walls; for of the encircling wall only small portions were left standing, and most of the houses were in ruins, only a few remaining in which the chief men of the Persians had themselves taken quarters.[44]

This devastation, so well attested in the literary sources, has left its mark on the monuments of the Agora. Building F was destroyed and never rebuilt, the Royal Stoa was severely damaged and had to be extensively rebuilt, and the lawcourt (Heliaia?) shows signs of later repairs as well. The Southeast Fountainhouse and the Bouleuterion presumably suffered also, though not enough survives to assess the damage. In addition, several large pits have been found full of debris (broken pottery, fragments of architecture and sculpture), which seems to represent the cleaning up of the area when the Athenians returned. Private houses were severely damaged, and eleven household wells were found to be full of similar debris, thrown in as the Athenians struggled to rebuild their shattered city.

What was to become common practice in later times, the plunder of art works, also occurred at this early date as the Persians made off with whatever they did not destroy. Among the most significant were the statues of the Tyrannicides: 'Of the statues, the one pair is the work of Kritios, the old pair was made by Antenor. Xerxes, when he took Athens after the Athenians had left the city, took away these last as spoils.'[45] The second pair was made by Kritios as soon as 477/6 BC to replace those plundered, and the original pair was returned to Athens years later by Alexander the Great or one of his successors. Of these two famous groups, only a small fragment of the inscribed base survives, apparently for the later pair and carrying part of the name of Harmodios.[46] Also removed and taken to Sardis was a small bronze statue of a water-bearer set up by Themistokles when he had been water commissioner.[47]

A particularly outrageous aspect of the Persian invasion for the Greeks was their treatment of sanctuaries. For centuries Greek polis had fought against polis, killing, enslaving, and inflicting all the horrors of war on one another. But rarely did they damage the temples, for all worshipped the same gods. The Persians had no such restraint and plundered and burned whatever temples and sanctuaries fell to them. In Athens, the temples of the Acropolis were burnt, and three small shrines along the west side of the Agora were also obliterated. As a result of this behaviour, the Greeks, after their victory in the final battle at Plataia in 479 BC, swore an oath not to rebuild the temples but to leave them in ruins as a permanent reminder of the barbarity of the Persians.[48]

With the end of the Persian wars, we close this chapter on the Archaic Agora, which has grown from a residential district and burial ground into the civic centre of the 6th-century city, a development which was disrupted but in no way halted as a result of the Persian sack of 480. Upon the ruins of the Archaic Agora rose the buildings which were to serve Athens during the flowering of the Classical period.

4 The Classical Agora

Historical background

Following the Persian wars, we find Athens in a position of leadership among the city-states of Greece, challenged only by Sparta. Indeed, the Classical period can be distinguished from the Archaic by the shift from a balance among the poleis to a period of Spartan and Athenian dominance. In the case of Athens this dominance was not just political and economic, but also artistic and literary so that, for better or worse, our view of Classical Greece has always been strongly Athenocentric.

Politically, Athens became the leader of an alliance against Persia, committed to following up the successes of Salamis and Plataia. Dozens of states joined the league, founded in 478 BC. The allies had the option of providing ships or money to maintain a fleet. Most contributed money, which allowed the Athenians to build a huge navy to be used, if necessary, against recalcitrant allies as well as Persians; over the years the alliance gradually became an Athenian empire. The war with Persia had mixed results: a great victory at the Eurymedon river in the 460s, a serious defeat in the 450s in Egypt. A peace of sorts was made with Persia sometime in the middle of the century, but Athens had to contend also with the Spartans and their Peloponnesian and Boeotian allies in a series of campaigns in the 450s and 440s. A peace made in the 440s allowed a period of respite during which the Athenians started a great building programme on the Acropolis, but the inevitable clash with Sparta broke out in 432/1 BC. Known as the Peloponnesian War, it raged all over the eastern Mediterranean, from Sicily to Asia Minor, until 405/4 BC, when the Athenian fleet was wiped out and Athens was forced to submit. Direct Spartan control of Athens was short-lived, and by 403/2 BC Athens was once again a democracy, vying for power with Persian help. In 378/7 BC a second Athenian league was founded and acted in concert with Thebes to reduce Spartan power and influence. This was followed by a brief period of Theban hegemony over Greece (371–62 BC), after which Athens was briefly in control once again, though soon to be confronted by Philip of Macedon.

It is against this historical backdrop that Athens flourished as the intellectual and cultural centre of the ancient world in the Classical period. During this remarkable time Athens produced or attracted genius in all fields of human endeavour, as even a short list makes clear: in drama, Aeschylus, Sophokles, Euripides, and Aristophanes; in history, Herodotos and

Thucydides; in philosophy, Sokrates, Plato, and Aristotle; in rhetoric, Demosthenes, Isokrates, and Aeschines; in sculpture, Pheidias and Praxiteles; in painting, Mikon and Polygnotos; and in architecture, Iktinos, Mnesikles, and Kallikrates. Through the works of such men, Athens of the 5th and 4th centuries was the scene of achievements against which all earlier and later cultures are judged. Also during this period democracy developed to a degree not seen before or since as all citizens took a direct hand in running the affairs of the city. Under Perikles the democratic reforms begun by Kleisthenes were brought to their fullest expression, resulting in the intellectual ferment and artistic accomplishment that has served as a model ever since.

Nowhere is the achievement of Classical Athens more readily appreciated than in the 5th century monuments of the Acropolis, where three temples and a 2, II   monumental gateway (Propylaia) were erected in the second half of the century. The earliest of these, the Parthenon (447–32 BC) and Propylaia (437–2), were certainly part of a great building programme initiated by Perikles. Possibly associated, though built somewhat later, were the Erechtheion and temple of Athena Nike. All four, for different reasons, are regarded as masterpieces of Greek architecture. The Parthenon is generally considered the outstanding example of the Doric order, built all of marble on a grand scale and with an innovative plan. Subtle architectural refinements allow the building to escape the static quality imposed by the rigid verticals and horizontals of most Doric buildings. A full sculptural plan featured themes appropriate to the building and its significance: the pediments depicted Athena, patroness of the city; the Doric frieze alluded to victory over the Persians by means of mythological scenes of civilization triumphing over barbarians; and the Ionic frieze showed the Panathenaic procession, glorifying Athens and her people at the height of their power. Inside was a colossal standing armed Athena, built of ivory and gold and other precious materials by Pheidias. The Erechtheion, immediately adjacent, is the most sacred building on the Acropolis; it housed a wooden cult statue so old it was said to have fallen from heaven. The architect wisely chose not to compete directly with the Parthenon and instead used the Ionic order, the lighter, more delicate and ornate style of Asia Minor. The unusual plan, with porches projecting off the side walls, may best be explained by the multitude of sacred spots which had to be either respected by or incorporated into the building. The monumental Propylaia, which served as the gateway to the Acropolis, was designed by Mnesikles. A detailed study of the building shows it to have one of the most sophisticated designs in all of Greek architecture, laid out in close relation to the Parthenon in terms of orientation, size, and proportions. Finally, the little Ionic temple of Athena Nike was built just outside the Propylaia, and the construction of the Classical Acropolis was completed, with the exception of some minor subsequent building.

This major work on the Acropolis in the second half of the 5th century might well be thought sufficient to have fully occupied the best sculptors, masons, and architects Athens had available, and yet the building programme comprised much more. In the lower city, the Hephaisteion was perhaps under construction at this time, and the Odeion south of the Acropolis certainly dates to the 440s. Religious structures were built in sanctuaries all over Attica as well, at Sounion, Eleusis, and Rhamnous, and probably at Acharnai, Thorikos, and Brauron. Plutarch preserves an ancient view of this activity:

So then the works arose, no less towering in their grandeur than inimitable in the grace of their outlines, since the workmen strove to surpass themselves in the beauty of their handicraft. And yet the most wonderful thing about them was the speed with which they arose. Each one of them, men thought, would require many successive generations to complete it, but all of them were fully completed in the heyday of a single administration.[49]

In all, as many as a dozen temples or related structures can be attributed to the Periklean building programme of the third quarter of the 5th century BC, though the monuments of the Acropolis are its most conspicuous element.

The architectural development of the Agora in the 5th century complements rather than parallels that of the Acropolis. After the Persian invasions the Agora was the scene of considerable activity at a time when the Oath of Plataia was in force, prohibiting the repair or reconstruction of the temples on the Acropolis. From 479 to mid-century the Painted Stoa, the Tholos, the Herms, and the aqueduct to the Academy were certainly built, and the Royal Stoa and Old Bouleuterion were presumably rebuilt. With the advent of the Periklean building programme in the middle of the century construction in the Agora was sharply curtailed, as attention shifted to the Acropolis and Attica. What little work was done concentrated on the shrines and sanctuaries, especially the repair of damage done by the Persians. During the Peloponnesian War construction on the monuments of the Periklean programme stopped, leaving several unfinished, some temporarily, some forever. The Athenians did not stop building, however; the emphasis simply shifted from religious structures to civic ones. The last third of the 5th century saw extensive activity in the Agora as the New Bouleuterion, Stoa of Zeus, South Stoa I, and the Mint were all erected. Generally more modest in their building materials, made of limestone and mud brick as opposed to marble, with simple floors of packed earth, these buildings nonetheless demonstrate the extent of Athenian resources and energy while engaged in a major war.

Concentrating on recovery of Athens' fortunes after the war was lost, her citizens abandoned most construction in the early 4th century. Except for the rebuilding of the fortification walls in the 390s, there was virtually no building activity in Athens. By the end of the 5th century all major aspects of civic activity were appropriately housed in the Agora, and the buildings sufficed until late in the 4th century. Here the business of the city was conducted, and here the great figures of Classical Athens could be found, serving in the Senate

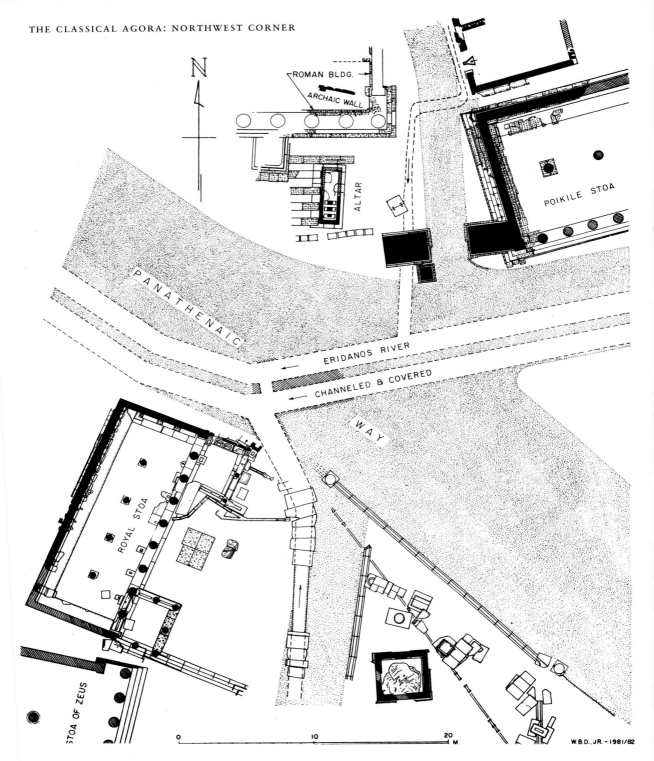

N

ROMAN BLDG.

ARCHAIC WALL

ALTAR

POIKILE STOA

PANATHENAIC

ERIDANOS RIVER

CHANNELED & COVERED

WAY

ROYAL STOA

STOA OF ZEUS

0   10   20 M.

W.B.D., JR. - 1981/82

40 *The northwest corner of the Agora in 300 BC, showing the Painted Stoa (Poikile Stoa), the Royal Stoa, the Altar of Aphrodite (centre above) and the crossroads enclosure (centre below). See also ills. 41, 55.*

41 *(opposite) Balloon view of the northwest corner of the Agora showing the Royal Stoa and the crossroads enclosure (below the modern street) and the Altar of Aphrodite and end of the Painted Stoa (above the street). Compare ills. 40, 55.*

or as a magistrate, pleading or acting as a juror in a lawcourt, perusing the notices or records at the archives, arguing business, politics, or philosophy in the shade of one of the stoas, or simply doing the daily shopping. Taking the monuments more or less in chronological order, we turn now to a more detailed account of the Agora in Classical times.

Kimonian Athens

Following the battle of Plataia in 479 BC the Persians fled back to Asia, never to return. The war itself continued, however, although the battlefield now shifted to the eastern Mediterranean. Leading Athens in this period was Kimon, whose father was Miltiades, the hero of Marathon. Of a wealthy and aristocratic family, Kimon was responsible for improving the city in a variety of ways: 'He was the first to beautify the city with the so-called "liberal" and elegant resorts of which they were so excessively fond a little later; for the Agora he planted with plane trees, and the Academy he converted from a waterless and arid spot to a well-watered grove, equipped with clear running tracks and shady walks.'[50] During an expedition against the island of Skyros in 476/5 he recovered the bones of Theseus and founded a shrine to house them somewhere east of the Agora;[51] in the 460s he fortified much of the Acropolis with spoils from the battle at the Eurymedon River;[52] and from its date it seems likely that the Klepsydra spring house on the slopes of the Acropolis was built during his administration.[53] In addition, several monuments in the Agora can be directly or indirectly associated with Kimon or his family.

The Painted Stoa

40, 41 Best known from this period was the Painted Stoa, among the most famous buildings of ancient Athens. An excellent candidate was discovered in the excavations of 1981; it has been only partially excavated up to now, and much of the building remains hidden under modern houses. It measures 12.5 m wide and, if the usual proportions for a stoa hold true, should be at least 36 m long and quite possibly more. It was of the severe Doric order outside, with a row of 43 Ionic columns inside. Most of the building was made of different limestones, though the Ionic capitals were of marble. The structure is well designed, carefully built, and one of the more lavish secular buildings in Athens. The step-blocks, for instance, were all cut to the same length, with the joints 42 fastened by means of iron double-T clamps leaded in, and alternate joints fall precisely under the centre of each column. According to the pottery associated with its construction it should be dated to the period 475–50 BC. Of all the stoas of Athens it holds the preferred location, along the north side of the Agora square, looking right up the Panathenaic Way to the Acropolis. It has the southern exposure recommended for stoas in order to take advantage of the warmth of the low winter sun while presenting its back wall to the cold north wind. Pausanias saw the Painted Stoa as he made his way along the north side

IV (opposite) *The Hephaisteion ('Theseion'), the 5th-century Doric temple which crowns the hill west of the Agora.*

V

VI

42 *Steps along the west end of the Painted Stoa. Note that the blocks are all cut to a uniform length of 3 Athenian feet (c. 1 m).*

of the square,⁵⁴ and this new stoa thus corresponds to what we know about the Painted Stoa in terms of size, date, and location; the identification of the remains as those of the Painted Stoa seems almost certain.

The building was first known as the Peisianaktios, after the man responsible for its construction, Peisianax, who may have been the brother-in-law of Kimon. Soon after its construction, however, it was decorated with a series of large paintings, and the building became known by the popular name Poikile (Painted), which appears as its official name in inscriptions by the 4th century BC.

The paintings were done on large wooden panels (sanides) by the outstanding artists of Athens: Polygnotos, Mikon, and Panainos. The works are referred to time and again by ancient authors and are described in some detail by Pausanias who saw them still in place after 600 years. They depicted scenes of Athenian military exploits, both mythological and historical: the Athenians against the Amazons, the Greeks at Troy, the Athenians defeating the Spartans at Argive Oinoe, and – by far the most famous – the Athenian victory over the Persians at Marathon. Pausanias' description is as follows:

44

The last part of the painting consists of those who fought at Marathon. The Boeotians of Plataia and the Attic contingent are coming to grips with the barbarians; at this

V *An ivory cosmetics box (pyxis) of the Mycenaean period (c. 1400 BC), found in the Agora and carved with scenes of griffins attacking deer.*

VI *Gold jewelry from the Agora excavations. (Upper right) A Mycenaean signet ring with the scene of a bull-headed man leading two female captives, c. 1400–1375 BC. (Left) A pair of earrings with filigree and granulation and pendant pomegranates, Geometric period, c. 850 BC. (Lower right) Two Hellenistic earrings in the form of Eros, from the crossroads well at the northwest corner of the Agora.*

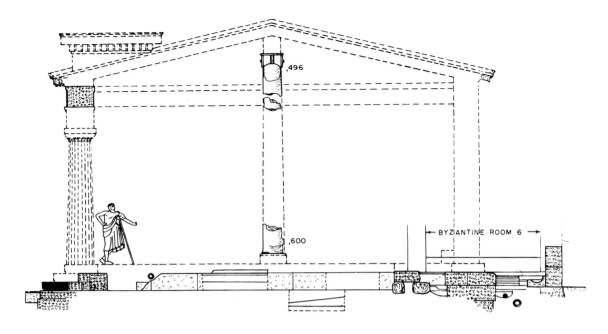

,496

,600

BYZANTINE ROOM 6

43, 44 *Restored cross-section (above) and perspective view (below) of the Painted Stoa.*
The building takes its name from the paintings which hung on the inner walls. Showing
scenes of Athenian military exploits, the paintings were executed on removable wooden
panels. It is from this famous stoa that Stoic philosophy takes its name.

W.B.D., JR. - 1981

point the action is evenly balanced between both sides. In the inner part of the fight are the barbarians fleeing and pushing one another into the marsh; at the extreme end of the painting are the Phoenician ships and the Greeks killing the barbarians who are tumbling into them. In this picture are also shown Marathon, the hero after whom the plain is named, Theseus, represented as coming up from the earth, Athena and Herakles – the Marathonians, according to their own account, were the first to recognize Herakles as a god. Of the combatants the most conspicuous in the picture are Kallimachos, who was chosen by the Athenians to be polemarch, and of the generals Miltiades[54].

After they were seen by Pausanias in the 2nd century AD, the paintings were all removed, apparently at the time of the bishop Synesios, who wrote *c*. AD 398:

May the ship's captain who brought me here perish miserably. Present day Athens possesses nothing venerable except the illustrious names of places. When the sacrifice of a victim has been completed, the skin is left as a token of the animal that once existed; in the same way now that philosophy has departed hence, all that is left for us is to walk around and wonder at the Academy and the Lyceum, and, by Zeus, the Poikile Stoa after which the philosophy of Chrysippos is named, now no longer many coloured; the proconsul took away the sanides to which Polygnotos of Thasos committed his art.[55]

In addition to these illustrations of Athenian exploits, the Stoa housed more tangible reminders of her military triumphs, which were seen by Pausanias: 'In the Poikile are deposited bronze shields. On some is an inscription saying that they were taken from the Skionaians and their auxiliaries; others, smeared with pitch to protect them from the ravages of time and rust, are said to be the shields of the Lakedaimonians who were captured at the island of Sphakteria.'[56] The battle of Sphakteria at Pylos in 425/4 BC was one of the great

45, 46 One of the bronze shields, nearly a metre across, taken from the defeated Spartans at Pylos in 425/4 BC. The text reads: 'The Athenians from the Lakedaimonians at Pylos.' A series of these shields were hung as trophies on the Painted Stoa, where they were seen by Pausanias almost 600 years later.

Athenian triumphs of the Peloponnesian War; 292 Spartans were captured alive,[57] and their armour apparently remained on public display for close to 600 years. One of the captured shields from the battle has been found in the

45, 46   excavations. It is round, measuring about 1 m in diameter, with a relief border decorated with a guilloche pattern. The bronze is badly corroded and damaged so the original weight cannot be determined; presumably there was an inner lining of leather, now missing. The shield was found in a cistern that was filled up in the 3rd century BC, and it cannot therefore have been seen by Pausanias, although it is certainly one of the same series. This is known because of the punched inscription across the front: 'The Athenians from the Lakedaimonians from Pylos'.[58]

As well as displaying paintings and captured arms, the Stoa was used for a wide variety of other functions. Unlike most of the other stoas in the Agora, it was not built for any specific purpose or activity or for the use of a single group of officials. Rather, it seems to have served the needs of the populace at large, providing shelter and a place to meet just off the Agora square. To be sure, it was used on occasion for official functions. A proclamation summoning those qualified to attend the Eleusinian mysteries was made from the stoa every year,[59] and it was used for legal proceedings as well. Demosthenes mentions an arbitration held here, and inscriptions of the 4th century BC refer to full courts of 501 jurors using the building.[60] In addition to this official use the stoa was also used informally by a mixed throng of people. This is clear from the abundant references in the written sources to the frequent use of the stoa by those whose trade depended on a crowd: sword-swallowers, jugglers, beggars, parasites, and fishmongers. Among those who came regularly were the philosophers, who could expect to find a ready audience in this convenient meeting place. There are references to cynicism and other unspecified philosophies being taught in the Stoa, but one branch of Western philosophy is particularly associated with the Painted Stoa. It was founded by the philosopher Zeno, who came from Kition in Cyprus in the years around 300 BC. He preferred the Painted Stoa and met here so regularly with his followers that they took their name from this particular stoa which served as their classroom. Diogenes Laertius, writing in the 3rd century AD, gives the clearest account: 'He used to discourse in the Poikile Stoa, which was also called Peisianaktios, and derived the name Poikile from the painting of Polygnotos. . . . Henceforth people came hither to hear him, and for this reason they were called Stoics.'[61] The stoa, filled with crowds from the Agora and frequented by philosophers, fits well the picture of the kind of liberal and elegant resorts that Kimon is said to have built for the city, a popular *lesche* where Athenians came together to discourse, argue, and learn.

The aqueduct to the Academy
A second element linking Kimon and his attempts to beautify the city to the Painted Stoa is to be found immediately behind the building. Here there is a

47 Alley behind the Painted Stoa, the back wall of which is on the left, viewed from the east. The terracotta pipeline is probably that built by Kimon to carry fresh water to the Academy.

narrow alley, no more than 1.3 m wide, running along the back wall. Within this alley was laid a carefully built water-pipe, similar to that which fed the Southeast Fountainhouse, though somewhat later in date. It is made of sections 0.65 m long, 0.28 m in diameter, with service holes and elaborately collared joints, and was decorated with glazed stripes. It flows westward, and where it passes under the street at the end of the stoa it was covered and protected by large slabs of dark grey stone. This same channel was found in excavations by Greek archaeologists some 70 m to the northwest and by the German excavators of the Kerameikos some 330 m farther on. It seems clear that this is an aqueduct built around 475–50 BC, designed to carry water out of the city to the northwest, that is, directly towards the Academy, which lies some 1,500 m beyond the Kerameikos. Once again, Plutarch's passage on Kimon comes to mind: ' . . . the Academy he converted from a waterless and arid spot to a well-watered grove . . . ' In all probability we have here the means of supply that made the transformation possible.

47

48 A herm of the early 5th century BC, found on the western steps of the Painted Stoa. Herms were stylized representations of the god Hermes and were used in Athens to mark entrances. A great many were found at the entrance to the Agora near the Royal and Painted Stoas. Height 31 cm.

The herms

The herms are a third major feature of the Agora associated with the name of Kimon. A herm was a typical Athenian dedication which consisted of a simple rectangular shaft with a set of male genitalia halfway up and a portrait of the god Hermes on top. They were used to mark entrances according to Thucydides: 'These square-wrought figures, in accordance with local custom, stood in large numbers both in private entrances and in shrines.'[62] The use of herms in Athens goes back to at least the 6th century BC, but the dedication of three large herms to celebrate Kimon's victories over the Persians at Eion in 476/5 BC was apparently very influential in their continuing popularity. Because they were designed to mark entrances, the appropriate place for the dedication of public herms was at the principal entrance to the Agora, where the Panathenaic Way led into the square at its northwest corner. Indeed, this entire area of town became known simply as 'the Herms', as we learn from

49 A herm found in the crossroads enclosure at the northwest corner of the Agora. It was deposited late in the 5th century BC and may well be one of the herms mutilated in 415/14 BC during the Peloponnesian War. Height 23 cm.

50 A herm found behind the Royal Stoa. It dates to the 2nd century AD and was knocked over during Alaric's attack on Athens in AD 395. Height 35 cm.

Harpokration: 'From the Poikile and the Royal Stoa extend the so-called Herms. Because they are set up in large numbers both by the private individuals and by magistrates they have acquired this name.'[63] The excavations have borne this out, and numerous fragments of herms or inscribed bases with the characteristic rectangular socket have come to light in the area, including two still *in situ* on the steps of the Royal Stoa and a head found on the steps of the Painted Stoa. They were apparently very conservative monuments, those as late as the 2nd century AD bearing a marked similarity to those of the 6th century BC.

48, 35

50

The herms feature also in a mysterious event in 415 BC during the Peloponnesian War that was recorded by Thucydides. On the eve of the departure of an Athenian fleet to Sicily, someone deliberately damaged the herms: 'The majority had their faces mutilated in a single night. No one knew the perpetrators, but great rewards were publicly offered for this detection. . . .

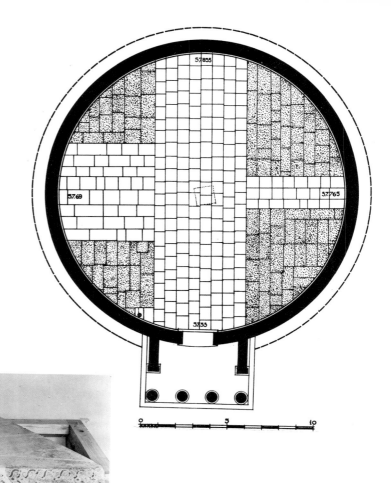

51 (right) The Tholos, originally built c. 470–460 BC; the flooring and columnar porch were later additions. Within this building the fifty senators (prytaneis) of the executive committee of the senate were fed at public expense.

52 (below) Eaves tiles and cover tile with floral finial (antefix) from the roof of the Tholos, c. 470 BC. The painted ornament is original. Height of antefix 30.6 cm.

53 Model of the Tholos showing one possible restoration of the roof with its diamond-shaped tiles.

The matter was taken very seriously for it seemed to be ominous for the expedition and to have been done in furtherance of a conspiracy with a view to a revolution and the overthrow of the democracy.'[64] Several of the herms recovered show signs of this mutilation; some were abandoned, others repaired and rededicated.

    49

    A topographical problem concerning the herms remains to be solved. Associated with them was a building referred to as the Stoa of the Herms; Aeschines wrote in *c.* 330 BC, 'The Demos gave them great honours as it seemed in those days – the right to set up three stone herms in the stoa of the herms.'[65] Despite this and other references to another stoa dating at least as early as the 5th century BC and standing somewhere near the northwest corner of the Agora, the building has thus far not been uncovered or recognized in the excavations. Both the Royal Stoa and the Painted Stoa would seem to be correctly identified, leaving little room for a third stoa in the immediate vicinity; only further excavation will shed light on this vexing question.

The Tholos

A fourth Agora building, the Tholos, should also probably be dated on the basis of ceramic evidence to the decade 470–60 BC. It was a large circular building, 18.32 m in outside diameter, with six interior columns to support the roof. The construction was simple, the walls rising in a plain drum with little evidence of architectural embellishment. The roof was made of a series of large diamond-shaped tiles set in an overlapping pattern which would have resembled a net or the scales of a fish. Its proper reconstruction continues to cause considerable difficulties, and the latest attempt features an *oculus* or opening in the centre which would have provided both light and air. A discussion of the function of this enigmatic building is best delayed until later in the chapter.

    51

    52, 53

Periklean Athens and the rebuilding of sanctuaries

Following the ostracism of Kimon in 461/60 BC, the statesman Perikles came to power, and it was under his guidance throughout most of the third quarter of the 5th century that Athens reached her apogee. In particular, Perikles is credited with instituting the great building programme which resulted in the handsome marble temples still crowning the Acropolis today. They were built after a peace was made with Persia – known as the Peace of Kallias after the Athenian negotiator – in 449 or perhaps the 460s. With a treaty signed, Perikles proposed to rescind the oath of Plataia and to rebuild the temples burnt by the Persians in 480; allied money of the Delian league would be used, though almost all the damaged temples were in fact Athenian. This raised something of an outcry both at home and abroad and led eventually to an ostracism, in which Perikles' rival Thucydides was exiled. The programme continued, and magnificent marble temples rose in Athens and throughout Attica.

54 North wall of the triangular sanctuary near the southwest corner of the Agora. The polygonal masonry dates to just after the middle of the 5th century BC. A boundary stone of the sanctuary is still in situ at the left (east) of the wall.

With such emphasis on the Acropolis and religious structures, the Agora, representing primarily civic life, was largely ignored during this period. What little attention it did receive was confined to cult buildings, perhaps including both the Hephaisteion and Stoa of Zeus. In addition, the Altar of the Twelve Gods and the altar of Aphrodite Ourania must have been damaged in the Persian sack, and both certainly show signs of repair in the third quarter of the 5th century. The sill of the enclosure around the Altar of the Twelve Gods is of the 5th century, and the crowning member and pedimental end pieces of the altar of Aphrodite were reset.

The triangular sanctuary

54, 120 A small shrine just outside the southwest corner of the Agora was extensively refurbished at this time. Numerous votive objects suggest that cult activity on the spot goes back to the 7th century BC. Architectural embellishment, however, dates only from the third quarter of the 5th century, when a handsome peribolos wall was built, defining a triangular area *c.* 8 m on a side. The wall is built of local Acropolis limestone set in a polygonal style. At the corner is a marble boundary stone, still *in situ*, with the laconic text '[Boundary] of the sanctuary'. The brevity of this marker is unfortunate, for it leaves us in the dark as to the deity in question, although the triangular form and the fact that it lies at a crossroads might indicate that it is a small shrine of Hekate.

The crossroads enclosure

A second crossroads enclosure was uncovered at the northwest corner of the *55, 57* square. It is very well preserved, taking the form of a square enclosure measuring 2.8 m on a side, made up of orthostats 1.22 m high of soft yellowish-tan poros standing on a sill. There is no access to the interior and the shrine was clearly an *abaton*, a sacred area not to be entered. Inside, the object of worship was an outcrop of hard bedrock. Excavation around the sanctuary and votives found within indicate that it was established in the third quarter of the 5th century BC. Unlike the southwest enclosure, no trace was found of earlier cult activity at this sanctuary. When excavated in 1971/2, the lower part of this enclosure was found to be full of votive offerings, with more pottery than earth from the top of the sill on down. In all, some 360 objects were recovered, including lekythoi (oil jars), drinking cups, loom weights, knuckle-bones, and gilded pebbles. Regrettably, none of these gifts were inscribed and the enclosure has no boundary stone, so we remain uncertain as to the deity worshipped here. Some of the votives (gold jewellery, loom weights, knuckle-bones) are appropriate for a female deity or deities, and this has led to the suggestion that the shrine be identified as the Leokoreion, dedicated to the daughters of Leos, who were sacrificed to save the city at the time of a plague or famine. The location is appropriate, in the Agora and by the Panathenaic Way, but the chronology is difficult. According to Aristotle, the Leokoreion was the scene of the murder of Hipparchos in 514 BC: Harmodios and Aristogeiton 'killed Hipparchos as he was marshalling the [Panathenaic] procession by the Leokoreion'.[66] Thus the Leokoreion must have been in use in the 6th century BC, that is, some seventy-five years earlier than any sign of cult activity around the crossroads enclosure.

56

The enclosure was allowed to silt up and apparently went out of use towards the end of the 4th century BC. It would seem, however, as though the cult itself continued, for similar dedications continued to be deposited in an adjacent well which should probably be regarded as sacred also. Lying just 2.5 m north of the abaton, it was excavated in 1971 and was found to be 13.45 m deep, closed on top by a stone well-head. When the ground level rose, a second well-head was added on top of the first to keep the shaft accessible. Lying as it does within the square itself, it must have served as a public well, available to those frequenting the Agora. Its use may not have been entirely unrestricted, and it may have been under the control of the deity or deities of the nearby shrine, perhaps Nymphs. An instance of such a public sacred well is attested in an inscription of the 5th century BC found on the west coast of Attica:

57, 58

. . . and to sacrifice to the Nymphs according to the Pythian oracle. Those drinking of the Halykon are to pay an obol a year to the sacred moneys of the Nymphs. Whoever does not pay down the obol, let him not drink from Halykon. If someone drinks by force, let him be fined five drachmai. If someone draws or carries off water and does not put down an obol for each amphora, let him be charged fifty drachmai for the sacred fund of the Nymphs.[67]

Although we cannot be sure, a similar situation may have prevailed here, for the well was found to be full of small votive offerings. In all, over 650 objects

The northwest corner of the Agora

55 A reconstruction of the northwest corner of the Agora as it would have appeared in about 400 BC. In the foreground is the crossroads enclosure and at upper left, the Royal Stoa. At the upper right is the Altar of Aphrodite Ourania and the Painted Stoa. Compare ills. 40, 41.

56 Detailed view of the interior of the crossroads enclosure, showing masses of broken votive pottery as found.

57 *Balloon view of the crossroads enclosure (centre below) and sacred well (centre) at the northwest corner of the Agora. Both the sanctuary and the well were found full of votive objects, mostly pottery but also knuckle-bones and gold jewelry. The well also produced numerous lead tablets from the archives of the Athenian cavalry which trained on the Panathenaic Way, the edge of which is defined by the stone gutter across the top of the photograph. Compare ill. 55.*

58 *The sacred well (centre) and crossroads enclosure (background) seen from the north.*

60, IV were recovered, the majority small squat lekythoi, but gold jewellery, inscribed knuckle-bones, and miniature votive pots were dropped down also. The composition of the material is very similar to that from the shrine, but the date of most of it is later, starting in the 4th century BC, when the sanctuary went out of use, and lasting until the 2nd century BC. The well may have been in use for a longer period, but the uppermost 5.4 m were cleaned out and reused in Byzantine times.

The Hephaisteion

Of all the religious buildings in or near the Agora, the most impressive is the marble temple which crowns the hill to the west. Though roughly contemporary with the other Periklean buildings, no trace of an earlier structure or any sign of earlier cult activity was found under or near the building. There is, therefore, no indication that it represents the rebuilding of a temple destroyed by the Persians and, strictly speaking, it should not be numbered among the monuments of the Periklean building programme. The structure was long identified as the Theseion, which remains its popular name, and recently it has been suggested that it should be identified as the temple of Eukleia (Artemis). Most scholars, however, accept its identification as the Hephaisteion, where Hephaistos, god of the forge, and Athena, goddess of arts and crafts, were worshipped together, appropriately enough, on the hill overlooking the commercial centre of the city. The best evidence for the identification comes from Harpokration who wrote: 'They used to call hired men *kolonetai*, since they stood by the *kolonos* (hill) which is near the Agora, where the Hephaisteion and the Eurysakeion are. This *kolonos* was called Agoraios.'[68] The location of the Eurysakeion is known from inscriptions found on the hill to the south of the temple, and Pausanias described the

59 The Hephaisteion, 5th century BC. The arrangement of the interior colonnades is conjectural.

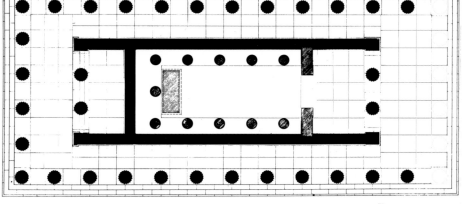

60 The Hephaisteion, here seen from the southwest, is the best-preserved Greek temple surviving from antiquity. The bushes around the temple are planted in ancient planting pits (cf. ill. 64).

61 Aerial view of the Hephaisteion, taken from 50 m, showing the coffered ceiling of the peristyle around the edges. The roof in the centre dates to medieval times.

Hephaisteion as above the Agora and the Royal Stoa. The discovery of bronze-and iron-working pits and slag on the hill suggests that the god's temple was placed in the neighbourhood where his mortal followers laboured.

By far the most lavish building of the Classical Agora, the Hephaisteion would receive far more attention than it has if it did not lie almost literally in the shadow of the Parthenon, the greatest example of the Doric order ever built. Except for the Parthenon, for instance, it carries more sculptural decoration than any other Doric temple. It is also the best preserved temple in the world, owing its fine state of preservation to two factors. First, Athens is not in a major earthquake zone, unlike the Peloponnese or central Greece, where many of the temples were thrown down by seismic activity at one time or another. Secondly, the temple was converted into a Christian church at a fairly early date (7th century AD?), rescuing it from the common fate of most ancient buildings, that is, to be used as a quarry for building material by later people. From the 3rd to the 19th century AD the Athenians were enthusiastic in their recycling of bits of ancient architecture, sculpture, and inscriptions, and most of the marble objects found in the excavations were actually recovered from the demolition of the late walls and houses overlying the site.

The Hephaisteion is built largely of Pentelic marble except for the lowest step, which is of limestone, and the sculpture and parts of the ceiling, which are of island marble. It had a peristyle of six columns across the front and back and 59 thirteen along each of the sides, surrounding the usual internal arrangement of the fully developed Greek temple of pronaos (front porch), cella (main room), and opisthodomos (back porch). Within, there seems to have been an interior colonnade of superimposed Doric columns, though little evidence of it remains today. The building is preserved to the level of the ceiling, which was made of wood inside while marble beams and coffered slabs were used in the peristyle.

61   The stone ceiling is one of the most elaborate in all of Greek architecture. The slabs were cut with deeply recessed coffers which lightened the load the beams would have to carry. This is normal for many stone ceilings. Unusual is the fact that all the coffer lids were carved as separate pieces which could be removed and each lid was cut so as to fit only one coffer. Presumably the small size and great depth of the coffers with the consequent difficulty in carving them is the best explanation for this elaborate and costly arrangement.

The temple is particularly rich in its sculptural adornment, which is placed in such a way as to emphasize the eastern end of the building. All across the front, the metopes of the frieze are carved with scenes of the labours of Herakles, now, sadly, battered and worn. Along both sides, the four 63 easternmost metopes, as far as the third lateral column, show the labours of Theseus. Over the pronaos there is a continuous sculpted frieze, carried all the way out to the same third column of each side, showing a battle watched by the gods. This eastern end of the peristyle is deeper than the west and is seen ringed with sculpture on all four sides when viewed from below and from the east, the usual view of the temple from the Agora square. At the back, over the

62 (above) Part of the sculptured frieze at
the west end of the Hephaisteion, showing
two centaurs hammering the Lapith
Kaineus into the ground with a boulder.
Note that the human, pagan, heads have
been deliberately mutilated, presumably by
Christians at the time of the conversion of
the temple to a church in the 7th century
AD, but that the monster, centaurs', heads,
though worn, are intact. Height 83 cm.

63 Metope at the southeast corner of the
Hephaisteion showing Theseus fighting the
bull-headed Minotaur of Crete. Note here
too, as in the preceding illustration, that
Theseus has had his head chopped off, but
the Minotaur has not. Height of metope 83
cm.

64 *Planting pits as found along the south side of the Hephaisteion, used in the original landscaping of the sanctuary in the 3rd century* BC.

opisthodomos, there is a frieze confined to the width of the inner building, showing the battle of Lapiths and Centaurs. A favourite theme of Greek artists, it was depicted over and over in sculpture and in painting, on vases and in bronze. The Centaurs had been invited to the wedding of the Lapith king's daughter. Centaurs and wine don't mix; the Centaurs got drunk and made off with the ladies at the feast, and the battle which ensued is shown here. In the centre is the Lapith Kaineus who is immortal. The Centaur solution to this problem is simple: two of them have taken a large boulder and are hammering Kaineus into the ground like a nail; buried to his hips already, he is fast disappearing. Both ends of the temple had pedimental sculpture as well, although only scraps have been recovered and their subject matter is uncertain.

Inside the temple stood a double cult statue of Hephaistos and Athena, done in bronze by the sculptor Alkamenes. According to Pausanias, the statue of Athena had blue-grey eyes, and according to Valerius Maximus

Visitors at Athens are impressed by the Vulcan [Hephaistos] made by the hands of Alkamenes; besides the other conspicuous signs of his supreme art there is one thing in particular which they admire; the god's lameness is masked; he stands there displaying some trace of it unobtrusively beneath his garment, and this is not a blemish with which fault could be found, but a definite and appropriate distinguishing mark of the god, becomingly represented.[69]

The temple is dated largely on the style of its architecture and sculpture, the pottery and ostraka from the building fill, and the letter forms of the masons' marks on the stone ceiling which ensured the proper placement of the coffer lids. It was apparently started in the mid-5th century BC, probably not earlier than c. 460 and no later than 450–448. Construction took a long time, perhaps because so many masons and sculptors were required for the Parthenon (447–432) and Propylaia (437–432) on the Acropolis, and perhaps because of the outbreak of the Peloponnesian War (432/1 BC). The upper parts of the building seem not to have been completed until c. 420 BC, and according to an inscription the cult statues were assembled in 421–415 BC, during a temporary lull in the war.

One other interesting feature of the sanctuary of Hephaistos is the evidence for landscaping. Excavations in the area around the temple, and especially to the south, uncovered a series of planting pits filled with large terracotta flowerpots. These were installed in the 3rd century BC and indicate the positions of two rows of shrubs or bushes along the north and south sides, and three rows along the west. They provide welcome physical evidence of something which has always been clear from inscriptions and literary sources, that is, that sanctuaries were well-watered and wooded. Nowadays, most excavated sanctuaries are hot and dusty places to visit, offering little in the way of shelter from the sun. In antiquity, just the opposite was true: a temple was usually deliberately sited at a spring or in a grove and if not, every effort was made to landscape and water the area. Kimon's watering of the Academy is a good example of the literary evidence (see above), and the garden of the Hephaisteion provides welcome corroboration.

64

The Peloponnesian War (431–404 BC) and its aftermath (404–401 BC)

In 431 the Peloponnesian War broke out, pitting Athens, her fleet, and her allies in the Aegean against Sparta, her army, and most of the poleis of the Peloponnese and central Greece. It was a long and bitter struggle, chronicled in detail by the historian Thucydides. The cost was very high, in both men and material, and yet both sides showed remarkable tenacity and resilience for the better part of a generation with only a brief respite, the so-called Peace of Nikias, from 421 to 415 BC.

Several remnants of this struggle have come to light in the Agora. We have already seen one of the shields taken from the Spartans at Pylos in 425/4 BC which were displayed on the Painted Stoa. A less glorious trophy is a bronze spear butt, dedicated to the Dioskouroi, which was taken when Athens put down an armed revolt of her allies on the island of Lesbos in 428/7 BC. Ostraka carrying the names of Nikias and Alkibiades from the final ostracism in 417 BC

45, 46

65

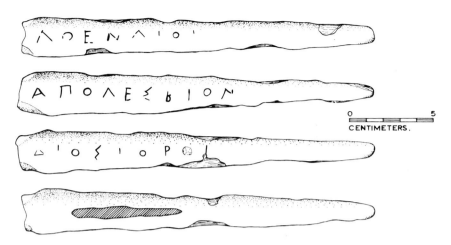

65 Four sides of a bronze spear-butt of the 5th century BC, showing traces of letters which read: 'The Athenians from the Lesbians [dedicated] to the Dioskouroi.' Taken by the Athenians in 428/7 BC when they quelled a revolt of their allies on the island of Lesbos during the Peloponnesian War.

remind us of the disagreements between the two generals over the conduct of the war. Alkibiades' erratic career during this period is also reflected in a series of eleven inscriptions known as the Attic Stelai. In 415/14 BC he and several dozen other Athenians were charged with the mutilation of the herms and also with profaning the Eleusinian Mysteries. Alkibiades, on campaign in Sicily at the time, deserted to Sparta rather than stand trial, and he was condemned to death *in absentia*. His property and that of the others were confiscated by the state and sold at public auction. The Attic Stelai are the records of this sale, originally set up in the Eleusinion, the sanctuary of Demeter on the slopes of the Acropolis above the Agora. As well as reflecting the severity of the punishment for these two acts of sacrilege, the inscriptions provide a fascinating glimpse into the private economy of 5th-century Athens as slaves, houses, crops, furniture, and pots and pans were auctioned off and listed in minute detail. Crops still in the field included figs, grapes, and olives, indicating that at least part of the auction took place in late summer or early fall. Of the slaves, 60 per cent came from Caria or Thrace, and the average price was 175 drachmai. Men and women brought roughly the same price, although there were wide variations depending on skills. A donkey-driver, for instance, cost much less, whereas a goldsmith sold for 300 drachmai. One list of property included 100 Panathenaic amphoras, specially made vessels that held the olive oil given as prizes in the Panathenaic games. We have here, almost certainly, some of the property of Alkibiades himself, whose stable of race horses won him an Olympic victory in 416 BC. They may well have won also at the Panathenaia of 418, the prize for which was 140 amphoras of oil.

At the end of the Peloponnesian War the victorious Spartans installed thirty

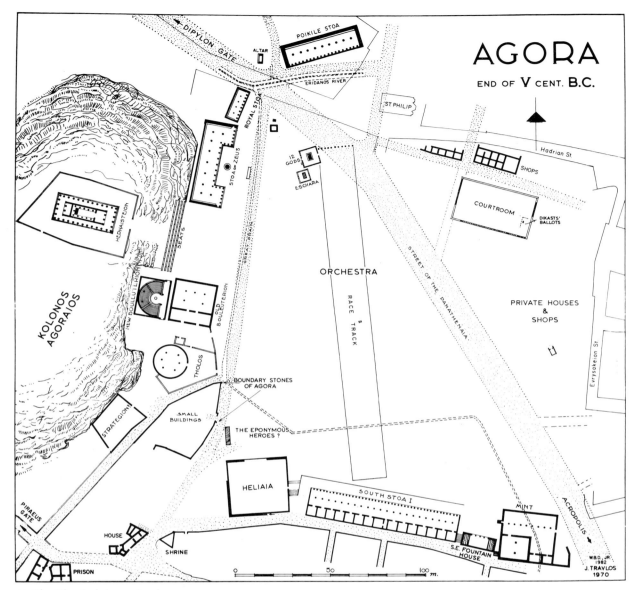

66 *The Classical Agora in about 400 BC.*

sympathetic Athenians to rule the city. Their reign was so harsh they soon became known as the Thirty Tyrants, and several of their more notorious acts were carried out in the Agora. They used the Tholos as their headquarters, and here they summoned Sokrates in a futile attempt to implicate him in their misdeeds: 'The Thirty summoned me with four others to the Tholos and ordered me to bring Leon from Salamis to be put to death . . . but when we had left the Tholos, while the other four went off to Salamis and brought Leon, I went off home.'[70] The arrest of the moderate Theramenes took place in the

Bouleuterion,[71] and the Thirty condemned 1,400 people to death in trials held in the Painted Stoa.[72] The Thirty were soon replaced by a more moderate oligarchy, but one that was still unacceptable to the democrats, many of whom had gone into exile. A band of these, under Thrasyboulos, seized the border fort at Phyle in 403 BC, a step which led first to civil war and ultimately to the restoration of full democracy. The story is told by Xenophon.[73] Most of the actual fighting took place in Peiraieus, but many of the laws concerning the restoration of the democracy were set up in the Agora. Most important was the decree listing the honours paid to those who first seized Phyle: crowns and grants of money.[74] Other inscriptions record grants of citizenship to foreigners who fought with the democrats,[75] grants of public support for the orphans of 'those of the Athenians who died a violent death in the oligarchy while helping the democracy',[76] and decrees of confiscation of the property of the Thirty and their associates.[77]

Public buildings of the Athenian democracy

CIVIC ACTIVITIES

66 By 400 BC most of the principal buildings needed to house the elements of the Athenian democracy were in place, though some were built slightly earlier and others were remodelled in the 4th century and later. This, therefore, seems the appropriate juncture to describe the public buildings of the Agora and the Athenian constitution, since all aspects of the government – legislature, administration, judiciary, and military – were accommodated in the area.

The New Bouleuterion

68, 91 In the years around 415–406 BC a new Senate House or Bouleuterion was built immediately to the west of the old one. Why a new one was needed is not clear, and not enough of the building is preserved to allow us to determine what advantages it offered over the Old Bouleuterion, which was still standing. The new building was rectangular in shape, measuring 16 m east–west by 22 m *67* north–south. Only a few blocks of the lowest courses of the foundation are preserved, and the arrangements for the seating can be restored in a variety of ways; most likely the senators sat on simple wooden benches, facing south. Pausanias described the building and its furnishings as follows:

Nearby is built a bouleuterion of the 'five hundred', who serve on the council of Athens for a year; in it stand a wooden image of Zeus Boulaios, an Apollo by Peisias and a Demos by Lyson. The Thesmothetai were painted by Protogenes of Kaunos; Olbiades painted the picture of Kallippos, who led the Athenians to Thermopylai to guard against the incursion of the Gauls into Greece.[78]

The five hundred members of the Boule were made up of fifty members from each of the ten tribes, and a study of the lists of senators has shown that seats

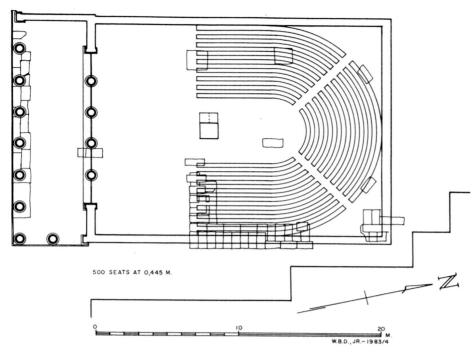

500 SEATS AT 0,445 M.

W.B.D., JR.-1983/4

67 The New Bouleuterion, c. 415–406 BC; restored plan superimposed over actual remains of foundations. The arrangement of the seating is conjectural and the columnar porch a later addition.

were awarded to the demes (townships) on the basis of population, assuring equal representation. The Senate met every day except during festivals and was one of two legislative bodies that were convened regularly. The other, the ekklesia (assembly), was composed of all the citizens (the *demos*) and met about every ten days to vote on the legislation proposed by the Boule. The meeting place for this group was the Pnyx, on the slopes some 400 m southwest of the Agora. The official Athenian decrees reflect this shared responsibility and always begin with the heading: 'Resolved by the boule and the demos of Athens . . . '.

The Metroon

The Old Bouleuterion did not go out of use with the construction of the New, but its function was limited. During the 5th century, when the Boule still met there, the building was used also as the official archives of the city, as is clear from an honorary decree for some Delphians in *c.* 450 BC: 'The Clerk of the Boule shall inscribe their names, on the Acropolis on a stele and in the Bouleuterion, as benefactors of the Athenians.'[79] When the Boule moved from the Old Bouleuterion to the New, perhaps but not certainly between 409 and 405 BC, the archives stayed behind in the Old Bouleuterion, and the building

68, 91

68 (opposite) *Aerial view of the civic buildings along the west side of the Agora. In the centre are the foundations of the Metroon/Bouleuterion. To the left of centre is the area of the New Bouleuterion and to the right are the foundations of the Monument of the Eponymous Heroes. The round shape of the Tholos is readily recognizable at the bottom. Compare ills. 71, 91, 151.*

69 *Small copy in marble of the statue of the Mother of the Gods which stood in the Metroon. The original statue, done by either Pheidias or Agorakritos, was of gold and ivory.*

became known by a new name, the Metroon (Sanctuary of Rhea, Mother of the Olympian Gods).

Just north of the Old Bouleuterion there had been a small archaic temple, burnt by the Persians, apparently dedicated to the Mother of the Gods, a deity imported early on from Phrygia and associated by the Athenians with Rhea. The temple was never rebuilt, but her cult was housed in the Old Bouleuterion: 'We see in the *Philippics* too that part of the bouleuterion the Athenians made the Metroon, the shrine of Rhea.'[80] Here stood a statue of the goddess, done either by Pheidias[81] or his pupil Agorakritos.[82] Arrian describes a similar statue as follows: 'She has a cymbal in her hands and lions beneath the throne and is seated as is the statue of Pheidias in the Metroon at Athens.'[83] Though the original has never been found it must have been popular and well known, for numerous small copies in marble, over one hundred in all, have been found in the excavations, scattered over the whole area.

Within Rhea's keeping were the official records of the city, and for some reason she was regarded as the appropriate protector of the laws, as we learn from Deinarchos in a speech delivered in 323 BC: 'He deposited an agreement with the people, in the keeping of the Mother of the Gods, who is established as guardian for the city of all the rights recorded in the documents.'[84] Over fifty such references in the ancient sources describe a full range of documents kept in the building: laws, decrees, records of lawsuits, financial accounts, lists of ephebes, sacred offerings, and weights and measures. None of the archives have actually been found since most of them must have been kept on papyrus or some such perishable material. These were the official texts, from which more permanent copies were often made on stone stelai to be set up in a public place.

150

The old complex was finally replaced in the years around 140 BC by a larger building which covered both the Old Bouleuterion/Metroon and the ruins of the archaic temple to the north, its foundations set right on the walls of its predecessors. The new building consisted of four rooms set side by side, the northernmost a peristyle courtyard open to the sky. Across the front of all four rooms, uniting them architecturally, was a colonnade of the Ionic order facing east, overlooking the Agora square. Only the heavy foundations of large reddish conglomerate blocks survive today, so the exact arrangement of the rooms is not clear, though from Pausanias and other late sources it is clear that the new building still housed both the shrine of the Mother and the archives of the city.

The Tholos

68, 51

Immediately to the south of the Metroon and New Bouleuterion lay the large round building known as the Tholos, or the Skias. The name is explained by Ammonios who wrote: 'The place where the Prytaneis eat is called Tholos; but by some it is called Skias, because it is built in this fashion, round like a sun-hat.'[85] It served an important civic function as the headquarters of the executive committee (prytaneis) of the Boule. Each contingent of fifty men from each of the ten tribes which made up the five hundred members of the senate served in rotation as its executive committee, responsible for day-to-day administration, the schedule, order of business, and so on. During the thirty-five or thirty-six days that a tribal contingent held this presidency its members were fed in the Tholos at public expense; it served, then, primarily as a dining chamber for fifty senators at a time. In addition, at least one-third of that tribal contingent was expected to be on duty in the building at all times, so at least seventeen senators actually slept there at night. This meant that if some emergency arose, either within the city or as a result of news from abroad, there were senators available at all times, ready to deal with it. Thus the Tholos in a sense represents the heart of the Athenian democracy, where common citizens were always on duty serving as senators.

If it is clear from the written sources that the building was used as a dining hall, it is difficult to find a suitable arrangement for its furniture. Greeks usually ate reclining on couches; at least that is the way diners are regularly shown on vase-paintings, and numerous rooms have been found all over Greece that were fitted with dining couches. There is, however, no good arrangement whereby fifty dining couches can be made to fit in the building. A recent suggestion offers a possible solution. In many sanctuaries where ritual dining occurred it seems likely that tents or round buildings were used and that the diners ate sitting up. If a similar practice were the case here then all fifty

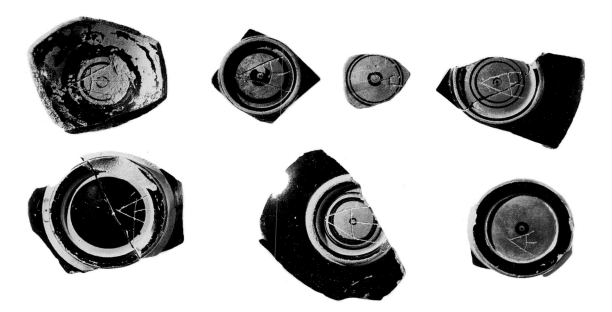

70 Fragments of public dining ware of the 5th century BC, marked with the ligature Æ for demosion, meaning 'public property'. Deposits of official dining sets, mostly drinking vessels, have been found near the Tholos, where the senators dined, and the Royal Stoa, where high magistrates ate.

diners could easily be accommodated, seated on a bench running around the inner face of the wall. Two small rooms built onto the north side of the Tholos may have served as the kitchen and pantry. The meals were probably fairly modest, if we may judge from the early menu known from the Prytaneion, where ambassadors, high officials, and priest were fed: in early times they were served simply cheese, barley cakes, olives, leeks, and wine, although by the late 5th century the menu also included fish and meat. Some of the crockery used at these public meals in the Tholos has been recovered from the vicinity of the building. The pieces, simple black-glazed cups, bowls, and pitchers, have a ligature scratched or painted on them, Æ , for *demosion* (public), presumably so that the senators would not inadvertently walk off with the official table settings.

   If we look backwards in time, the function and location of the Tholos help to shed light on the history of Building F, which lies immediately below. As suggested earlier, Building F, with its plan of a large private house, may well have served originally as the palace of the Peisistratids. Following their expulsion in 510 BC and the institution of the constitution of Kleisthenes in 508/7, how appropriate that the tyrants' very dining hall should now be used to feed the senators of the new democracy! Building F was then burnt by the Persians in 480, to be replaced soon after on the same spot by the Tholos, where senatorial dining continued for hundreds of years.

70

22, 27

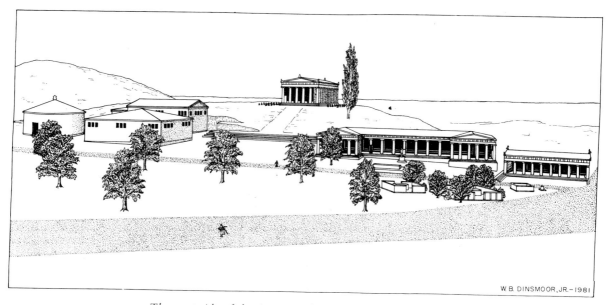

W.B. DINSMOOR, JR. – 1981

71 The west side of the Agora in about 400 BC, looking across the square and the Panathenaic Way. Restored view showing, from left to right, the Tholos, the Metroon/Old Bouleuterion, the New Bouleuterion behind, the seats of the 'Synedrion' or meeting-place, the Hephaisteion (above), the Stoa of Zeus, and the Royal Stoa. Together these buildings represent the centre of the Athenian democracy, housing high magistrates, the senate, and the archives.

71   Thus in the Tholos/Bouleuterion complex we have what may rightly be regarded as the centre of the Athenian democracy. In one the representatives of all the people met every day, and in the other a group of senators representing the rule of the people were on duty twenty-four hours a day. The significance of the Tholos as the actual seat of government was not lost on the Thirty Tyrants when they were installed in power by the Spartans at the end of the Peloponnesian War in 404 BC. As we have seen, while they used the Painted Stoa as a tribunal from which they sentenced 1,400 people to death, their headquarters during their short-lived administration was the Tholos.

Pausanias had little to say of the Tholos; he remarked only that he saw some small silver statues in it. Other sources record that it was also the repository of official weights and measures, the standards against which commercial weights and measures were made and tested in the Agora.

The Tholos is also of value in our understanding of the topography of the Agora. As the only round building of appropriate date, it provides a secure fixed point in determining Pausanias' route along the west side. With the Royal Stoa at the beginning and the Tholos at the end of his account, the other buildings such as the Metroon and Bouleuterion can be identified. Without Pausanias, the Bouleuterion would be hard to recognize because of its poor state of preservation, and there is nothing about the plan of the Metroon that would allow us to know that it once housed the archives of the city.

The Eponymous Heroes

Associated with the Metroon and its permanent archival collection was an unusual monument used for more ephemeral record-keeping, the monument   68
of the Eponymous Heroes. The earliest references to such a monument go back to Aristophanes in the 420s BC, although the monument in its present location immediately east of the Metroon, along the west side of the Agora square, dates only to the years around 330 BC.

The monument of the Eponymous Heroes is yet another indication of the significance of the Kleisthenic reforms of 508/7 BC for the development of full Athenian democracy. In his attempt to break up the old power structure, Kleisthenes abolished the use of the four old Ionian tribes and created in their stead ten new ones. All the citizens were assigned to one of these tribes, which   6
were made up of members from each of the three geographical regions of city, coast, and inland. All rights and many of one's privileges depended on membership in one of the new tribes. Citizenship in Athens required prior enrolment in one of the tribes, and such membership was hereditary. One served in the Boule as a member of a tribe, and one fought in the army – where one's life literally depended in part on the shield of the next man in line – in a tribal contingent. There were certain privileges as well: common grazing land, for instance, reserved for members of a given tribe, as well as sacrifices conducted by a tribe in honour of its eponymous hero. The significance of the common sacrifices should not be underestimated since sacrifices in antiquity often meant a feast, one of those rare occasions for many Athenians when meat was eaten. The killing of the animal represented the actual sacrifice, and the gods generally seem to have been content with the smell of roasting flesh; what became of the cooked meat seems not to have concerned them greatly. Usually the officiating priest was given a share as a fee, and the rest of the animal was eaten by the participants in the sacrifice. Fighting, feasting, and enjoying the privileges of citizenship together forged new bonds of loyalty with fellow tribesmen, even though they were from different areas of Attica and belonged to different clans, and the tribal system should thus be seen as an essential feature of the Athenian democracy.

Having created his ten tribes, Kleisthenes then sent to Apollo's oracle at Delphi the names of one hundred early Athenian heroes, and the oracle picked ten, after whom the ten tribes were named. Hence the term eponymous, which means giving one's name to something; for example, the tribe Leontis is named after the hero Leos. The ten original tribes were Hippothontis, Antiochis, Aiantis, Leontis, Erechtheis, Aigeis, Oineis, Akamantis, Kekropis, and Pandionis.

The 4th-century monument of the Eponymous Heroes was a long statue   72, 73
base which carried bronze statues of the ten heroes, with tripods at either end

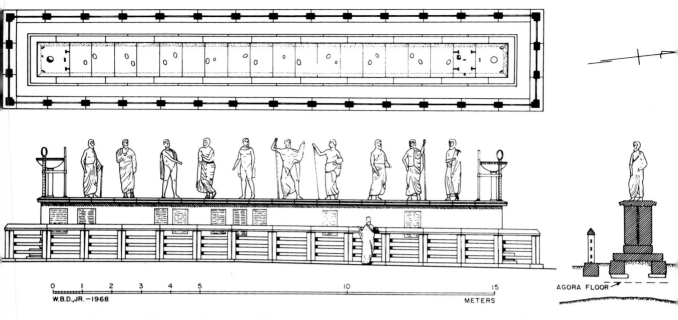

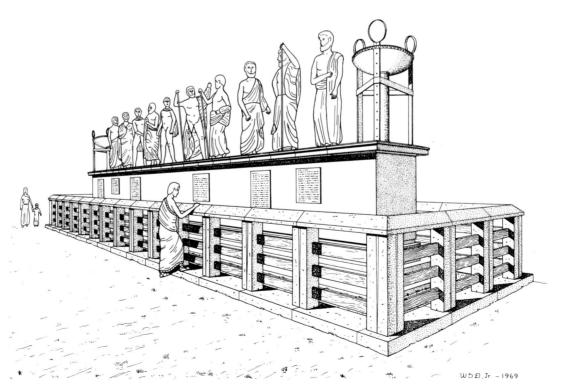

72 Restored plan and elevation of the Monument of the Eponymous Heroes, c. 330 BC, showing public notices hanging on the base beneath the statues. The statues are long gone and only two of the original twenty blocks which made up the top of the base survive.

73 Restored perspective of the Monument of the Eponymous Heroes.

presumably to reflect the Delphic role in their selection. They stood on a high pedestal, *c.* 16.64 m long and 1.87 m wide, and the whole base was surrounded by a barrier of stone fence posts with wooden railings. Preserved today is most of the sill of the surrounding fence, several posts of marble and limestone, five blocks from the lower part of the base, and two marble blocks from its top.

The monument was one of the few permitted to stand within the limits of the Agora square, near the seat of government, as an embodiment of the Athenian tribal system. It fulfilled a practical function as well, for it served as a public notice board; notices concerning members of the tribes would be hung on the front of the base beneath the appropriate tribal hero. Thus under the statue of Leos a member of the tribe of Leontis would find relevant notices, such as lists for military conscription, public honours, upcoming court hearings, and the like. More general announcements were also posted; in particular, legislation to be submitted to the ekklesia (assembly) was published at the Eponymoi several days before the meeting so that citizens would have an opportunity to consider and discuss the proposals before voting.[86] In the days before radio and television, newspapers and the telephone, the monument of the Eponymous Heroes was a crucial element in the dissemination of official information and yet another reason why the average citizen who lived in the city itself would have occasion to visit the Agora almost every day.

74 Monument of the Eponymous Heroes viewed from the south, showing the sill of the fence which surrounded the base for the statues. In the foreground is the addition made for the statue of Hadrian when he was made an Eponymous Hero in the 2nd century AD.

Major changes were made to the monument starting as early as the generation after its erection. These modifications reflect changes in the tribal system itself and will be noted when we come to consider the Agora of Hellenistic and Roman times. The long history of the monument indicates that it remained an important focal point of civic administration for over 500 years.

The 'Synedrion'

Just to the north of the Old Bouleuterion there was another meeting-place. Set into the east slope of Kolonos Agoraios were four rows of yellowish soft poros blocks, each row some 25 m in length and 1.6 m wide. Altogether they could easily have seated well over 200 people. They were installed in the 5th century BC and remained in use at least until the late 4th century, at which time the area in front was greatly restricted by the construction of a small temple identified as that of Apollo Patroos. Though of modest construction, these seats are in a central location and presumably served some important function. Indeed, it has been suggested that they were used as a lawcourt. An inscription[87] and literary references[88] suggest the location of a synedrion (meeting-place) in the vicinity and it might be well to regard these seats as such a place, used not only as a lawcourt but also by various groups sitting in an official capacity.

The Royal Stoa

As we have already seen, the Royal Stoa or Stoa Basileios was probably first built in the Archaic period, apparently towards the end of the 6th century BC. If so, it was badly damaged in the Persian sack of 480, and extensively rebuilt in the 5th century.

Here the second in command of the Athenian government, the king archon (basileus) held office. Assisted by two *paredroi* (assessors), he was responsible for religious matters and the laws as is clear from Aristotle's description of his role:

The *basileus* is first responsible for the Mysteries, in conjunction with the overseers elected by the people . . . also for the Dionysia at the Lenaion, which involves a procession and a contest. . . . He also organizes all the torch-races and one might say that he administers all the traditional sacrifices. Public lawsuits fall to him on charges of impiety, and when a man is involved in a dispute with someone over a priesthood. He holds the adjudications for clans and for priests in all their disputes on religious matters. Also all private suits for homicide fall to him.[89]

These religious and legal aspects of the king's duties are reflected in the furnishings of the building itself. The herm base set up on the steps of the building in about 400 BC to commemorate Onesippos' term as king archon is a good example, for it records also the winners in the theatrical contests of the Lenaia held in that same year. Under the notations 'Comedy' and 'Tragedy' we read the names of the winning producers (Sosikrates in comedy, Stratonikos in tragedy) and playwrights (Nikochares and Megakleides). The comic poet

75 *The lithos, or oath-stone, which stood in front of the Royal Stoa, where all incoming magistrates swore an oath of office. In the background is the north wall of the stoa, and in the foreground a terracotta drain of the 4th century BC.*

Nikochares is known to be a contemporary of Aristophanes, having lost to the latter's *Plutus* in 388 BC, so we may date Onesippos' term of office to the late 5th or early 4th century BC. The base thus stands as one of our earliest recorded 'Academy Awards', in the days when theatre was sacred to Dionysos and administered by the king archon, Athens' chief religious magistrate.

Immediately in front of the building there is a large unworked block of hard limestone, measuring 0.95 m by 2.95 m, of no particular distinction or merit. 75 Despite its unprepossessing appearance we must assume that the stone had some special significance, given its prominent location, placed in such a way as to block access to almost a quarter of the length of this important old building. Several ancient sources refer to an oath taken by various magistrates and tell us that it was administered at a *lithos* (stone), near the Royal Stoa in the Agora: 'They took the oath near the Basileios Stoa, on the stone on which were the parts of the victims, swearing that they would guard the laws.'[90] Plutarch wrote: 'The council took a joint oath to ratify the laws of Solon, and each of the thesmothetes swore separately at the stone in the Agora.'[91] This, then, would seem to be the lithos where all incoming magistrates swore allegiance before taking office, and it may well be that the stone, which has an early look to it, actually goes back to the time of Solon or earlier, in which case it would predate the stoa and may have actually determined its placement. The

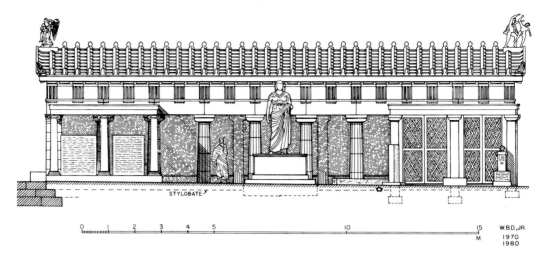

76 *The Royal Stoa in about 300 BC, showing the addition of two wings at either end, built in part to display the inscribed law-code. In front is the monumental marble statue of Themis, goddess of justice, erected in about 330 BC.*

attractive suggestion has been made that the lithos is in fact a lintel block from a Mycenaean tholos tomb.

Aristotle, writing in the 4th century BC, actually says that the laws were inscribed and set up in the building at the time of Solon:

He [Solon] established a constitution and made other laws, and they ceased to observe the ordinances of Drako, except those relating to homicide. They wrote up the laws on *kyrbeis* and set them up in the Royal Stoa and all swore to observe them. The nine

77 *A fragment of the inscribed law-code or constitution of Athens which was set up in the Royal Stoa at the end of the 5th century BC. The section illustrated here is a calendar of official state sacrifices to the gods.*

78 Monumental statue of an allegorical figure, probably Themis (goddess of justice), set up in front of the Royal Stoa in about 330 BC. Compare ill. 76.

archons, taking an oath at the stone, declared that they would set up a golden statue if they transgressed any of the laws.[92]

The archaeological evidence does not seem to indicate that the building is as old as the time of Solon (though the stone might well be), but it is clear that both Stoa and stone were firmly connected in Athenian minds with the earliest laws of the city. Indeed, towards the end of the 5th century, after the city had undergone several changes from democratic to oligarchic constitutions and back again during the Peloponnesian War, it was decided to draw up an official version of the laws, based on the old laws of Drako (7th BC) and Solon (6th BC), and to inscribe them on stone and set them up at the stoa. The man in charge, Nikomachos, was attacked in a speech by the orator Lysias for being too slow, and the process seems to have taken up much of the last decade of the 5th century, a time of further constitutional crises. Andokides mentions this new codification of the laws several times[93] and we have also a copy on marble of the old law concerning homicide by Drako (? 621 BC), which was set up in 409/8 BC;[94] the publication clause reads as follows: 'The law concerning homicide is to be inscribed by the inscribers of the laws, after they have received it from the secretary of the Boule for the prytany, on a stone stele, and placed in front of the Stoa Basileios.' Other pieces of the revised law code have come to light in the excavations and are housed in the store-rooms; they list official state sacrifices and a law concerning administration of the fleet. The building itself shows evidence of the placement of these laws. Traces of a later fire indicate that a row of large marble stelai were set up against the back wall of the building, forming a continuous wall or revetment which carried many of the laws; Andokides refers specifically to this wall of inscriptions: 'The laws which are approved shall be inscribed on the wall, where they were inscribed before, for anyone who wishes to examine.'[95] In addition, two wings were built on to either end of the façade to provide additional display areas. They take the form of columnar porches, and between the columns were set more stelai, opisthographic (inscribed on both faces), which could be read from inside or outside the annexes. Thus by the years around 400 BC the Royal Stoa was the repository of an official copy of the constitution of Athens, inscribed on stone and set up in public where it could be consulted by any citizen.

Other furnishings accommodated the king archon, his paredroi (assistants), and others taking part in the official proceedings. These included several sets of thrones which originally stood inside or in front of the stoa. An early set was made of limestone, replaced in the 4th century by a series in marble. Just how many people may have had to be provided for is not clear, but by the 4th century BC as large a body as the council of the Areopagos is known to have met in the building. If we may trust Aristophanes, the stoa was also used for official dining: 'The herald will make a proclamation that those from Section Beta shall follow to the Stoa Basileios to dine . . . '.[96] That this is not mere fantasy by the comic poet is clear from the discovery behind the building of a pit full of official dining ware similar to that usually associated with the

77

Tholos. Fragments of hundreds of vases were recovered, including cooking ware and animal bones of the sort discarded in a kitchen dump. By far the greatest number of vases were for drinking, however, and parts of 600 cups were found, along with sixty-eight mixing bowls for wine, together with amphoras in which the highly prized wine of Chios was transported. The official nature of all this partying is attested by the ligature scratched on several of the cups: Ⅎ for demosion (public property), the same symbol as was used in the Tholos dining ware. Much of the material is high-quality painted red-figure ware, and the deposit as a whole dates from about 465 to 425 BC. Just where the diners ate is not clear, though it is worth noting that in the original plan there was a foundation c. 0.79 m wide which ran around the interior face of all three walls and could easily have held benches or couches for dining.

The Stoa was also the setting for events which led to the trial and death of Sokrates. What occurred in the Royal Stoa in 399 BC was the indictment, the preliminary arguments which led to the trial, as we learn from Plato, who quoted Sokrates himself: 'Now I must present myself at the stoa of the Basileus to answer the indictment which Meletos has brought against me.'[97] The philosopher was tried for impiety, for importing new gods into the city, for corrupting the youth of Athens. These were religious matters and as such fell under the jurisdiction of the king archon, who would hear the charges and, if there was sufficient cause, collect the evidence, assign the case to a court, and so on. The actual trial took place in one of the lawcourts of the city, at a spot not as yet identified, and the eventual execution was carried out in the prison.

A large base of four squared blocks of conglomerate was installed in a central position immediately in front of the Stoa in the second half of the 4th century BC. These clearly represent the foundations for the base of a large statue, and the probable occupant was found built into a Byzantine wall immediately above. She is a large draped lady of Pentelic marble, preserved from neck to knee and originally about 3 m tall. She probably represents an allegorical concept of the kind that became popular in the 4th century. Two suggestions have been made for her identification: Themis, goddess of Justice, or Demokratia, a statue of whom is known to have stood in the Agora. Either goddess would be suitable here in front of this building so intimately associated with the laws by which the Athenian democracy was ruled, though Themis is to be preferred.

The Stoa of Zeus Eleutherios
Immediately adjacent to the Royal Stoa was the Stoa of Zeus, which Pausanias described as follows:

Behind is built a stoa with paintings of the gods called twelve. On the wall opposite is painted Theseus, and also Demokratia and Demos. . . . Here is also a picture of the exploit at Mantineia of the Athenians who were sent to help the Lacedaimonians. . . . In the picture is a cavalry battle, in which the most notable figures are, among the

79 The Stoa of Zeus Eleutherios, c. 430–420 BC, in a restored view.

Athenians, Grylos, the son of Xenophon, and in the Boeotian cavalry, Epaminondas the Theban. These pictures were painted for the Athenians by Euphranor, who also made the Apollo called Patroos in the temple nearby.'[98]

79   The stoa was a handsome building of the Doric order with two projecting wings. The style of the preserved architectural fragments and the pottery found in its construction fill suggest that the stoa was built in the decade 430–420 BC. Unlike most of the Classical buildings around the square, its façade was of Pentelic marble. This may be explained by the unusual nature of the building itself. It was dedicated to Zeus Eleutherios (Freedom) and thus was a religious structure, yet it takes the form of a common civic building, the stoa, rather than that of a temple. The cult of Zeus Eleutherios is said to have been founded after the final battle of the Persian wars at Plataia in 479, when mainland Greece was freed from the threat of Persian dominance. This association with freedom was maintained by the Athenians, who adorned the building with the shields of those who died fighting for the freedom of Athens. Pausanias recorded two different examples of dedications of shields from the early 3rd century BC: 'When he fell in battle, honours were paid to him by the Athenians; amongst other things they dedicated his shield to Zeus Eleutherios, inscribing on it the name of Leokritos and his achievement';[99] and

The Attic contingent surpassed the other Greeks in valour that day [Thermopylai, 279 BC] and of the Athenians the greatest prowess was shown by Kydias, a young man then going into battle for the first time. He was killed by the Gauls, and his family dedicated his shield to Eleutherios Zeus, with the inscription, 'Here am I dedicated, yearning for the young manhood of Kydias, the shield of an illustrious man, an offering to Zeus, the first shield through which he stretched his left arm, on the day when furious war against the Gaul reached its height.' This was the inscription on the shield, until Sulla's men removed [86 BC], amongst other things at Athens, the shields in the stoa of Eleutherios Zeus.[100]

Like the Painted Stoa, this stoa too was decorated with pictures. Including the Bouleuterion, we have three buildings in the Agora described by Pausanias as adorned with paintings, and many other Athenian buildings (Propylaia, Prytaneion, Pompeion, Erechtheion) were also decorated this way. While almost no examples of this major branch of Greek art survive, one should try to reconstruct them in the mind's eye when imagining many ancient buildings.

The stoa was used by the Athenians as an informal meeting place and it is clear from several passages in Plato and Xenophon that Sokrates would meet his friends and pupils here. Whether it served any official function is not clear. As a religious building, framing a statue of Zeus Eleutherios, it need have had no further use. Its location among the administrative buildings along the west side of the square is suggestive, however, and it may well have housed some administrative boards. If so, it is a good candidate for the Thesmotheteion, where the six thesmothetai (judicial archons) came together to deliberate and, apparently, to dine.

Lawcourts and furnishings

The major political, administrative, and legislative buildings of the Athenian state can be seen to have clustered along the west side of the square. Also associated with the Agora, but more difficult to identify with certainty, were the lawcourts. The Athenians were a litigious people, and many issues, both private and public, were referred to the courts, which played an important role in the government. In describing the constitution of Solon and the new role of the lowest class (Thetes), Plutarch explained the significance of the courts:

All the rest were called Thetes; they were not allowed to hold any office, but took part in the administration only as members of the assembly and as jurors. This last privilege seemed at first of no account, but afterwards proved to be of the very highest importance, since most disputes finally came into the hands of these jurors. For even in

cases which Solon assigned to the magistrates for decision, he allowed also an appeal to a popular court when anyone desired it. Besides, it is said that his laws were obscurely and ambiguously worded on purpose to enhance the power of the popular courts. For since parties to a controversy could not get satisfaction from the laws, the result was that they always wanted jurors to decide it, and every dispute was laid before them, so that they were in a manner masters of the laws.[101]

These courts were large, the smallest Athenian jury comprising 201 men, with much larger courts attested. Sokrates was tried before 501 men, and juries of 1,000, 1,500 and 2,500 are not unheard of. There is considerable documentary evidence concerning the courts: Aristotle in his *Constitution of the Athenians* described an elaborate complex of courts in the 4th century BC, Pausanias included a long list of courts scattered around the city,[102] and we have dozens of speeches of the 5th and 4th centuries BC that have survived from the careers of Demosthenes, Isokrates, Lysias, Aeschines, Hypereides, and Lykourgos. In all, there are over 300 references to Athenian courts in the ancient literature, making them one of the better understood governing bodies of the city.

When it comes to identifying one of these courts physically, however, we run into considerable difficulty, for we do not know what form they took. The actual panel could, and apparently did, meet in a variety of buildings. Nothing has yet come to light which matches Aristotle's description, and Pausanias is unusually disappointing, for he discusses Athenian courts all together in a single passage rather than in his usual manner, in topographical order as he saw them. From the sources, however, it is clear that a few elements were necessary for any court. They must have been large buildings to accommodate the large juries; they usually had seats (of wood); and the juries were separated in some way from outsiders who could nonetheless often overhear the proceedings. Courts were roofed or unroofed, the latter used for cases of homicide, which had to meet in the open.[103] In general, large stoas seem to be the most appropriate form for a lawcourt, and both the Painted Stoa and Basileios are known to have been so used on occasion. The association of at least some of the courts with the bustle and business of the Agora is suggested by a fragment of the comic poet Euboulos: 'You will find everything sold together in the same place at Athens – figs, summoners, bunches of grapes, pears, apples, witnesses, roses, medlars, haggis, honeycombs, chickpeas, lawsuits, beestings, beestings-pudding, myrtle, allotment machines, hyacinth, lambs, water-clocks, laws, indictments.'[104]

29, 99 Two areas of the Agora have some claim to having housed courts. One, in the southwest corner, is the large rectangular enclosure built in the 6th century BC. Poorly preserved, it offers no clue to its function though its size, location, and early date suggest it is an important public building and a lawcourt seems the likeliest identification. A second complex at the northeast corner has a better claim. Here, three large buildings of irregular shape were built at the end of the 5th century BC and replaced in the late 4th century by a large peristyle

80 (opposite) Bronze ballots used in the lawcourts of Athens inscribed 'psephos demosia' ('public ballot'). The ballots were held with thumb and forefinger over the ends of the axles for a secret vote; pierced axles were for guilty and solid for acquitted.

81 'Ballot box' found at the northeast corner of the Agora, under the Stoa of Attalos. The container in which the six bronze ballots (ill. 80) were found is made of two terracotta drain tiles set on end.

courtyard. Any or all of these are large enough to have housed one or more courts. The reason for supposing they might have are the furnishings found in one of the early buildings. Here an installation consisting of two drain tiles set on end formed a crude container or support. In and around it were scattered six bronze disks which can be identified as public ballots, as is clear from the inscriptions incised on them (*psephos demosia*). These ballots came with a central axle which could be solid or pierced all the way through. Each juror entering the court would be issued one of each type of ballot. Having heard the case he would then vote, holding thumb and forefinger over the ends of the axles so that his vote was secret. A pierced axle meant guilty (there's a hole in his story) and solid, acquittal. As the minimum Athenian jury was 201 men and only six ballots were found, we do not know if the last individual tried was guilty or innocent, but their discovery suggests that this is one of the Athenian lawcourts.

Other scattered finds from the excavations apparently represent furnishings of other lawcourts around the Agora. These include allotment machines,

129

81

80

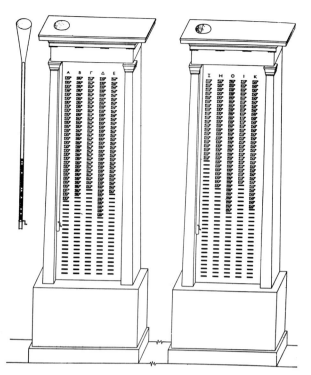

82, 83 Reconstruction (right) and lower half of an actual allotment machine (below), used for the random selection of jurors and magistrates, and a vivid example of the lengths to which the Athenians went to forestall corruption in their democracy. There are vertical rows of slots, one for each of the tribes of Athens, with jurors' tags (pinakia) inserted in them. On the far left is the hollow bronze tube which was placed down the side of the machines, and which contained a random mixture of white and black marbles. If a turn of the crank at the bottom produced a white marble, the first horizontal row of plaques would be selected and those jurors – one from each of the tribes – would be allocated to the court for that day. A black ball meant that those jurors were dismissed for the day. The crank continued to be turned until enough jurors had been appointed.

84 A bronze juror's identification ticket (pinakion) of the 4th century BC, used in an allotment machine for the selection of a jury. The ticket carries the man's name (Demophanes), his father's name (Phil . . .) and deme (Kephisia), as well as an official validating stamp.

water-clocks, and jurors' tickets and identification tags. Most interesting, perhaps, are the *kleroteria* (allotment machines) used both to assign jurors to the courts and to select magistrates. The procedure worked as follows. Each man on jury duty for a given year would be issued a bronze plaque (*pinakion*) which carried an official stamp, the juror's name, his father's name, and the deme or township he belonged to. On the day a trial was to be held the juror would appear before the magistrate in charge of the allotment who was stationed at one of these machines, at the base of which were ten baskets, one for each of the ten tribes. The pinakion would go into the appropriate tribal basket, which would be clear from the deme of the juror. When the time for allotment had come, the magistrate would take all the pinakia from tribe 'A' and put them in the first vertical row of slots in the machine, all the pinakia from tribe 'B' in the second row, and so on until he had placed all the pinakia into slots. Along the side of the machine was a hollow bronze tube, with a funnel at the top and a crank at the bottom. Into the funnel would be poured a mixture of white and black marbles which would line up in the tube in random order. A turn of the crank at the bottom would produce a single ball. If it was white, the ten jurors whose pinakia were set into the first horizontal row would be assigned to the jury for that day and would proceed at once to the court. If it was a black ball, all members in that row were dismissed for the day. The procedure was repeated until a court was filled, selecting ten jurors with every white ball. The machine assured absolutely random selection, both in the order in which the pinakia were placed in the kleroterion and in the order

82, 83

84

85 Working model of the 5th-century water-clock found in the Agora. Such small clocks were used to time speeches in the courts. The example here, belonging to the tribe Antiochis, held 2 choes (6.4 litres) of water and ran for about 6 minutes.

in which the balls appeared. There was no easy way to bribe an Athenian jury, made up as it was of at least 201 men chosen immediately before the court sat. At the same time, the kleroterion chose one juror from each of the ten tribes with each white ball, so that there was equal tribal representation on every court. The machine could also be used to appoint magistrates as well, simply by using a single white ball. As much as any object left to us from antiquity, the kleroterion indicates the lengths to which the Athenians went in trying both to ensure equality and to forestall corruption in their governmental affairs.

Athenian jurors were paid, another democratic procedure designed to ensure that all could afford to serve. Small round bronze tokens or *symbola* were issued to jurors who had been allotted to assure proper payment to the right individuals. Payment was made only at the end of the trial and only upon presentation of the symbolon. Numerous symbola have been found scattered over the whole area; they carry different devices and letters to indicate to which court the juror was assigned.

85 Also recovered from the excavations was a single example of a water-clock or *klepsydra*, used to time speeches in the courts, as we learn from Aristotle: 'There are klepsydras which have small tubes for the outflow; into these they pour the water by which the lawsuits must be conducted.'[105] It is a simple clay vessel with flaring walls, an overflow hole near the top, and a small bronze outlet at the bottom. It would be filled with water, and the speaker spoke until time literally ran out. The limits thus imposed were used for rhetorical effect by the orators, such as Isokrates, who, claiming he could not list all the sins of his opponent, stated, 'Not even if there were twice as much water would it be enough.'[106] The example recovered dates to the years around 400 BC; it carries a painted inscription indicating that it belonged to the tribe Antiochis, and two painted XX's presumably indicate the volume of water it held: 2 *choes* or 6.4 litres. It runs for only 6 minutes and thus represents a short speech, perhaps the second rebuttal in a minor divorce case or the like. The preserved speeches of Demosthenes and other orators, whether on public or private matters, run much longer and there must have been larger clocks to time them. This is clear from the speeches themselves; testimony of witnesses or citation of official documents did not count as part of a speaker's time,[107] and there are repeated requests to stop the water as witnesses take the stand. The experienced orators would keep an eye on the jet of water at the outlet, and as the pressure fell they would bring their speech to an end just as the last drops ran out.[108]

86 A final item of dikastic equipment was discovered in the 1970s and only recently interpreted. It is at first glance the most modest of artifacts, the simple lid of an unglazed clay cooking pot, known as an *echinos*, of the 4th century BC. However, the letters painted on the top which refer to the contents are unusual. Though the text is fragmentary, it seems to list documents stored in the pot until needed for a trial. The text reads: 'Of the written copies, the following four are inside: testimony [*diamartyria*] from the arbitration [*anakrisis*], law on the abuse of heiresses, challenge of testimony, oaths of

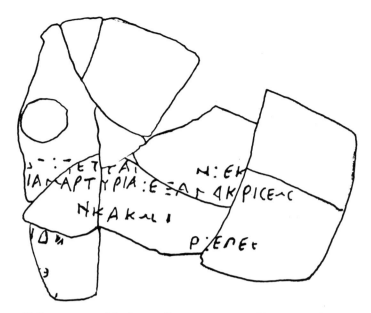

86 Fragmentary lid of a small coarse-ware cooking pot with a painted inscription listing the documents sealed inside for presentation as testimony in a trial, 4th century BC.

litigants. Antenor put the lid on.'[109] These would seem to be the documents resulting from an arbitration at which conflicting testimony was given, leading to a full trial for false witnesses. Such documents had to be officially sealed so that different testimony could not be given at the trial, as we learn from Plato: 'When a witness' testimony is challenged, the magistrates are to keep the challenges, which have been sealed up by both parties to the action, and produce them at the trial for false witness.'[110] Thus this lid joins the kleroteria, pinakia, symbola, ballots, and klepsydras as part of the furnishings of those Athenian lawcourts which lay near the Agora.

The state prison

Associated with the lawcourts was the prison, which may have stood near the Agora, although we are not told so specifically by any ancient source. A possible candidate for the building is located outside the southwest corner of the square, not far from the 6th-century lawcourt (?). The large size of the building, *c.* 40 by 17 m, suggests that it probably served a public function, though its ground-plan is not like that of any known public building. More often than not in Greek architecture form and function are related, and temples, theatres, stoas, and gymnasia are readily recognizable from their form, even when in ruins. Here, a long corridor leads back to a large courtyard; five square rooms open off one side of the corridor, and three off the other. At the entrance there is a complex of four rooms, built on a different

87
88

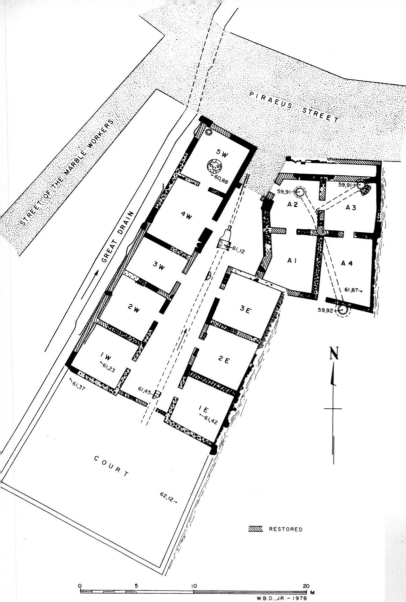

The state prison

87 A restored plan of what may have
been the state prison, mid-5th
century BC. Provisions for bathing
were found in the northwest room
(5W), and thirteen medicine bottles
in the northeast room (A3), perhaps
containers for the draughts of
hemlock used to dispatch prisoners.

88 (right) General view of the
building from the north after
excavations in 1977. The large jar
(pithos) set into the floor at the
lower right was used for the storage
of water.

89 Medicine bottles from a cistern
in the prison, perhaps used to
hold the hemlock employed in
executions.

90 Small marble statuette, possibly of Sokrates, found in the ruins of the prison, where the philosopher died after being poisoned with hemlock in 399 BC. Height, as preserved, 10 cm.

orientation but apparently contemporary. Set in an industrial area, the structure has a plan suitable for a market building or *xenon* (hostel), but the arrangement would work nicely for a prison as well. The square rooms would serve as cells, the large courtyard for multiple arrests, and the single entrance is controlled by the complex of four rooms that could be the guards' quarters. Built in the mid-5th century BC, the building fronts on a major street, lies down in a hollow, and had provisions for bathing, all of which correspond to what we know of the prison from ancient sources.

While the Athenians did not generally sentence people to long jail terms, usually preferring fines, exile, or death as penalties, the prison housed some notable figures, including at least some of the 292 Spartans captured at Pylos in 425/4 BC,[111] Andokides and thirty-nine others accused of mutilating herms or profaning the Mysteries in 415 BC,[112] and Phocion and other generals in 318 BC.[113] By far the most famous detainee, however, was Sokrates, who was executed in 399 BC by means of a draught of hemlock, an infusion made from a herbaceous plant of the carrot family. His confinement and execution in the prison are described in some detail by Plato, whose dialogues shed considerable light on the building where Sokrates was held. The identification as the prison is strengthened by the discovery within the building of thirteen little clay medicine bottles, thrown down an abandoned cistern. In all the years of excavating in the Agora only twenty-one such bottles have come to light; thirteen in one place is a suspicious concentration. One cannot argue that they indicate the building was a hospital or the like; if one were really sick in antiquity one went to the local shrine of Asklepios to be cured, in Athens south of the Acropolis by the theatre. It has been suggested that the bottles were used to hold the hemlock with which the prisoners were dispatched, since we know that the doses of poison were individually mixed and carefully measured out. A small statuette of Sokrates himself found in the ruins of the building perhaps indicates a small memorial to the philosopher, set up in the building by the Athenians, who soon realized their mistake in executing one of the great thinkers of Classical Athens.

89

90

MILITARY ACTIVITIES

The Strategeion

Another important element in the administration of the Athenian state was the military. The fleet was administered in the port at Peiraieus although under the supervision of the Boule in Athens. The army was managed by the polemarch, third archon of Athens after the eponymous and king, together with ten generals, one elected from each of the tribes. In their attempt to ensure equality, the Athenians by the 5th century allotted most offices, even the highest archonships. Some positions, however, such as treasurers and the water commissioner, were simply too important to be left to the luck of the

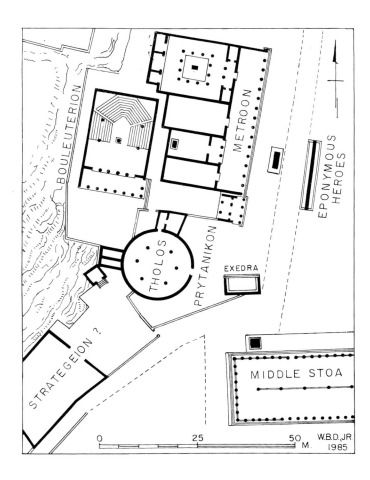

91 *The southwest corner of the Agora, showing the Metroon/Bouleuterion/Tholos complex. The location of the building tentatively identified as the generals' headquarters (Strategeion) is at the lower left. To judge from the numerous inscriptions found in the area, the state auctioneers (poletai) also held office somewhere in the vicinity.*

draw; these remained elective and therefore became the real positions of power whereby a politician demonstrated popular support and remained in office for many years. The generalships are the clearest example of this practice, and many of the leading statesmen of Athens held the position. Perikles, for instance, never served as eponymous archon – nominally the highest post in the state – but he was elected general of his tribe year after year, and from that position guided Athenian affairs for decades.

The generals (*strategoi*, leaders of the army) held office in a building known 91 as the Strategeion, which stood in or near the Agora apparently not far from the other public office buildings. Several inscriptions honouring military officers which were set up in front of the Strategeion have been found near the southwest corner of the square, and the building should probably be sought somewhere in the vicinity. Though we have no firm candidate, the scanty remains of a building of the 5th century just southwest of the Tholos are of an appropriate date and location and have been tentatively identified as the headquarters of the strategoi. Nikias, one of the generals during the

Peloponnesian War, worked hard in the building: 'He did not dine with any of his fellow-citizens, or take part in gathering for discussion or recreation; he had no leisure for any such activities; when in office he remained in the strategeion till night-fall.'[114] One of his fellow generals was the playwright Sophokles: 'The story is told that once in the Strategeion when he and his colleagues were discussing some question, he bade the poet Sophokles give his opinion first, as being the senior general; "I" said Sophokles, "am the oldest in years, but you are senior in honour."'[115]

The army was made up primarily of Athenian citizens, though mercenaries were used also, particulary in Hellenistic times. Citizens were enrolled at the beginning of the new year after their eighteenth birthday. They spent their first two years as ephebes (cadets) during which period they served full-time, training and on guard duty. Thereafter they returned to daily life, though they remained liable for conscription for the next forty years, until their sixtieth year. Lists of the ephebes were posted near the Eponymous Heroes, first on painted boards, and by the 4th century on bronze stelai.[116] When an army was being conscripted, the lists of citizens drafted would also be posted by year of enrolment at or near the Eponymoi, not far from the Strategeion.

Other small finds from the Agora remind us of the administration of the army. Among these are two small rectangular plaques of clay, tokens stamped with the name and title of a military officer: 'Xenokles of Perithoidai the Peripolarch'. The peripolarch was the military officer responsible for frontier garrisons and patrolling the borders. The tokens, which date to the 4th century BC, must have been used in some official way, perhaps as the credentials of messengers going to and from the frontier.

The Hipparcheion

An important, élite element of the Athenian army was the cavalry (*hippeis*). Throughout antiquity and the Middle Ages it was a mark of honour and prestige to fight on horseback, a privilege of the upper classes, or knights. We have seen evidence of this distinction in the early Agora graves of the 9th and 8th centuries BC, and in later times this corps was administered by its own officers, the hipparchs, who sat in a separate office known as the Hipparcheion. To judge from the find-spots of inscriptions which were set up in front of this building, it should be sought somewhere not far from the northwest corner of the Agora. Indeed this whole part of town has very close connections with the cavalry, and it appears as though the knights actually trained along the broad Panathenaic Way at this point, near the herms. The open spaces of any agora were ideal for training horses, and Pausanias wrote that in the city of Elis, 'The present name of the Agora is the Hippodrome, and the natives train their horses there.'[117] That the Athenian Agora was also used in this way is clear from a fragment of the comic poet Mnesimachos, who wrote in the 4th century BC: 'Go forth, Manes, to the Agora, to the Herms, the place frequented by the phylarchs, and to their handsome pupils, whom

92 (left) *Terracotta token of the 4th century* BC *belonging to the border commander (peripolarch), Xenokles of Perithoidai. Such tokens were presumably used as passports to the border and for messengers reporting to and from military headquarters.*

93 (right) *Terracotta tokens of Pheidon, the cavalry commander (hipparch) at Lemnos, who was responsible for training the cavalry recruits along the Panathenaic Way; 4th century* BC, *found in the crossroads well.*

Pheidon trains in mounting and dismounting.'[118] In a remarkable example of a correlation between literary and archaeological evidence, the name of the trainer Pheidon appears on a series of small round clay tokens which were found discarded in the well along the Panathenaic Way at the northwest corner of the square. In all, some thirty disks were found, carefully stamped 'Pheidon the hipparch at Lemnos', an island dependency of Athens. Presumably the tokens were used in some messenger system, similar to that of Xenokles the Peripolarch, and they surely refer to the same cavalry officer mentioned in the comedy of Mnesimachos.

57
93

Nor are these tokens the only material relevant to the cavalry to have been recovered from the crossroads well. Found with them at two separate levels were the actual archives of the cavalry. These take the form of thin lead tablets inscribed with a man's name, the colour of his horse, a description of the horse's brand, and a price: 'Of Arkesos, black, with a snake, 700 drachmas' or 'Of Konon, a chestnut, with a centaur, 700 drachmas'. Such tablets were clearly used for the annual assessment of the cavalry, which apparently would then form the basis of a reimbursement by the state should the horse be lost in battle. At the end of the year, of course, these records would become obsolete and could be reused or discarded, as in the case of those found in the well. Two

94

94 *A lead strip from the cavalry archive of the 4th century* BC *recording the registration of a horse belonging to Konon, chestnut in colour, bearing the brand of a centaur, and valued at 700 drachmas. The horses of the cavalry were assessed in this fashion every year. Several dozen of these tablets were found in the public well at the northwest corner of the Agora.*

95 Bronze tokens of the mid-3rd century BC showing items of armour (helmet, breastplate, greaves) distributed by the state to members of the cavalry; found in the public well at the northwest corner of the Agora.

series were recovered: one group of twenty-six tablets dating to 350–340 BC, and a second group of eighty-five, dating to *c.* 250 BC. These could be supplemented by a similar group found by German archaeologists at the Dipylon gate, some 400 m to the northwest. Together they reveal much about the composition of the Athenian cavalry. We learn, for instance, that the corps, which numbered 1,000 men by law in the 5th and 4th centuries BC, showed a rapid decline in numbers in the 3rd century, a time of civil war and foreign domination. In 282/1 BC there were 300 knights, but by *c.* 250 BC barely 200 men are listed. One learns a bit about ancient horse-trading as well: the maximum assessment was 1,200 drachmas, well below the value of many horses and representing the maximum limit of the state's liability; the minimum amount was 500 drachmas (1 drachma equalled a day's wage). When an ageing horse reached that lower limit, we find the owner returning the following year with a new horse. On average, an Athenian horse of the 3rd century BC depreciated at the rate of 100 drachmas a year.

95   Still more material relating to the cavalry was recovered from the crossroads well: a series of nine round lead tokens dating to the mid-3rd century BC. On one side they are stamped with representations of armour: helmet, shield, breastplate, or greaves; on the other side, a single large letter: A, Γ, or Δ . These apparently served for the issuing of armour owned by the state to members of the army or, in this case, the cavalry. The Athenian state owned huge amounts of armour either donated by individuals or captured in battle. While members of the army were usually expected to arm themselves, there are numerous instances recorded of the state providing some if not all of their equipment and these tokens must have come into play in such circumstances.

Hippic activity in the northwest corner is further suggested by the discovery in the area of several sculptured monuments set up to celebrate victories in cavalry displays. One was found just behind the Royal Stoa in 1891 during work on the extension of the Athens–Peiraieus railway. It is signed by Bryaxis, one of the sculptors of the Mausoleum of Halicarnassos, and shows on each of

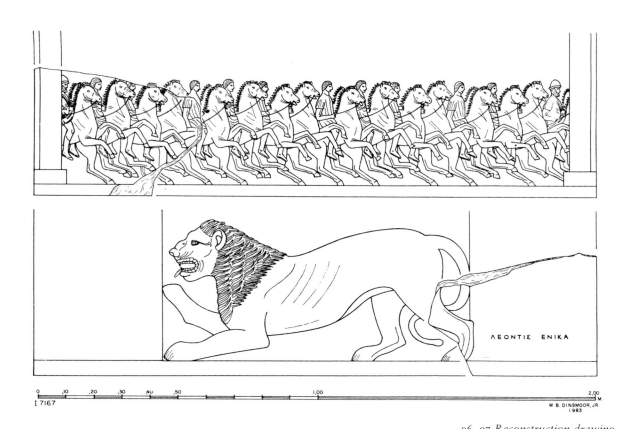

ΛΕΟΝΤΙΣ ΕΝΙΚΑ

I 7167

W. B. DINSMOOR, JR.
1983

96, 97 Reconstruction drawing (above) and surviving fragment (left) of the victory monument showing a display of the Athenian cavalry. On one side is depicted the winning troop of horsemen, and on the other a lion, a punning reference to the name of Leontis, the victorious tribe.

121

three sides a mounted horseman approaching a tripod, symbol of victory. The fourth side carries the artist's signature along with the inscription which says that the monument celebrated a victory by Demainetos and his two sons, Demeas and Demosthenes, in the *anthippasia*, a cavalry display which was part of the Panathenaic games.

A second cavalry piece, built into a late wall just behind the Royal Stoa, came to light in 1970. It is a relief, carved on both sides. One side carried the figure of a lion, only partially preserved today, intended as a punning reference to the name of the winning tribe, Leontis, which is inscribed alongside the lion together with the word *enika* (was victorious). The other side shows the cavalry display itself, several young men riding forth, followed by a bearded older man. Presumably we have here an illustration of normal cavalry procedure: the best man is up front, leading the contingent, and the second officer rides at the rear, well positioned to be in the lead should a sudden about-face become necessary.[119]

Pausanias recorded a trophy set up by the Athenian cavalry in this part of town,[120] and several more fragmentary reliefs and inscriptions concerning the cavalry have also been found in the same area. Together with the archives, Pheidon's tokens, the armour tokens, and the sculpted reliefs, they form a significant concentration indicating that the Hipparcheion should in all probability be sought just outside the northwest limits of the square.

COMMERCIAL ACTIVITIES

The state had a role in the commerce and finances of the city; here too the Agora was the focal point as the true business centre or market-place of the city. Much of this commercial activity took place in small private shops and workrooms immediately outside the square. Temporary booths or stalls set up in and around the square were the scene of other business transactions, and we hear also of simple tables where bankers and money-changers conducted their business. At some point, apparently as early as the 5th century BC, there were large public market buildings as well, both in Athens and Peiraieus.

South Stoa I

A building which seems to have served an official commercial function during
99, 29   the Classical period was built along the south side of the square. It takes the form of a long stoa and in the absence of any evidence of its original name it is called South Stoa I, to distinguish it from a later stoa which occupied much the same area in the Hellenistic period. It was of the Doric order outside and
100   consisted of a double colonnade with sixteen rooms behind. Pottery found beneath the lowest floor indicates that the building should be dated to the decade 430–420 BC, that is, during the Peloponnesian War. A certain degree of economy is evident; the lower parts of the walls are all built of large squared
98   blocks, but the upper parts are of simple sun-dried mud brick. Such bricks are a

much cheaper building material than stone and if covered and plastered will last for decades. South Stoa I stood for some 270 years, until about 150 BC, when it was dismantled to make way for South Stoa II. In the absence of any ancient references, we must rely on the excavation and the plan of the building itself to reveal its function. These would seem to indicate that the stoa was a large public commercial building of some sort, as suggested by the inordinately large number of coins, some 240 altogether, mostly of bronze, found in the building. Perhaps the bankers' tables, referred to as early as the 5th century BC, stood in the building.[121] Not far away was the Mint where Athenian bronze coins were produced; possibly they were put into circulation from South Stoa I. The rooms of the stoa itself are of interest, for all the preserved doorways are set off-centre. This is not poor architectural design but deliberate, in order to fit in dining couches. As is clear from descriptions of parties and representations on vases, the Greeks often ate while reclining rather than sitting up. If the door were on-centre in one of the small rooms of South Stoa I there would be no room for a couch against the door-wall. By shifting the door a foot or so to the east a couch could be accommodated to the west of the door. Two more couches fit against each of the three remaining walls, with the head of the seventh couch just filling the narrower space east of the door. One of the rooms was even equipped with the characteristic raised cement border that kept the wooden legs of the couches free of the water used to swab the floor

101

98 *A wall in South Stoa I, c. 430–420 BC, the lower part of stone, the upper parts of mud brick. Such bricks were used in most Greek buildings, though they rarely survived once the roof collapsed.*

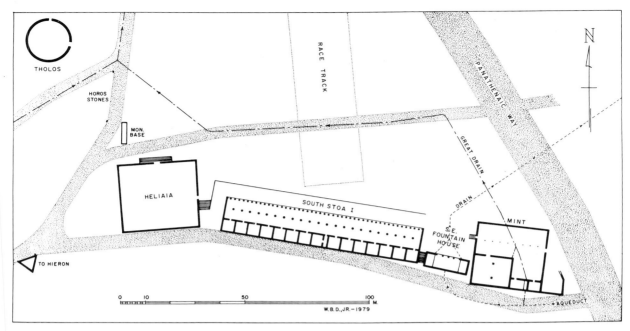

99 *The south side of the Agora in about* 400 BC, *showing from left to right the lawcourt (Heliaia), South Stoa I, the Southeast Fountainhouse, and the Mint. The Tholos appears at the upper left.*

100 *Aerial view of the east end of South Stoa I, showing the dining rooms along the back wall,* c. 430–420 BC.

after a meal. Thus some of the rooms were originally designed and built to serve as dining rooms, though at a later date several were converted and fitted with simple benches.

As members of the Boule and the archons were fed at public expense, it was suggested in the 1930s when South Stoa I was first uncovered that it may have served as a public office building where some of the dozens of small boards and commissions charged with running the city on a day-to-day basis may have held office. This would seem to have been borne out by the discovery in one of the rooms in 1967 of an inscription so fresh that the red paint used to emphasize certain words was still visible, indicating that it stood inside, perhaps within the building itself. It is a record of the *metronomoi*, the inspectors of weights and measures, of whom Aristotle wrote: 'There are ten *metronomoi* appointed by lot, five for the city and five for Piraeus. They are responsible for all measures and weights, to ensure that the salesmen use honest standards.'[122] The inscription dates to 222/1 BC and records the handing over of the official weights and measures to the incoming board of the

101 A dining room in South Stoa I designed to accommodate seven diners on couches. Note how the door is set off-centre to allow space for a couch against the wall on that side. The stoa was apparently used for small boards and commissions, the members of which were fed at public expense.

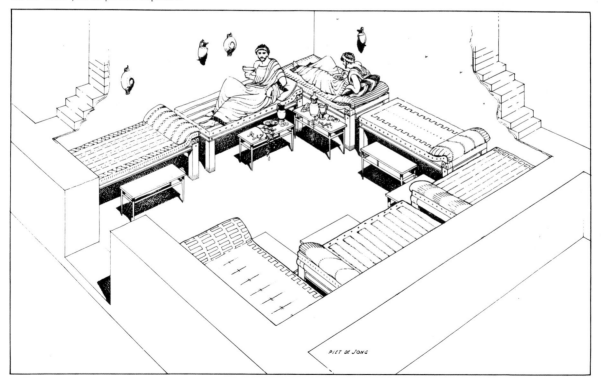

following year; listed before the stone breaks off are twelve bronze grain measures of 1 hemiekt (4.32 litres) each, two one-choinix measures (1.08 litres), and an indeterminate number of half-choinix measures (.54 litres). Also listed are the names of the five metronomoi, together with their two secretaries, one allotted, one elected, that is, a total of seven men, just the number which could be accommodated in one of the dining rooms of the stoa. Thus South Stoa I would seem to be one of the public market buildings of Athens, where business was transacted and where those officials directly concerned with the administration of the commercial life of the city held office.

Official weights, measures, and standards

The decree of the metronomoi leads to the actual weights and measures used to regulate trade in the Agora every day. As we have seen, one set may have been kept in South Stoa I; another set is known to have been kept in the Tholos:

> So that the measures and weights may remain for future time the man appointed for the provision of measures and weights, Diodoros son of Theophilos of Halai, shall hand them over to the public slave appointed in the Skias [Tholos, p. 94], and to the one in Piraeus along with the overseer, and to the one at Eleusis. These shall preserve them carefully, giving equivalents of the weights and measures to the officials and to all others who may require them, and not having power to make any change nor to take anything out of the rooms provided except the lead and bronze equivalents which have been made.[123]

102 Several of these lead and bronze weights have been found, most in the vicinity of the Tholos. The bronze weights, dating as early as *c.* 500 BC in some cases, carry inscriptions identifying them as official weights with symbols in relief on the top (knuckle-bone, turtle, shield) allowing immediate identification for those unwilling or unable to read. The lead weights, dating to the 4th century, also carry inscriptions and devices to indicate the weight of the piece.

103 A series of dry measures has also been found. One, of bronze and dating to the 5th century BC, was found in a well just north of the Mint and not far from South Stoa I. It holds only a half kotyle (126 cc) and carries a punched inscription (public) and will presumably have served for spices and precious commodities. Other dry measures for grain and nuts have been found,

104 carefully made cylindrical vessels of clay with painted inscriptions and official validating stamps. The nut measure in particular, which dates to the 2nd

105 century BC, conforms to a description preserved in the inscription concerning official weights and measures of the same period:

> Sellers of Persian nuts, almonds, hazelnuts, pine-nuts, chestnuts, Egyptian beans, dates and any other dried fruits normally sold with these, also lupines, olives, and pine kernels shall use a measure of the capacity of three half-choinikes of grain levelled off, selling them heaped up in this choinix which shall be five fingers deep and have a lip one finger wide. . . . If anyone sell in a smaller container, the appropriate authority shall immediately sell the contents by auction, pay the money to the public bank, and destroy the container.[124]

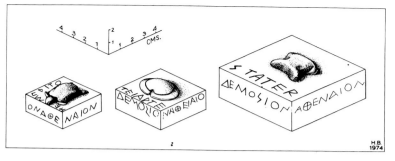

102 A set of official bronze weights inscribed and with symbols (turtle, shield, knuckle-bone) denoting their values, c. 500 BC. These weights represent a stater (795 gm), a quarter (190 gm), and a sixth (126 gm); they are also inscribed with the phrase, 'Public [property] of the Athenians'. Sets of such weights, used to check those used in the market, were kept in the Tholos and perhaps South Stoa I.

103 A bronze measure, dating to the 5th century BC and found in a well north of the Mint. The punched inscription says that it is official (demosion); it holds 126 cc.

104 A set of official dry and wet measures of clay used to regulate trade in the marketplace. They carry painted inscriptions indicating that they are official (demosion) and validating stamps guaranteeing their capacities.

105 An official container of the 2nd century BC with the broad lip specifically called for in an inscription for nut measures.

106 A marble tile standard for measuring terracotta roof tiles of curved Laconian type. The narrower tile (right) was used to cover the joints between the main pan tiles (centre).

Liquid measures were also used and a dozen examples, olpai and oinochoai, carrying painted inscriptions indicating their official nature have been found.

Not only was the sale of commodities subject to regulation in the market-place, but standards for other goods sold in the area were maintained as well. *106* Large marble plaques were found near the Tholos carved in such a way as to show the correct size and shape of terracotta roof tiles of the curved Laconian type, both pan tiles and the cover tiles which sealed the joints. Similar standards for roof tiles have been found also at Assos, in Asia Minor, and at Messene, in the Peloponnese. Thus whatever he bought, whether grain, wine, or building supplies, the Athenian frequenting the Agora had access to some measure of official quality control.

The Mint and Athenian coinage

99 Close to South Stoa I and perhaps loosely associated with it in function is a building first excavated in the 1950s and identified then as the Mint of the city. Further excavations carried out in 1978 clarified the plan of the building and produced abundant new evidence to support the identification. It is a large *107, 108* square building measuring 27 by 29 m, placed between the Panathenaic Way and the old Archaic fountainhouse. Its identification as a mint is based on finds

107 Restored plan of the Mint, after the excavations of 1978. The furnaces were in the southwest corner room.

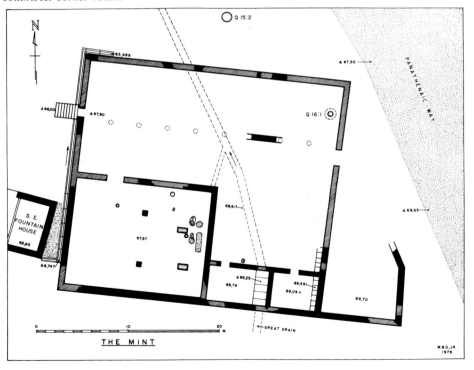

108 Aerial view of the southwest corner of the Mint, showing the large number of later disturbances which have damaged the remains. The Church of the Holy Apostles is at the upper left.

from within the building itself, where furnaces for bronze-working and other signs of industrial activity such as slag and water basins were found. In addition, dozens of bronze flans or unstruck coin-blanks were found scattered over the southwest quadrant of the building, and it seems clear that Athenian bronze coins were being struck in the building in the 3rd and 2nd centuries BC.

The building itself is earlier, however, and according to pottery found under the lowest floor its construction should be dated to the years around 400 BC. This is somewhat earlier than most numismatists are willing to accept for the introduction of bronze coinage in Athens, although there are references in the literature of the late 5th century BC to fractional coins known as *chalkous* (bronzes) and to an emergency issue of silver-plated bronze coins in 407/6 BC. Furthermore, analysis of the industrial debris from the building has produced no trace of any materials other than bronze and lead being prepared. If one is unwilling to accept a late-5th-century date for bronze coinage in Athens, then one should perhaps think of the 'mint' as a sort of public foundry, used to produce a variety of official items, including bronze coins, once the need for them was recognized in the 4th century BC. Even without coins there was a wide range of official material in bronze required by the state: bronze measures *103* (two of which were found in a well immediately north of the building), official bronze and lead weights,[125] and jurors' pinakia and symbola which carried an official validating stamp similar to the coin types. Ancient references claim that the statesman Hyperbolos' father was a lamp-maker in the Mint,[126] and at least one example of a bronze lamp has been found in the excavations.

Much of the building has been badly damaged, particularly along the north, where the southeast temple (2nd century AD), the Nymphaion (2nd century AD), and the Church of the Holy Apostles (*c.* AD 1000) were built directly on the ruins of the Mint. As far as can be determined, much of the northern half was given over to a courtyard, open to the sky. A large room in the southwest corner seems to have been the scene of much of the actual industrial activity, and it is here that the furnaces and cement-lined water basins were found. Two small rooms in the southeast corner may have been used for storage or to house the *epistatai* (overseers), the ten officials in charge of the administration of the Mint.

Thus with the construction of South Stoa I and the Mint in the latter part of the 5th century BC the south side of the square became the official commercial area, just as the west side served as the administrative/political centre.

Still to be considered briefly is the evidence concerning coinage and the circulation of money in the Agora. Altogether the excavations have produced huge quantities of coins, close to 100,000 in all, dating from the beginning of Greek coinage in the 6th century BC down to modern times. The vast majority of the coins are bronze; time was taken to recover any silver or gold coins which were dropped. Coins could be carried in purses or in the folds of a garment, but often they were kept under one's tongue. Most have been found packed into the gravel surfaces of the roads, many others were dropped in shops, and a fair number found their way into wells, cisterns, and drains. Only a few have been found in hoards deliberately buried.

The Athenians minted their best coins out of silver from the mines at Laureion, in southeast Attica, a source of wealth for the city for centuries. Themistokles used the silver of Laureion to build the ships which defeated the Persians at Salamis; the Spartans actively encouraged the thousands of slaves working the mines to desert in an attempt to put economic pressure on Athens during the Peloponnesian War; and the mines provided the basis for Athenian economic recovery in the mid-4th century BC. The actual mineral rights were the property of the state, and special officials, the *poletai*, who held office in the Agora, were responsible for leasing them to individuals: 'Poletai and Poleterion. The Poletai are magistrates at Athens, ten in number, one from each tribe. They deal with everything which is auctioned by the city, taxes and mines and rents and confiscated property. . . . Poleterion is the name given to the place where the Poletai hold their meetings.'[127] A large number of inscriptions recording the leasing of the silver mines have been found in the excavations, clustered in the area of the Tholos and Bouleuterion, suggesting *91* that the Poleterion stood in that part of the Agora. The inscriptions date from the period of the revival of the mines from 367 to 307/6 BC, and a better preserved one reads in part:

Mines were leased: in the first prytany, that of Hippothontis, Dexiakon [name of mine] in Nape at the Lookout, of which the boundaries are on all sides [the property of] Nikias of Kydantidai, the lessee: Kallias of Sphettos, the price: 20 drachmai. Diakon [name of mine] at Laureion of which the boundaries are on the east the fields of Exopios, on the west the mountain, the lessee: Epiteles of Kerameikos, the price: 20 drachmai.[128]

The prices of other leases vary greatly, depending on whether the lease is for an old mine or a new exploration.

Because of their high silver content Athenian coins were much admired in antiquity and were used throughout the Mediterranean, almost as a form of international exchange. Athenian coins have been found in hoards as far away as Bulgaria, Algeria, and India. The coin type was appropriate to Athens and easily recognizable: Athena, patroness of the city, on one side and her sacred *109* symbols, the owl with olive sprig, on the other. These figures were used with only the slightest changes for centuries. The Athenians carefully guarded the quality of their coins against any sort of fraud. A law of 375/4 BC describes in detail the procedures used to ensure the high quality of the coins circulating in the Agora. The text is of sufficient interest to quote it in full; missing words are restored in square brackets.

Resolved by the Nomothetai, in the archonship of Hippodamas; Nikophon made the proposal: Attic silver currency is to be accepted when [it is shown to be] silver and bears the official die. Let the public Tester (*dokimastes*), who sits among [the] tables, test in accordance with these provisions every [day except] whenever there is a cash payment; at that time let him test in [the Bouleuterion]. If anyone brings forward [foreign silver currency] which has the same device as the Attic, [if it is good,] let the Tester give it back to the one who brought it forward; but if it is [bronze at the core,] or lead at the core, or counterfeit, let him cut it across [immediately] and let it be sacred to the Mother of the Gods and let him [deposit] it with the Boule.

If the Tester does not sit at his post or if he does not test according to the law, let the Collectors of the people beat [him] fifty lashes with the [whip]. If anyone does not accept whatever silver currency the Tester has approved, let everything that he offers for sale on [that] day be confiscated. Let denunciations for offences in the grain-market be laid [before] the Sitophylakes, for those in the agora and in [the rest] of the city before the Collectors of the people; those [in the] market and in Peiraieus before the [Epimeletai] of the market, except for offences in the grain-market; offences [in the] grain-market are to be laid before the Sitophylakes. For [all those] denunciations

109 *Athenian silver tetradrachms of the 5th century* BC *(top row) and the 2nd century* BC *(above), with the helmeted head of Athena on the obverse, and an owl on the reverse.*

which are up to ten drachmai the magistrates [are to be] competent to give a verdict; for those over ten [drachmai] let them bring them into the lawcourt and let the Thesmothetai assist them by allotting a court whenever they request one or let them be subject to a fine of [?] drachmai. Let [the one who] makes the denunciation receive a share of one-half, if he wins a conviction. If the seller is a slave or a slave woman let [him] be beaten fifty lashes with the whip by [the magistrates] to whom the various denunciations have been assigned. If anyone of the magistrates does not act in accordance with the written instructions, let anyone of the Athenians who wishes, and to whom [it is permitted], bring [him] before the Boule. And if he is convicted, let him cease serving [as a magistrate] and let the Boule fine him up to [five hundred drachmai].

In order that there may also be a Tester in Peiraieus for [the] shipowners and the merchants and [all] others, let the Boule appoint one from among the public slaves or let it purchase one. Let the Apodektai [allot] the price and let the Epimeletai of the market see to it that he sits at the stele of Poseidon and let them apply the law in the same way as has been stated in the case of the Tester in the city.

Inscribe this law on a stone stele and place one in the city among the tables, another in Peiraieus in front of the stele of Poseidon. Let the Secretary of the Boule report the price to the Poletai and let the Poletai introduce it into the Boule. Let the payment of the salary for the Tester in the market begin from the time he is appointed in the archonship of Hippodamas. Let the Apodektai allot the same amount as for the Tester

VII (opposite) *Terracotta vase in the form of a kneeling boy tying on a ribbon, indicating a victory in the games, c. 540* BC.

in the city. For the future let his salary come from the same source as for the mint workers.

If there is any decree recorded anywhere on a stele contrary to this present law, let the Secretary of the Boule tear it down.[129]

The procedure of rendering a coin permanently invalid was to slash it (end of paragraph one), and several examples of such coins, slashed and removed from circulation, have actually been recovered in the excavations.

After three centuries of almost no changes at all, the Athenians finally altered the style of their tetradrachms (4-drachma pieces) in the 2nd century BC, although the basic symbols of Athena and the owl were retained. The coins were struck on larger, thinner flans, Athena wears a more elaborate helmet, and the owl is now perched on an amphora. This type survived until Athenian minting of silver coins stopped in *c.* 40 BC. The location of the mint or mints which produced the silver coins of Athens for 500 years is not known.

109

If the widespread distribution of Athenian coins indicates the far-flung economic power of Athens, then the foreign coins found in the Agora tell the same story. A gold coin from Kyzikos in the Hellespont and a large bronze one from Olbia in the Crimea (South Russia) reflect Athenian dependence on a steady supply of grain from the Black Sea, while a Persian daric and coins from Carthage (North Africa) and Gela (Sicily) indicate the wide range of people and/or goods which made their way into the market-place of Athens.

Private industry and commerce

In addition to the public buildings associated with the commercial centre of the Agora, the excavations have brought to light numerous private business establishments which shed considerable light on the economic life of the city. A large area southwest of the Agora was found to be crowded with workshops, and others have come to light east and northeast of the square. Like the public buildings, these shops also served as social centres, particularly those referred to by Lysias as being close to the Agora: 'For each of you is in the habit of frequenting some place, a perfumer's shop, a barber's, a cobbler's, and so forth; and the greatest number visit those who have their establishments nearest the Agora, and the smallest those who are furthest from it.'[130] A wide range of industrial and commercial activity is represented in the establishments excavated thus far.

Pottery

Of all the industries of ancient Athens perhaps her pottery was the best known. There was in any case a tradition that Athenians 'invented the potter's wheel

---

VIII (opposite) *Red-figure cup showing a youth carrying a hare, signed by the potter Gorgos, c. 500 BC.*

110 Fragment of a black-figured cup of the 6th century BC, *showing a man and spectator at a board game. The inscription reads 'and I have four'. The height of the figures is only 2.5 cm.*

and that useful house-maid, born of clay and kiln, well-renowned pottery'. Excellent reddish clay from beds near Marousi, several miles north of Athens, and skilled painters made Athenian pottery famous throughout the ancient world. Except for a brief period in the 7th century, when the Corinthians dominated foreign markets, Athenian pottery was widely exported from 1000 to 300 BC; indeed, many of the finest surviving examples of Classical Attic pottery come not from Athens or even Greece, but from Italy and South Russia. The decorative style of painting, using figured scenes from Greek mythology or daily life, developed slowly out of the rigid decoration of the Geometric style (9th–8th centuries) and the exuberant experimentation of the Proto-Attic style (7th century). By the 6th century the standard method of decoration was the black-figured style, the figures shown in black silhouette with details added in incised lines and white and purple paint. In the years around 530 BC the process was reversed: the background was painted black and the figures were left the natural reddish colour of the clay with details done in delicate thin lines of glaze. This style, which lasted until sometime after 300 BC, is known as the red-figure style. Both painters and potters were extremely skilled, and their pride in their work is reflected by both men signing a single pot. The scale of painting ranges from miniature figures no more than 3 cm high to a grand style with figures 30 cm or more in height, giving some sense of great wall paintings now lost.

In addition to the handsome painted wares Athenian potters produced large amounts of simpler pottery: dozens of different shapes, used mostly for drinking, storing, and pouring wine, oil, and water, all decorated with a plain

14, 18
20
110

VIII

111

136

111 (above) A selection of typical undecorated black-glazed table ware of the 5th century BC, found in a well.

112 Unglazed cooking pots of the 5th century BC. The lower vessels were portable braziers, which carried coals to cook and heat the food.

113 Part of a hemispherical mould-made bowl (right) and the mould for its manufacture. Such bowls were apparently first made in metal in Egypt. The clay examples were made in Athens near the Agora in the 3rd and 2nd centuries BC.

114 A terracotta hedgehog carrying off grapes. Length c. 7 cm.

112 lustrous black glaze of great durability. Another large series of pots was made of coarser, unglazed clay, a wide variety of handmade cooking pots for the preparation and serving of food.

While the main workshops for pottery production lay to the west, not far from the Dipylon gate, the Agora was also a centre for the ceramic industry. The area designated as the Kerameikos (potters' quarters) by a series of handsome marble boundary stones ran up along the Panathenaic Way to a point just behind the Royal Stoa, and Pausanias uses the term Kerameikos to refer to the area as a whole in his description of what we know as the Agora. Indeed, pottery production is the earliest industry in the Agora for which we have clear evidence. A well of about 1000 BC, excavated near the centre of the square, stands at the beginning of the long tradition of Attic pottery. It was found to contain numerous test pieces: irregular scraps of pottery with swabs of glaze on them and pierced with holes so they could be fished out of the kiln in order to check the firing. The remains of an actual pottery kiln dating to the 7th century BC were found just southeast of the Tholos, and dumps of the 7th and 6th centuries contained test pieces and wasters (misfired pieces), indicating production on the spot. A well of the early 5th century produced pottery in such huge amounts that it can only have come from a potter's shop, apparently destroyed by the Persians in 480 BC. In Hellenistic times, when the preferred

113 pottery carried mould-made relief decoration in imitation of metal shapes, the moulds used in their manufacture indicate that potters worked in the area at least as late as the 2nd century BC.

Terracotta figurines

Closely related to the potters were the coroplasts, the manufacturers of the small terracotta figurines which were so common in antiquity. Illustrating the close correspondence between the two arts is a magnificent and unique piece

VII found in a well near the Hephaisteion. It is a small oil vase made in the form of a kneeling youth tying a fillet around his head, to be dated to the decade 540–530 BC. Most products of the coroplasts' shops were not so elegant, but they were especially popular throughout Classical and Hellenistic times and examples from the Agora actually date from as early as 1400 BC to as late as AD 400. The little figurines were used as votive gifts to the gods, as offerings to the dead in graves, and as toys. As inexpensive, common objects they often reflect the interests and humour of the common man, such as the grotesque masked figures from the theatre or the little hedgehog which illustrates a poem from the Palatine Anthology: 'Bristling with the sharpest of spikes and with arrogant pride, this fruit-stealing hedgehog was caught rolling grapes on his spine.'

114

Once again, the excavations have made it clear that the coroplasts worked in the vicinity, especially to the south and southwest of the Agora where several wells and cisterns were filled with dozens of moulds used in the manufacture of these small figures.

Metalwork

Considerable evidence of the activity of metalworkers, mostly in bronze and iron and dating from 500 BC to AD 500, has come to light in the area as well. In all, some twenty foundries or smithies have been uncovered, nine of them clustering around the Hephaisteion, apparently indicating that those who worshipped the god of the forge actually toiled near his sanctuary. Casting pits can be recognized by the masses of charcoal, slag, lumps of metal, tools, and fragments of terracotta moulds used in the casting process. In general, the

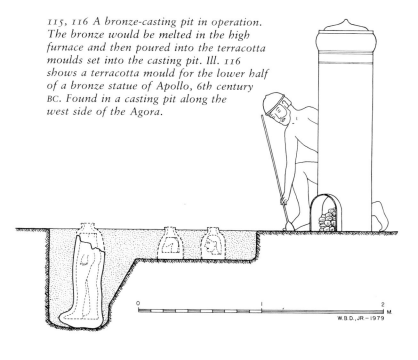

115, 116 A bronze-casting pit in operation. The bronze would be melted in the high furnace and then poured into the terracotta moulds set into the casting pit. Ill. 116 shows a terracotta mould for the lower half of a bronze statue of Apollo, 6th century BC. Found in a casting pit along the west side of the Agora.

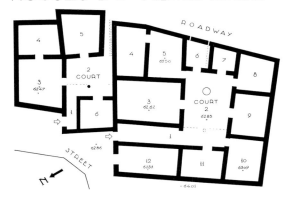

HOUSES D·C V CENTURY PRE-DRAIN

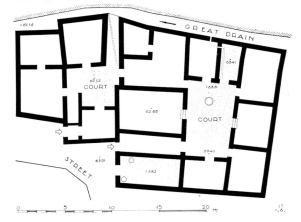

HOUSES D·C' AFTER MID. IV CENTURY

117 (above) *Two private houses of the 5th century BC, and their remodelled state in the 4th century. The smaller house D, at left, is the find-spot of the curse tablet against bronzeworkers.*

118 *A lead curse tablet. Usually deposited in wells or graves, such tablets called on the gods and goddesses of the underworld to inflict terrible troubles and sicknesses on the cursed individuals.*

'lost-wax' method was used, whereby the intended object was done in wax, built up around a core; more clay and sand were then added to the outside and metal pins were inserted to hold mould and core in place when the wax was melted out. Molten bronze was then poured in to take the place of the wax between mould and core and a hollow-cast piece of metal or sculpture was the result.

One of the earliest bronze-casting pits was apparently for a statue of Apollo which stood in a small temple along the west side of the Agora in about 500 BC. The pit lay just south of the temple, and the fragments of the mould preserve most of the lower part of the statue and pieces from the face. The roles of sculptor and the man who actually cast the piece were separate and in Rhodes at least regarded as almost equal: several statue bases there were signed by both artist and bronze-caster.

The home and perhaps workshop of other bronzeworkers, active in the 4th century BC, can be identified in the industrial district southwest of the Agora.

*119 An ancient clay impression
taken from the metal clasp of a belt,
with Odysseus mourning Ajax, c. 430 BC.*

The identification has been made on the basis of a lead curse-tablet found in the ruins of one of the houses. Scratched on it is the following inscription: 'I condemn Aristaichmos the bronzeworker to those of the underworld, and Pyrrias the bronzeworker and his work and their souls, and Sosias the Lamian and his work and soul, and Ages(ion) the Boeotian.'[131] Numerous curse-tablets of this sort have been found in the excavations. Usually they are written on lead sheets and rolled up, a nail is driven through them, and they are dropped into a grave or a well in order to reach the spirits of the underworld most directly. They call down awful things on the individual cursed, and if a bit of hair or something belonging to the individual can be included, so much the better. The tablet cited above is unusual in that it was buried or hidden in the house rather than in a grave or well; the fortuitous use of the professions of the cursees allows us to identify the establishment with a fair degree of probability.

In addition to sculpture, bronzeworkers created thousands of objects: various tools, armour, metal vessels, and the like. Hundreds of scraps of bronze objects have been recovered in the excavations representing only a tiny fraction of what was originally in use. The reason for this is obvious; unlike marble or terracotta, bronze can be melted down and reused, and this was clearly done over and over again. Some idea of the skill of these ancient metalworkers can be found in terracotta impressions of the decorative work *119* on some metal objects long lost.

Sculptors and marble-workers

In addition to the metalworkers, we have ample evidence for the sculptors who produced so many marble statues in antiquity. As in a great number of fields Athenian sculptors were well known, and hundreds of works survive, done in the white marble of nearby Mount Penteli. A principal location for marble-working was apparently the industrial district to the southwest, where layers of marble dust and chips were found scattered over much of the area. A house *120* somewhat closer to the square, just west of and across the street from the triangular crossroads enclosure, was certainly a marble-working establishment. Here were found floor levels full of marble dust and working chips, chunks of unfinished sculpture, and tools of lead, bronze, and bone. The house was in use from about 475 until 275 BC, apparently occupied by sculptors throughout its history. The name of the first owner, Mikion, is preserved on a *121* small bone tool found on the lowest floor of the house. The last occupant of the house, Menon, inscribed his name on much of his simple black-glazed crockery. It was in just such shops and probably in this very area that Sokrates' father and the youthful Sokrates himself plied their craft of marble-working.

A second marble-worker's atelier, also full of fragments of unfinished sculpture, dates to the 1st century AD and was found in one of the rooms of the western stoa of the library of Pantainos.

120 The area just outside the southwest corner of the Agora as excavated. At the right is the triangular sanctuary (cf. ill. 54), at the left the house of the sculptors Mikion and Menon, 5th to 3rd centuries BC.

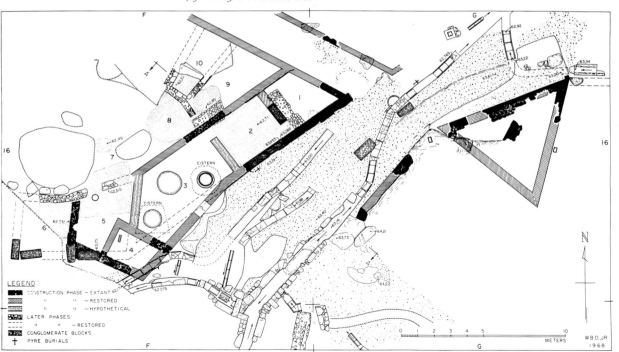

LEGEND
CONSTRUCTION PHASE – EXTANT
" " – RESTORED
" " – HYPOTHETICAL
LATER PHASES
" " – RESTORED
CONGLOMERATE BLOCKS
PYRE BURIALS

W.B.D.,JR
1968

121 (above) A well-used bone stylus inscribed with the name of the sculptor Mikion.

122 Amphora handle from the island of Rhodes, stamped with the head of the sun-god Helios and the name of the magistrate Sostratos.

Wine and wineshops

The Athenians were great lovers of wine and imported a great deal, even though the land of Attica has always produced excellent grapes of its own. Wineshops and taverns were to be found all over town, and several must have been within easy reach of the square. In a small group of shops just east of the Agora a well was found which was filled up with debris in the years around 400–380 BC. Much of the material consisted of black-glazed drinking cups and pitchers, enough to suggest that the pottery was dumped in from a tavern in the vicinity. Also found were parts of 350 of the large coarse-ware amphoras in which wine was usually transported in antiquity. This particular shop apparently dealt in wine from Mende, Chios, Lesbos, Thasos (?), and Corinth. This is apparent from the amphoras themselves, which can usually be identified from their shapes and the composition of the clay. Often, particularly in the Hellenistic period, the handles of the jars were stamped with the name or symbol of the city of manufacture, as well as magistrates' names to date the container and presumably the wine within. Such handles can usually be dated to within a few years, and they thus provide, like coins and pottery, important evidence for the date of a building, well, or whatever deposit they are found in. A careful analysis of the amphoras allows one to study ancient trade and economics, at least in terms of a common and widely traded commodity. The jars themselves might break, but the fragments were virtually indestructible; this is especially true of the thick handles, which have been found by the thousands in the excavations. Over 20,000 have been catalogued so far, and we know that in Hellenistic times the wines of Thasos, Kos, and especially Rhodes (23 per cent), and Knidos (62 per cent) were favoured.

122

In addition, some 870 whole jars have been set up in the museum   *123*
storerooms, arranged by area and date, so the development of the shapes can
be studied easily. The jars themselves have two handles at the top, and their
bodies taper to a pointed knoblike toe. They cannot stand on their own; their
primary use was for transport. An average amphora stands 76 cm tall, carried
about 7 gallons, and weighed 35 kilos when full. The small knobby toe served
as a convenient and necessary third handle for lifting and moving the
amphora. When in transit the jars were simply stacked against the hull of the
ship; thousands still lie stacked in this way on the floor of the Mediterranean. If
used in a house or shop, the jars would be set into a special tripod stand or a
hole in the ground. Since the Greeks almost always drank their wine mixed
with water, the wine would usually be transferred from the amphora to a
krater (mixing bowl) before serving. Oinochoai (pitchers) were then used
actually to serve the wine, which was drunk from a variety of drinking cups,   *111*
the kylix and skyphos (6th and 5th centuries), kantharos (4th and 3rd
centuries), or hemispherical bowl (3rd and 2nd centuries).   *113*

Shoemaking

Another industry for which good evidence has come to light is shoemaking. A
small house of the 5th century BC was found just outside the square, adjacent to   *124*
the Agora boundary stone by the Tholos. From its floors came dozens of iron
hobnails of the sort used in shoemaking, along with many bone eyelets for   *125*
laces. It seems clear that a cobbler was at work in this house, and in fact he may
well have been one of the best-known shoemakers of 5th-century Athens. In
the street just outside, apparently discarded from the house, was found the
base of a simple black-glazed drinking cup which carries the scratched
inscription 'of Simon' on the bottom. We learn from Xenophon that Sokrates,
when he wished to converse with those pupils or friends who were too young
to go into the Agora, would meet them in a leather-working shop near the
square.[132] Diogenes Laertios wrote: 'Simon, an Athenian, a shoemaker. When
Sokrates came to his workshop and discoursed, he used to make notes of what
he remembered, whence these dialogues were called "The Shoemaker's".
Thirty-three were gathered into a book.'[133] And Plutarch presumably had this
same man in mind when he wrote: 'I wish I were a shoemaker in ancient
Athens so that Sokrates would come and sit beside Perikles in my house and
chat with him.'[134] We have a 5th-century cobbler by the name of Simon,
working as close to the Agora as possible; the archaeological evidence would

*123 (opposite) Part of the collection of almost 900 amphoras now held in the storerooms
of the Stoa of Attalos. Used for the transport of wine – and occasionally oil – the jars have
a pointed toe for ease of handling. Different cities produced amphoras of different and
recognizable shape. Those in the top row are all from Lesbos, those in the middle from
Mende, and those at the bottom from Thasos.*

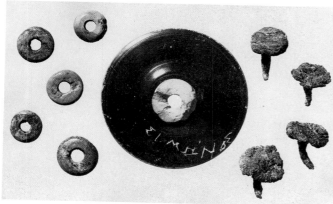

124 (above) *Remains of the house of Simon the cobbler. An Agora boundary stone is visible in the foreground and the courtyard of the house in the area behind. The street lies to the right.*

125 *Material from the house of Simon the cobbler, 5th century BC. From left to right: bone eyelets, the base of a black-glazed cup inscribed with the name of Simon, and iron hobnails.*

suggest that this is the very shop, visited by Perikles, which Sokrates used as an informal classroom, meeting here those pupils too young to frequent the square.

As we try to picture the scene in Simon's shop we turn once again to the literary sources and another find from the Agora. The text, from Xenophon, describes a large shoemaker's shop: 'One man makes shoes for men, another for women, and there are even places where one man earns a living by only stitching shoes, another by cutting them out, another by sewing the uppers

126 Dedication by the shoemaker Dionysios to the hero Kallistephanos, showing a cobbler's shop. First half of the 4th century BC.

together, while there is another who performs none of these operations, but only assembles the parts.'[135] For an illustration of such a shop we have a handsome relief dedicated by the cobbler Dionysios to the hero Kallistephanos 126 in the first half of the 4th century BC.[136] It shows a scene in the shop itself: on the right, and partially broken away, two figures sit at work behind a cobbler's bench, while next to them, seated frontally, is a young man hard at work on a sandal. At the left edge an elderly man, bearded and bald, reaches up towards a beam which runs across the top, where numerous sandals hang from pegs. In front of him a small boy crouches, cutting strips of leather. An altogether lively, busy scene, with three generations hard at work in the small shop. Beneath the relief runs the inscribed dedication: 'Dionysios the cobbler, son of [. . .]onos, and his children dedicate this to the hero Kallistephanos'. Below are three lines of hexameter verse: 'Having seen a divine vision in his sleep, Dionysios adorns the hero and the children of Kallistephanos; do you give in return for these things wealth and happy health.' The name of the father of Dionysios is only partially preserved; it was seven or eight letters long and a plausible restoration is [Sim]onos: '[son] of Simon'. This may be a dedication by the descendant of the old friend of Sokrates, carrying on his shoemaking trade.

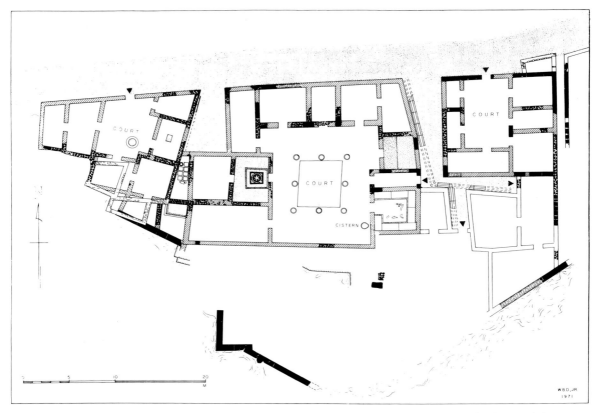

127 Plan of three private houses of the 5th and 4th centuries BC on the slopes of the Areopagos. Note how the rooms are all grouped around a central courtyard.

Private houses

As we have seen, much of the commerce of Athens took place in workshops which were part of the private dwellings of the artisans and tradesmen. It *127* might be well to consider here some aspects of a typical Athenian house, several dozen of which have been excavated, especially to the south and *117* southwest of the Agora. One should say at the outset that they have no *120* standard size or arrangement, either internally or within a given block, as is the case with several other cities (Peiraieus, Olynthos), which show a marked degree of urban planning. This irregularity was noted even in antiquity: 'The whole city is dry, not well-watered, badly laid out on account of its antiquity. Most of the houses are mean, the nice ones few. A stranger would doubt, on seeing it first, if this were really the renowned city of the Athenians.'[137] The average Athenian house was small, a series of rooms grouped around a central courtyard which provided light and air. For reasons of security there will have been few if any external windows, and only one, or occasionally two, external doors. By modern standards the rooms were poor and sparsely furnished. The floors of most of the rooms were simply packed earth or clay. The main room of the house was used for entertaining and was known as the *andron*. It was often set on the north side of the court, facing south to take full advantage of the warmth of the low winter sun. It would usually have a mosaic floor of pebbles set in lime mortar with a slightly raised border around the sides of the room to carry the dining couches. The functions of the other rooms are less easy to recognize, although occasionally the finds give some indication: a small room with a drain might be either bathroom or latrine, a concentration of cooking ware and crockery indicates the position of a kitchen or pantry, and a collection of loom weights locates the women's quarters. Water was available in the courtyard, usually from a well which was cut down into bedrock to a depth of as much as 15 m, though the average depth was generally round 12 m. Starting in the middle of the 4th century there was a shift in private water supply from wells to cisterns, apparently as the result of a drought or protracted dry spell. The water table dropped and wells were abandoned in favour of cisterns which stored rain-water caught off the roof. Good clean drinking water will have been fetched by women or slaves from a public fountainhouse which had water piped in from fresh springs.

In general it would appear that Athenian men spent little time at home. Certainly most social life took place in the stoas and shops of the Agora, or in the gymnasia where the youth of the city gathered. The houses around the Agora correspond to the references in Demosthenes who claimed that the leading men of 5th-century Athens lived in modest houses, identical to those of their neighbours.[138] Excavations have not yet brought to light the aristocratic houses also described in the literature, those with two colonnaded courtyards and second storeys. Not surprisingly, the environs of the Agora were apparently not regarded by the upper classes as a particularly desirable residential area.

The building materials used for the houses were similarly modest. The foundations and lower parts of the walls were usually made of rubble, simple field stones set in clay. This socle would rise a foot or so above ground level, and above that the walls were of sun-dried mud bricks. This is by far the *98* cheapest and easiest of building materials. The wall would be stuccoed and further protected from the elements by the overhanging eaves of the roof. The roof itself was made up of wooden beams and boards supporting roof tiles of baked clay. The materials used will explain how so many Greek buildings were buried in those instances when erosion does not seem a satisfactory explanation. When the roof collapses, as a result of either deliberate destruction or neglect following abandonment, the floor is littered with the debris of the fallen beams and roof tiles. With no protection from the roof and exposed to the elements, the mud-brick walls will begin to disintegrate, turning back into clay or mud, and the ruin thus buries itself. Should one then wish to build on the same site, one had the option of digging out and carting off several tons of debris, or of simply bringing in a few loads of earth, levelling the ground, and starting to build again, at a somewhat higher level. This same process holds true not just for private houses but also for many public buildings, a large number of which were built of similarly modest materials.

Recovery after 400 BC

Athenian recovery after the Peloponnesian War was surprisingly quick in some ways. With Persian help the Athenian general Konon defeated a Spartan fleet off Knidos in 394 BC, and land battles were fought around Corinth at about the same time. Athenian fortunes had improved sufficiently to allow her to rebuild her city walls and those of Peiraieus in the period from 394 to 390 BC without fear of Spartan interference. In general, however, Athenian energies and resources were committed to maintaining her political and military position first in relation to Sparta and Thebes, and then in relation to several allies over the administration of Delphi. As a result, little building activity took place in Athens in the first half of the 4th century. The next phase of significant building in the Agora and elsewhere in the city coincided with renewed activity at the Laureion mines and did not occur until the middle of the century, at a time when Athens was confronting the rising power of Macedon.

IX (*opposite*) *Bronze head of the goddess Nike (Victory), originally gilded, 5th century* BC.

X

XI

5 Macedon and the Hellenistic period

Philip II came to the throne of Macedon in 359 BC. His early years were absorbed with the consolidation of power in order to hold his unruly kingdom and to secure the borders with Epiros and Thrace. Once these matters were under control, he looked both eastward and southward. To the east he took the city of Olynthos, a close Athenian ally, in 348 BC. Attempts to take Byzantium and Perinthos in 340/39 further threatened Athens' vital shipping routes to the Black Sea. Since the time of Solon, Athens had not been self-sufficient in grain, and by the 4th century half her imported supply came from the Black Sea, especially the Crimea.

In the 340s Philip also began to concern himself with affairs in southern Greece and in 338 intervened directly, moving into central Greece. His first overt move south, an attack on the Phocian town of Elateia, caused great dismay in the Agora of Athens, at least according to Demosthenes:

It was evening and someone came to the Prytaneis with the report that Elateia had been taken. At this the Prytaneis immediately arose in the middle of their meal and began to shut out their occupants from the booths about the Agora and to burn the wicker-work constructions, while some of them sent for the Strategoi and summoned the trumpeter. The city was full of confusion.[139]

Harpokration's explanation of the burning of the stalls indicates that perhaps not all the Athenians were as concerned as they might be: 'In the present instance Demosthenes says that the coverings and screens of the booths were burnt so that people might not gather together about the wares in the Agora or spend their time on other matters.'[140]

Later in the same year the Athenians and Thebans were routed by Philip at the battle of Chaironeia in Boeotia. With this success Philip was effectively master of mainland Greece. His treatment of Athens in defeat was unusually mild, brought on by his respect for her distinguished history and reputation as a centre of culture and learning. Despite his overtures, Athens remained hostile, spurred on by the implacable hatred of the orator Demosthenes, who

---

X *Watercolour of the restored upper parts of the Middle Stoa, mid-2nd century BC, showing the colours used to decorate this and most Greek buildings.*

XI *Ionic Capital of the 5th century BC with traces of the original painted ornament. From an unknown building reused in the Agora in the early Roman period.*

throughout his long career personified Athenian antipathy towards Macedon. He is said to have written the epigram himself which was inscribed on an honorary statue set up in the Agora after his death. The statue is said by other sources to have stood by a plane tree, near the Altar of the Twelve Gods.

129

A little later the Athenian people, rendering worthy honour to him, set up a bronze statue and decreed that the eldest member of his family should have public maintenance in the Prytaneion. The much-quoted epigram was inscribed on the base of the statue, 'If you had had power equal to your resolution, Demosthenes, the Macedonian Ares would never have acquired dominion over the Greeks.'[141]

128

The Athenian attitude towards Philip and their uncertainty concerning the future of their democracy can be read in a decree passed in the year following Chaironeia (337/6 BC), which was found in the Agora:

In the archonship of Phrynichos, in the ninth prytany of Leontis for which Chairestratos, son of Ameinias, of Acharnai, was secretary; Menestratos of Aixone, of the proedroi, put the question to a vote; Eukrates, son of Aristodimos, of Peiraieus, made the motion: with Good Fortune of the Demos [people] of the Athenians, be it resolved by the Nomothetai: If anyone rise up against the Demos for tyranny or join in establishing the tyranny or overthrow the Demos of the Athenians or the democracy in

128 Anti-tyranny decree of 337/6 BC calling for the acquittal of anyone accused of murdering a tyrant. The relief shows a seated Demos (People of Athens) being crowned by Democracy.

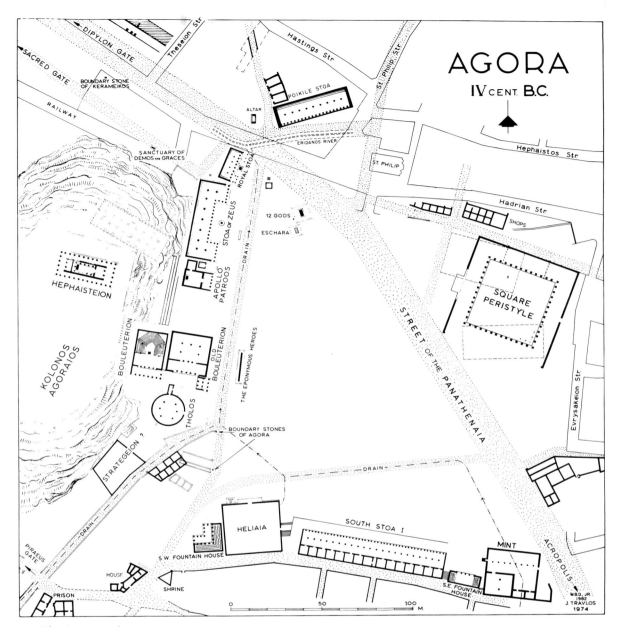

129 *The Agora in about 300 BC.*

Athens, whoever kills him who does any of these things shall be blameless. It shall not be permitted for anyone of the Councillors of the Council from the Areopagos – if the Demos or the democracy in Athens has been overthrown – to go up into the Areopagos or sit in the Council or deliberate about anything. If anyone – the Demos or the democracy in Athens overthrown – of the Councillors of the Areopagos goes up into the Areopagos or sits in the Council or deliberates about anything, both he and his progeny shall be deprived of civil rights and his substance shall be confiscated and a tenth given to the Goddess. The secretary of the Council shall inscribe this law on two stelai of stone and set one of them by the entrance into the Areopagos, that entrance, namely, near where one goes into the Bouleuterion, and the other in the Ekklesia. For the inscribing of the stelai the treasurer of the Demos shall give 20 drachmai from the moneys expendable by the Demos according to decrees.[142]

The copy of the decree is crowned with a handsome relief, usually interpreted as a representation of Democracy crowning the seated Demos (people) of Athens. In the following year Philip was, in fact, assassinated, though in Macedonia and apparently by Macedonians. He was succeeded by Alexander who, like his father, was inclined to treat Athens with considerable respect. Alexander's interests lay elsewhere, however, and after quelling a short-lived revolt in Greece, he crossed over into Asia in 334 BC to begin his phenomenal conquest of the East.

During the reign of Philip (359–336) and Alexander (336–323), Athens was able to recover her fortunes after the difficulties of the early 4th century. Under the financial administration of Euboulos and Lykourgos the treasury, depleted during the Sacred War, was replenished. A major element in this recovery was the silver mined at Laureion, and the numerous poletai accounts found in the Agora indicate the extent of activity in this period. Improved revenues allowed the Athenians to build a new stadium for the Panathenaic games, a new theatre in the precinct of Dionysos on the south slopes of the Acropolis, and perhaps to enlarge the meeting-place on the Pnyx. With these major building projects under way, little attention was paid to the Agora, though some construction took place.

129

The Southwest Fountainhouse

29 A large fountainhouse was constructed in the southwest corner of the square.
129 The building is in a pitiable state of disrepair, and its very identification as a fountainhouse depends on the great stone aqueduct which brought water to the building from the east. Built of large slabs of poros limestone, the channel
149 was large enough for a man to walk through, doubled over, for maintenance and cleaning. It has been traced to the east for some 220 m, at which point it disappears under the modern city. Of the fountainhouse it supplied, only the foundations and a few blocks of the superstructure survive. A small square court at the northwest corner gave access through a colonnaded porch to a large L-shaped draw basin with a floor area of just over 100 square m. Pottery found under the floor suggests a construction date of 350–325 BC. Despite its poor preservation and the lack of any ancient reference to it, the Southwest Fountainhouse with its aqueduct represents a major addition to the Athenian water supply. It lay in a prominent location by the Agora, near a major cross-roads, and its dimensions show it to be the largest known fountain in the city.

The new fountainhouse is one indication among several that Athens may have suffered a period of severe drought in the years between 350 and 325 BC. The excavations of the Agora have provided further evidence. An analysis of the wells serving the private houses in the area shows that they became progressively deeper from the 6th to the 4th centuries, presumably because of a gradually falling water table. Then, starting about 350, wells were replaced by cisterns as the standard source of supply in most houses, as we have seen. Cisterns then remained the favoured source throughout the Hellenistic period (140 cisterns, as opposed to 40 wells excavated). Apparently the water table sank too low to be tapped easily, and whatever rain that fell was collected off the roofs and carefully saved. Thus both the Southwest Fountainhouse and the pattern of private water supply suggest a period of drought beginning near the middle of the 4th century. This drought was not without effect, for by 330 BC it had caused a severe famine in Athens and elsewhere in Greece. Large emergency shipments of grain were made from Cyrene in North Africa and elsewhere to help the city survive, and 'Those of you who dwelt in the city were having their barley meal measured out to them in the Odeion, and those who dwelt in Peiraeus were receiving their loaves bit by bit in the dockyard and in the long stoa, having their meal measured out to them a twelfth of a medimnos at a time and being nearly trampled to death.'[143]

The water-clock

Also built at some point in the second half of the 4th century was a monumental klepsydra or water-clock. It was set up against the north face of the old lawcourt (?) at the southwest corner, drawing its water from the recently built aqueduct which supplied the Southwest Fountainhouse. The device was at first a simple outflow clock, a stone tank or cistern holding just under 1000 litres of water with a small bronze outlet hole at the bottom which allowed the tank to drain slowly. Some flotation device would record the passing hours as the water level fell. The full tank would take some 17 hours to empty, more than enough to record the longest summer days which last just under 15 (60-minute) hours. The Greeks reckoned time not in 24-hour cycles, but by means of 12 hours of sunlight a day calculated as equal divisions; this means a 45-minute hour in winter and a 75-minute hour in summer. The plug would be pulled at dawn each day and specified times could be set for starting a meeting or a trial, or for the opening and closing of the market. The Agora clock is well placed, in a prominent location at the southwest corner of the square near a major crossroads and on the street leading from the Agora through the residential district and up to the Pnyx. Such monumental outflow clocks are rare in Greece and only two other examples are known, one in the Arcadian town of Stymphalos and the other at Oropos, which lay just beyond the northeast border of Attica. The Oropos example is far better preserved than the Agora clock and so similar that it seems probable that they were designed by the same man.

Great innovations were made in the technology of water-clocks in Alexandria in the early 3rd century BC, involving the change to an inflow system with new valves for the improved regulation of the flow of water, thereby avoiding difficulties inherent in an outflow system with its constantly

130
131

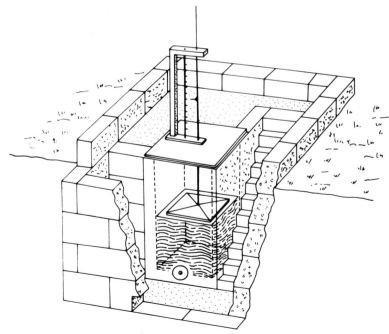

130, 131 Excavated remains (above) and cut-away view (left) of the Agora water-clock (klepsydra), late 4th century BC. The large central tank would be filled and as the water drained slowly through the outlet hole at the bottom its falling level indicated the passing hours. The full tank took some 17 hours to empty.

changing water pressure. The Agora clock was apparently modified to take account of these technical advances if we may judge from a new outlet hole which replaced the old, allowing the tank to be emptied in about 40 minutes and presumably used to drain the tank after it had filled gradually during the course of the day.

The mechanism of the clock itself has not survived, but it should be noted that as early as the 3rd century and perhaps earlier the Greeks were capable of quite sophisticated machinery including the use of interlocking gears, as is clear from the descriptions of Vitruvius and other technical authors.

The temple of Apollo Patroos

Another building dating to the second half of the 4th century is the small temple of Apollo Patroos built along the west side of the Agora between the *132* Stoa of Zeus and the Metroon. It was a small plain structure measuring *c.* 10 by 16.5 m, with four columns *in antis* across the east façade only. Pausanias saw several statues of Apollo by major artists when he visited the temple: 'Euphranor also made the Apollo Patroos in the temple nearby. In front of the

132 Plan of the temple of Apollo Patroos, c.330 BC, along the west side of the Agora.

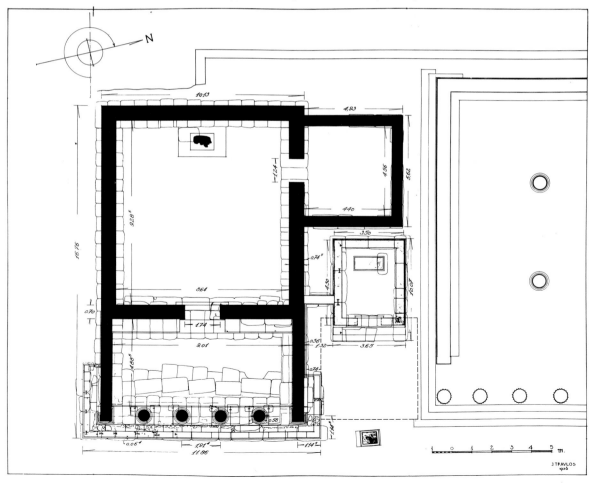

134 A reconstruction of the early temple of Apollo Patroos, with an apsidal end, 6th century BC.

temple the one Apollo was made by Leochares, the other, whom they call Alexikakos (Averter of Evil), by Kalamis. They say that the god received the name because by an oracle from Delphi he stopped the plague which was afflicting them at the same time as the Peloponnesian War.'[144] A large marble statue of a draped Apollo playing a kithara was found some 20 m to the south of the temple in the 19th century and is usually identified as the work of Euphranor. The significance of Patroos (Fatherly) Apollo is explained by Harpokration: 'Apollo Patroos is the Pythian Apollo. This is a title of the god who has many others too. The Athenians have a public cult of Apollo as paternal deity, because of Ion. Ion having settled Attica, as Aristotle says, the Athenians were called Ionians and Apollo received the name Patroos among them.'[145] The 4th-century temple sits on the scrappy remains of an earlier building identified as the 6th-century predecessor, associated with the bronze-casting pit for a late Archaic bronze kouros. There is no evidence concerning the cult from the period of the destruction of the earlier temple by the Persians in 480 BC to that of the new temple of c. 330 BC, though the sculptor Kalamis worked in the 5th century BC and the plague struck in 429–427/6 BC.

133

134
116

133 (opposite) A colossal marble statue found near the temple of Apollo Patroos, and thought to be by the sculptor Euphranor. The figure originally held a large kithara, a stringed instrument. Height 2.5 m.

Also to the years around 330 BC, apparently, should be dated the new Monument of the Eponymous Heroes (p. 97) in a different location, along the west side of the Agora square, in a convenient location near the Metroon and the more permanent archives stored there.

Macedonian rule: Demetrios Poliorcetes (The Besieger)

Following the death of Alexander in Babylon in 323 BC, Athens, along with most of Greece, rebelled against Macedonian rule. The revolt, known as the Lamian War, was short-lived and by 322 BC Athens and most of Greece had lost their last hopes of independence. The city became a pawn in a series of

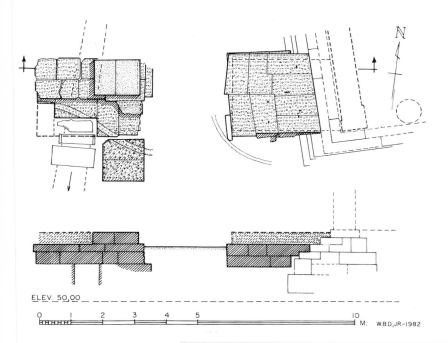

ELEV. 50,00

135 Actual-state plan and cross-section of the piers for the gate just west of the Painted Stoa. The gate was set up to celebrate an Athenian victory over the Macedonian cavalry in 303/2 BC. Compare ills. 136 and 137.

136 (below) Foundations of the gate beside the Painted Stoa. The west end of the stoa steps are at the right. The Ionic column base on the left pier is a much later addition.

137 Reconstruction of the gate next to the Painted Stoa. Pausanias records that the gate carried a trophy to celebrate the cavalry victory. Such trophies were usually made of captured weapons. The position of the equestrian statue and the use of the arch for the span are both conjectural.

wars fought among the successors of Alexander as each laid claim to parts of his vast empire: Demetrios and Antigonos, Ptolemy, Seleukos, Eumenes, Lysimachos, and dozens of lesser pretenders and claimants. The Athenians fell first under the control of Cassander, who set for them an aristocratic government with Demetrios of Phaleron as tyrant in 317 BC. This regime was overthrown in 307/6 by Demetrios Poliorcetes who liberated Athens and proclaimed her free, re-establishing a democracy. In return for this Demetrios and his father Antigonos were awarded extraordinary honours by the Athenians: 'The Athenians, on the proposal of Stratokles, passed a decree to set up gold statues of Antigonos and Demetrios in a chariot, near Harmodios and Aristogeiton, and to crown them both at a cost of two hundred talents, and to establish an altar and call it "the altar of the Saviours"; and to add to the ten tribes two more, Demetrias and Antigonis.'[146] The golden statues, now lost, must have stood in the Agora since they were to be set up by the old statues of the Tyrannicides. Most extraordinary was the creation of two new tribes named after them, for it meant an increase in the Boule to 600 members and a reassigning of demes among twelve rather than ten tribes. This constitutional change left its mark on the monument of the Eponymous Heroes, the physical embodiment of the tribal system. Two new statues had to be added, and the traces of the lengthening of the base to accommodate them can be seen on the southern sill of the surrounding fence and in the clamp cuttings which indicate the resetting of the two preserved marble crowning blocks of the base.

Liberation certainly did not mean an end to hostilities, and Cassander and his brother Pleistarchos continued to contend with Demetrios for control of Athens. In 303/2 the Athenian cavalry, campaigning with Demetrios in the Peloponnese, defeated Pleistarchos. In commemoration of the victory the Athenians set up a trophy on a gate seen by Pausanias as he made his way to the Painted Stoa: 'As you go to the stoa which is called Poikile because of the pictures, there is a bronze Hermes called Agoraios, and a gate nearby. On the gate is a trophy erected by the Athenians when in a cavalry fight they defeated Pleistarchos, who was the brother of Cassander and was entrusted with the command of his cavalry and mercenaries.'[147] What seem to be the foundations of this gate have come to light immediately west of the Painted Stoa, partially resting on its steps. Preserved are two square foundations measuring 2.7 by 3.3 m which presumably supported the two piers of the gate; the foundations are set 2.5 m apart, spanning a narrow street. Nothing of the superstructure survives and the restoration above the foundation is conjectural; in this period either an arch or a straight lintel could be used. Despite the unprepossessing state of the ruins, a glance at the plan will confirm their significance. The northwest corner of the Agora where the Panathenaic Way enters the square was bounded by two stoas (Painted and Basileios) and two sanctuaries (crossroads and Aphrodite Ourania). All four monuments were built in the 6th or 5th century BC, the latest (crossroads shrine) in place no later than c. 430 BC. Nothing further was allowed to be constructed in the area for over a century, until the gate came to occupy what is clearly a significant, prominent location. The trophy on top will have consisted of captured arms or a sculptural representation of them. Given its size and prominence the gate and trophy must have been meant to honour more than just the Athenian cavalry at this time, and the monument should probably be thought of as yet another attempt on the part of the Athenians to honour and please Demetrios.

Dating to about this same period and perhaps associated in some way with the gate and trophy are the remains of a gilded bronze statue almost certainly of Demetrios himself. All that is preserved is the left leg, a fragment of drapery, and the sheathed sword of a life-size figure on horseback. The leg is hollow-cast and wears a thonged sandal tied up to the ankle. The sword is solid bronze. All three pieces have narrow grooves traversing them in which the thin plates of gold used to gild the statue were anchored. Some pieces of the

135, 136

137

40, 55

138

138 Sword and leg from a bronze equestrian statue of Demetrios Poliorcetes, set up in c. 300 BC and torn down by the Athenians and thrown into a well in 200 BC. The statue was originally gilded, and traces of the gilding still remain. Length of sword 88 cm.

gold still adhere in places, though most was stripped away before the pieces were discarded. In addition to the gold statue of Demetrios set up with his father's next to the Tyrannicides, we learn of a second, equestrian, statue set up in the Agora: 'Resolved by the picked volunteers, to honour King Demetrios, son of King Antigonos, with a [gold or silver] statue on horseback in the Agora by the statue of Demokratia, where the other Greeks stand, and to establish an altar to him.'[148] Where in the Agora this may have stood is unknown, for we are uncertain as to the location of Demokratia, but we may well have here the pieces of this statue. Alternatively, the statue represented by these fragments may be associated in some way with the gate. They were found just across the street, 26 m to the south, in the crossroads well in a layer dating to about 200 BC, a time when the Athenians were disposing of all reminders of their Macedonian overlords.

40

The 3rd century BC: civil wars

The years of Demetrios' reign and the following ones were difficult for Athens as full-scale civil war broke out between nationalist and pro-Macedonian factions. The government changed hands seven times between 307 and 261, often violently. One such revolt, in 287 or 286 BC, is described in an honorary inscription for one Kallias, son of Thymochares of Sphettos. It was found in 1971, reused as a cover for the large drain east of the Royal Stoa. Part of it reads:

Whereas Kallias – when the revolution of the Demos [people] took place against those who were occupying the city, and they expelled the mercenary soldiers from the city, but the fort of the Mouseion was still occupied, and the countryside was in a state of war at the hands of the troops from the Peiraeus, and while Demetrios with his army was approaching from the Peloponnese to attack the city – Kallias learned the impending danger to the state and choosing a thousand of the mercenary troops stationed with him on Andros, paying their wages and providing rations of grain, he came at once to the city to help the Demos, acting in accordance with the good will of King Ptolemy toward the Demos; and he marched his troops into the countryside and made every effort to protect the harvest of grain so that as much grain as possible could be brought into the city.

And whereas, when Demetrios had arrived and encamped to besiege the city, Kallias fought on the side of the Demos, and attacking with his troops, although a wounded man, he did not shrink from any danger, not at any moment, for the sake of the deliverance of the people.[149]

Characteristic of such civil wars, Phaidros, the brother of this democrat Kallias, was one of the city's leading pro-Macedonian figures; he also was honoured by the Athenians, though some fifteen years later when Athens was again under Macedonian control. Both men were honoured with bronze statues in the Agora along with inscribed stelai recording their benefactions.

The effects of these wars can actually be seen in the buildings of the Agora. The Tholos/Bouleuterion complex shows signs of damage at this time, early in the 3rd century BC, as do a number of private houses which lie to the southwest in the industrial district, that is, between the Agora and the Mouseion hill, garrisoned by the Macedonians. Among them were houses C and D where the *117* bronzeworkers lived (p. 140) and the house of the sculptors Mikion and *120* Menon (p. 142). These and several others were subsequently abandoned as death, exile, and emigration took their sad toll.

This gloomy picture of 3rd-century Athens is further substantiated when one considers public building activity in the Agora and the rest of Athens. Almost no new buildings are to be found anywhere in the city. The grim political and economic circumstances clearly affected urban development, and for all intents and purposes private and public building activity ceased until near the end of the century. In the Agora only two buildings can be dated to the 3rd century, and both of them are modest indeed.

The Square Peristyle

In the northeast corner of the Agora a huge peristyle courtyard was laid out *129* and construction started in the years around 300 BC. It measured over 35 m on a side, covering and presumably meant to replace in function the series of earlier buildings on the spot identified on the basis of the 'ballot box' as lawcourts. Much reused material was incorporated into the structure and its appearance can best be described as shoddy; proper foundations were not always laid, and the west side was never finished. Indeed, the whole building seems never to have been properly brought to completion, though it seems to have been used, and its construction reflects the difficult times.

The Arsenal

A second building which may be dated to the early 3rd century BC lies on the *151* slopes of Kolonos Agoraios, just north of the Hephaisteion. It is in terrible disrepair, with only a few foundation blocks preserved; however, cuttings in bedrock give some idea of the plan of a large rectangular building measuring 17.62 m by 44.4 m with two rows of eight interior supports in each row. Given its large size and plan, the most probable identification of the building is an arsenal, used by the state for the storage of armour, weapons, and other military equipment. We have noted elsewhere that the Athenian cavalry, though much depleted, trained just below this building, and the group of tokens used for the distribution of armour was found in a well less than 70 m *95* away (p. 120).

More and more, Athens came under the influence of one or another Hellenistic kingdom in an attempt to counterbalance the strong Macedonian control. King Ptolemy Soter of Egypt is mentioned in the decree honouring Kallias, and in 223 BC King Ptolemy Euergetes was awarded the extraordinary honour of being named an eponymous hero. The tribes were thus increased to thirteen in number, and a thirteenth statue was added to the Monument of the Eponymous Heroes.

At the end of the 3rd century war broke out again, with Rhodes, Pergamon, and Rome aiding Athens against Philip V of Macedon. Failing to take Athens in 200 BC, Philip carried out a savage attack on the buildings and grave monuments in the suburbs outside the walls and in the demes of Attica. These outrageous and unnecessary acts of vandalism angered the Athenians, and a decree was passed which Livy records:

All statues and pictures of Philip as well as of all his ancestors in both the male and female line should be taken and destroyed; that all holidays, rites, and priesthoods instituted in his honour or that of his forefathers should be disestablished; that the places, too, in which a dedication or an inscription of this import had been placed should be accursed. A final clause made valid against Philip all the decrees formerly voted against the Peisistratidae.[150]

That this *damnatio memoriae* of the royal house of Macedon was actively carried out can be seen in several of the monuments of the Agora. First, the two tribes named after Demetrios and Antigonos were disbanded and their statues removed from the Monument of the Eponymous Heroes, reducing their number to eleven; within months, however, King Attalos I of Pergamon was added, bringing the number of tribes and statues back up to twelve. Not only were the tribes disbanded, but also all references to the Macedonians were expunged from the record. Several inscriptions which refer only in passing to the honours paid Antigonos and Demetrios had those references carefully and deliberately erased by chipping away the surface of the stone. Furthermore, we have the fragments of the gilded bronze equestrian statue, almost certainly of Demetrios, thrown into the crossroads well in 200 BC. Though the gold was stripped, the bronze too had considerable value and could have been melted down and reused. This is the fate of most bronze statuary, and the circumstances of preservation have left us a distorted view of the ratio of marble to bronze statues. Marble statues or fragments thereof tend to survive, whereas only a handful of bronze examples have survived being melted and reused. The cuttings for feet on statue bases indicate, however, that bronze statues were as common as marble in antiquity. The fact that the leg, sword, and drapery were tossed down the well presumably reflects the violent anti-Macedonian sentiment gripping Athens at this time as recorded by Livy; cool consideration and common sense would have prompted their reuse for monetary gain.

The 2nd century BC: recovery

The 2nd century BC saw the direct intervention in the Aegean of the power of Rome, drawn in by the various Hellenistic monarchs as they contended against each other. Victory over Macedon and Philip V was achieved by Rome and her allies in 197 BC, opening up for Athens a period of relative independence and stability. Soon one can sense the real significance of Athens in the Hellenistic and Roman periods, and one sees clearly its effect as early as the 2nd century. As a result of her great traditions, the teaching of Sokrates, Plato, Aristotle, and Zeno, and the founding of the philosophic schools of the Academy, the Lyceum, and the Stoa, Athens claimed to be and was in fact regarded as the educational and cultural centre of the Mediterranean. Anyone aspiring to be regarded as an educated and intellectual man came to study under the philosophers and teachers of rhetoric and logic who crowded into Athens and especially the Agora. Princes of the royal houses came also, and Antiochos IV Ephiphanes was in the city in 176 BC, shortly before becoming king of Syria. In the 2nd century this royal interest in Athens gained substance in the form of large public buildings paid for by foreign benefactors in appreciation of Athenian pre-eminence as the cultural centre of the ancient world. Once one or two monarchs made such a gift, then that healthy spirit of rivalry which

139

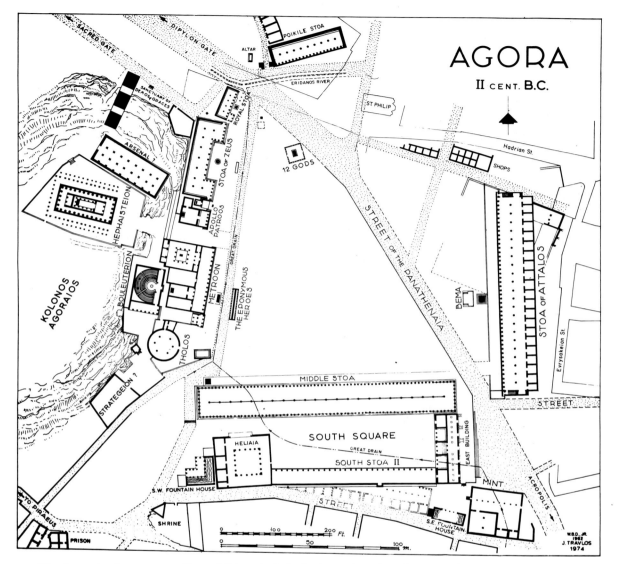

139 *The Agora in about 150 BC. New additions include the Stoa of Attalos, the stoas of the South Square, and the Arsenal north of the Hephaisteion.*

permeated so much of the ancient Greek life took over and many monarchs followed suit. The royal houses of Egypt, Syria, Pergamon, Cappadocia, and the Pontus are all known to have contributed to Athenian resources in the Hellenistic period, and particularly in the 2nd century. Buildings were seen as the most appropriate and permanent gift, and there was a tremendous burst of activity which resulted in several large edifices the city herself could never have afforded. In the Agora this represents a major renaissance following the troubled and impoverished 3rd century.

140 The Stoa of Attalos soon after its reconstruction in 1956. The remains of the Roman Odeion, or concert hall, are visible in the foreground.

The Stoa of Attalos

The most impressive of the new buildings of the 2nd century Agora was built
along the east side of the square by King Attalos II, who ruled Pergamon from
159 to 138 BC. The identification is based on a large dedicatory inscription
carved on the architrave: 'King Attalos, son of King Attalos and Queen
Apollonis, built the stoa . . . to the demos of the Athenians'.[151] It was a large
stoa or colonnaded building of marble and limestone, measuring over 115 m
long by 20 m wide, and rising to two storeys. There was a double colonnade
downstairs with twenty-one rooms behind, and the same arrangement was
repeated on the floor above. This stoa thus represents the fullest development
of this important architectural type. The forty-two rooms were shops: the Stoa
served as the ancient predecessor of the modern shopping mall, with numerous
stores all housed under a single roof. After centuries of casual and temporary
shelters, the commercial aspects of the Agora were housed in very elegant
surroundings. The individual shops were presumably rented out by the state,
and the revenues could pay for the upkeep of the building with money to spare.
Doric and Ionic columns were used, along with a particularly Pergamene
capital adapted from the Egyptian palm variety. The columns are spaced more
widely apart than in most Classical buildings, especially temples; here they fall
under every third triglyph of the frieze rather than under every other triglyph.
This is undoubtedly to ease access to the building which, unlike a temple with
its closely spaced columns, was intended to be used by large numbers of
people. Also because of this heavy traffic the bottom third of each exterior
column was left unfluted, since there was every reason to expect they would
become worn or chipped by the passage of goods and people in and out of the
building. The interior columns were left unfluted since their position
precluded the effective play of light and shadow across the shaft.

The Stoa stood for over 400 years and was destroyed by the Herulians (p.
197) in AD 267. The ruins were then incorporated into the line of a new
fortification wall, and as a result parts of the north and south ends stood to
their full height into modern times. In the 1940s several attempts were made to
find a suitable location for a site museum, with no good results because of the
wealth of ancient remains uncovered at every turn. In the end the only solution
was to reconstruct an ancient building and the Stoa of Attalos was the obvious
candidate: it was large enough, and sufficient pieces remained to ensure an
accurate reconstruction. The building was reconstructed between 1952 and
1956, using the same materials as the original for the visible parts and a fair
amount of reinforced concrete elsewhere. Towards the south end original
pieces were incorporated to allow the visitor to check for himself the
correctness of the rebuilding. Only one mistake was made. None of the
original lion-head spouts which drained rainwater off the roof had its muzzle
preserved. As a result all the new lions were made without tongues and instead
of throwing water clear of the building the lions tend to drool, the water
dripping off their chins and spattering on the steps below. With this one

141 Reconstructed view of the north end of the ground floor of the Stoa of Attalos.

142 The Stoa of Attalos, c. 150 BC. Plan of the foundations (below), ground floor (centre), and first floor (top). The forty-two rooms were used as shops, making the stoa one of the principal market buildings of Hellenistic Athens.

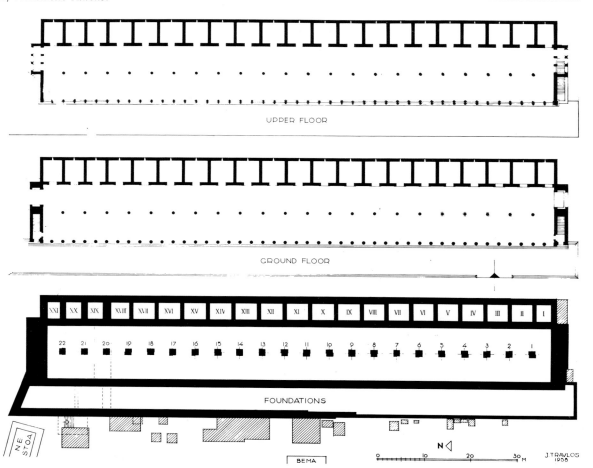

UPPER FLOOR

GROUND FLOOR

FOUNDATIONS

NE STOA

BEMA

N

0   10   20   30 M

J. TRAVLOS
1956

143 An example of an interior column capital from the upper storey of the Stoa of Attalos. This type, which originated in Pergamon, the capital of king Attalos, is an adaptation of the Egyptian palm-leaf variety.

144 (below) A view down the length of the ground floor of the reconstructed Stoa of Attalos. Such colonnades, providing shelter with ample light and air for vast numbers of people, were a favoured architectural form in public buildings.

145 (opposite) Cut-away model of the Stoa of Attalos, showing the arrangement of the colonnades, rooms, and roofing.

exception, however, the Stoa is an accurate replica of the original, and here the visitor may sense for himself the effects of light, shadow, space, and air in an ancient stoa. Cool in summer and sheltering in winter, the stoa was and is well-suited to the Greek climate, and it is easy to see why it was such a popular form for a public building.

144

The South Square

Other stoas too were begun at about this same time, in the first half of the 2nd century BC. Three buildings, two of them stoas, were laid out in a planned complex which effectively cut off the south half of the square from the north. The earliest of these components was the great Middle Stoa, which ran east–west and divided the Agora into two unequal parts. This represented a major encroachment on the integrity of the old square, and one of the early boundary stones is buried – still in place – deep within the foundation of the building at its western end. The effect of this division was made less abrupt by the plan of the new stoa, which had Doric colonnades facing both north and south. A screen wall connecting the interior columns divided the Stoa into two distinct halves. The Stoa is a large one, measuring *c.* 147 m long by 17.5 m wide. Despite its great size it was relatively modest in its building material, the columns and entablature all of limestone, except for marble metopes in the frieze, and the sima (gutter) of terracotta. Their surfaces have preserved

139, 146,
147

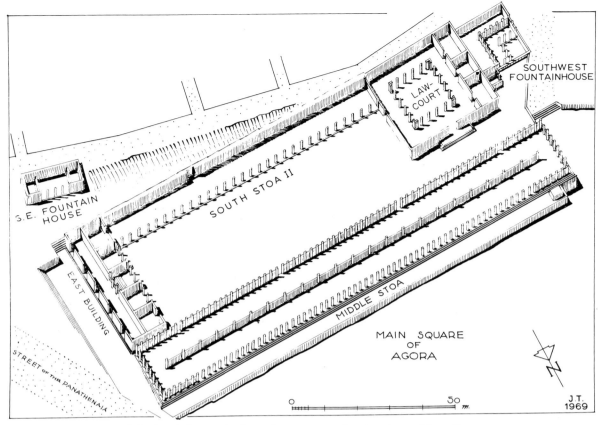

146 *A cut-away view of the South Square in the 2nd century* BC, *showing the position of the Middle Stoa, the East Building, and South Stoa II.*

147 *A view of the South Square, seen from the east. The Middle Stoa starts in the foreground and recedes towards the upper right.*

remarkably well the traces of bright paint with which this and most Greek buildings were decorated in their upper parts. The Doric columns were unfluted. If the building had a royal donor we do not know his identity, though Pharnakes I of Pontus has been suggested.

X

The second element of the South Square is the so-called East Building, which connected the two new stoas at their eastern end. It was a relatively small building (12 by 40 m) divided longitudinally with the east half facing the Panathenaic Way and the west half opening onto the square to the west. The east half is a single long room, with a mosaic floor of marble chips. Set into this floor at regular intervals are marble base blocks with cuttings in their upper surfaces for the feet of tables or some similar piece of furniture. Only four are preserved, though originally there were twelve, set 3 m apart. The floor level of the west half of the building lies *c.* 1.7 m lower than the east half; here there were five square rooms, with the central one serving as a staircase joining the two levels.

148

The third element, South Stoa II, formed the southern limit of the South Square. It replaced, at a slightly different orientation and at a much lower level, old South Stoa I, which was demolished after some 270 years to make way for the newcomer. This stoa too was of the Doric order, with only a single colonnade and no rooms behind. A small fountain was built into the back wall, its source the large stone aqueduct which fed the southwest fountainhouse. Most of the building material and particularly the Doric façade of South Stoa II came from the square peristyle at the northeast corner of the Agora, which was demolished at this same time to make room for the Stoa of Attalos.

146, 149

The order of construction of the South Square seems to have been as described: the Middle Stoa was laid out first, apparently as early as *c.* 180 BC, with the East Building and South Stoa II constructed in the years around the middle of the century. To the west, the old lawcourt still stood, though with an interior peristyle and new rooms along its west side, perhaps added at this same time. The monumental water-clock along its north wall went out of use, its functions taken over by the clock and sundials of the elegant Tower of the Winds. Beyond, the old Southwest Fountainhouse was embellished with a new annex.

The function of the South Square has been a problem which has plagued the excavators since its discovery. Gymnasium, lawcourt complex, and sanctuary have all been proposed and ultimately rejected. On the whole an early suggestion still seems the best, that is to regard the South Square as essentially a commercial centre and the two new stoas as market buildings. They are appropriate for this function and, as we have seen, there is reason to suppose that earlier South Stoa I was an official commercial building in this southern part of the Agora. The buildings which replaced it might reasonably be expected to have fulfilled a similar function. If so, the tables in the East Building should perhaps be thought of as the bankers' tables where money-changers conducted business in a convenient location for those entering the

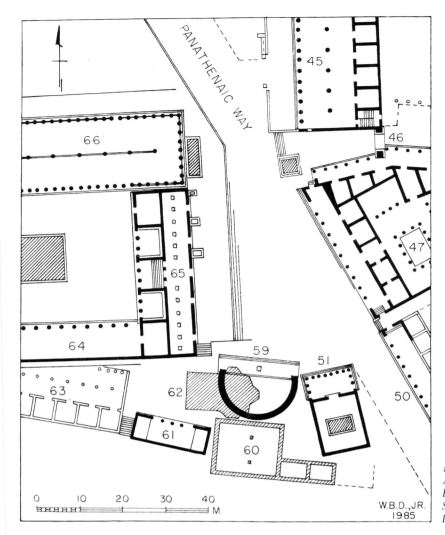

PANATHENAIC WAY

148 *The southeast corner of the
Agora in about* AD *150. No. 65,
East Building; 59, Nymphaion; 51,
Southeast Temple; 47, Library of
Pantainos.*

W.B.D.,JR.
1985

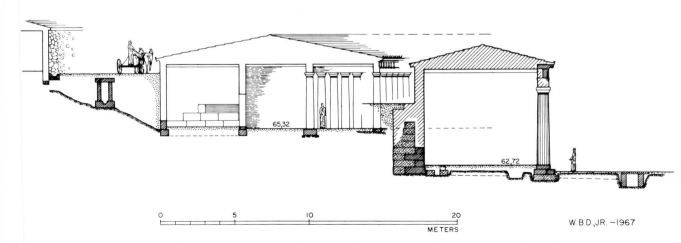

65,32

62,72

W.B.D,JR. —1967

149 *Cross-section of the south side of the Agora. From left to right: south road with
aqueduct to Southwest Fountainhouse; room and double colonnade of South Stoa I; and,
at a much lower level, South Stoa II.*

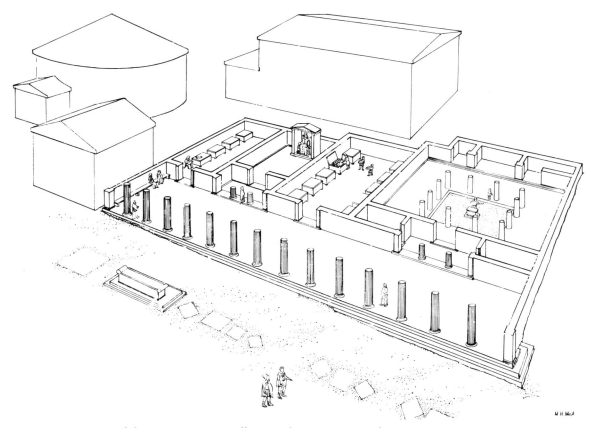

150 Cut-away view of the Metroon in its Hellenistic phase, c. 140 BC. The exact arrangement of the shrine of the Mother of the Gods and the archives is conjectural. The Tholos and New Bouleuterion are shown in outline behind.

market area from the Panathenaic Way. The Mint lay nearby, of course, and the tables may have been the place where the bronze coinage was actually put into circulation.

The new Metroon

Also built at this same time, in the years around 140 BC, was a new Metroon, four rooms set side by side with an Ionic colonnade along the east façade. The interior arrangement is unclear, and there is no way of knowing with certainty where the archives were stored or where the gold and ivory statue of the Mother described by Pausanias may have stood. Indeed, the form of the building gives no hint as to its function, and its identification as archives and sanctuary depends entirely on the traveller's account.

68, 91, 150, 151

With all these building operations completed, the old Agora took on a very different appearance in the second half of the 2nd century BC. The open square

139

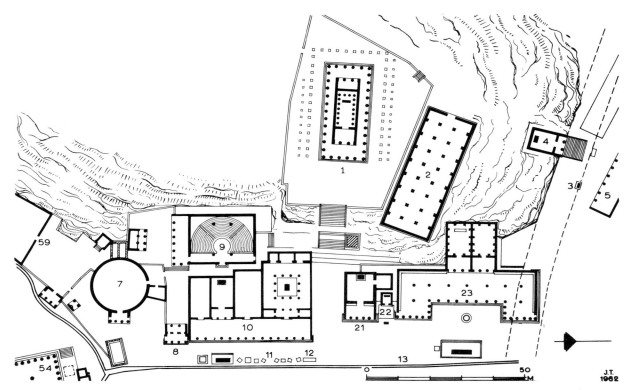

151 Civic buildings along the west side of the Agora in the Hellenistic period. No. 2, Arsenal; 10, Metroon. For the south (left) half, compare the aerial photograph ill. 68.

was very much smaller, divided into two unequal halves by the Middle Stoa. Furthermore, each half was now more clearly defined by the architecture set around its edges, especially the northern half. With the rebuilding of the Metroon all sides were now closed with colonnades, approximating the great squares being laid out in newly founded Hellenistic cities in the east, which regularly had stoas on all four sides. On the west the Royal Stoa, Stoa of Zeus, Temple of Apollo, and Metroon made up an irregular but nonetheless almost continuous colonnaded border, while the other three sides were defined by the Painted Stoa, the Stoa of Attalos, and the Middle Stoa. An attempt was made to impose the appearance of order and grandeur on the somewhat quaint, irregular, and unplanned arrangement of the old Classical Agora.

6 The Roman period

Historically speaking, one should probably date the beginnings of the 'Roman period' in Greece to 146 BC. In that year the Roman general Mummius smashed the Achaean League, completely destroying the capital city of Corinth, and from that time on Greece was ruled as though a Roman province. Archaeologically, one would never know it in Athens: the citizens did not change immediately to togas, start speaking Latin, or begin building vaults and using baked bricks. The Stoa of Attalos, for instance, was built just during this period (159–138 BC), as we saw in the last chapter, and it is a pure Hellenistic building, like most other Athenian monuments of the 2nd century BC.

More significant for our purposes is the year 86 BC. In 88 the Athenians made the mistake of siding with King Mithradates of Pontus in his revolt against Rome, and they paid for it. In 86, Athens and Peiraieus were besieged in a long and bitter campaign by the Roman general Sulla. Much damage was done to the city during this siege, and several large stone catapult balls found in the Agora serve to remind us of Roman power and the sophistication of her siege machinery. The Agora itself seems to have been beyond the initial reach of the catapults, estimated to have a range of *c.* 400 m, but the Romans did break through the walls in the northwest part of the circuit, near the Agora, and several monuments, particularly those of the South Square, show signs of damage. South Stoa II, the Heliaia, and the East Building all seem to have been destroyed, and the evidence of potters' kilns, metalworkers' casting pits and slag, and sculptors' marble dust, emery pits, and saw marks suggest that the area was used thereafter for mixed industrial activities. From 86 BC on, Athens' fate is inextricably linked to her relations with Rome, whose civil wars in the 1st century BC were all fought on Greek soil. The several battles brought numerous prominent Romans to Greece and to Athens in particular: Julius Caesar, Pompey, Brutus, Cassius, and Mark Antony all visited and supported the city, and several were honoured by the Athenians, including those whom history and Shakespeare have since depicted as evil. Brutus and Cassius, for instance, were honoured as tyrant slayers for their assassination of Julius Caesar, and 'The Athenians also voted them bronze statues beside the statue of Harmodios and the statue of Aristogeiton, on the ground that they had emulated these men.'[152] Mark Antony, too, was honoured by the Athenians before his disastrous loss with Cleopatra to Octavian at the Battle of Actium in

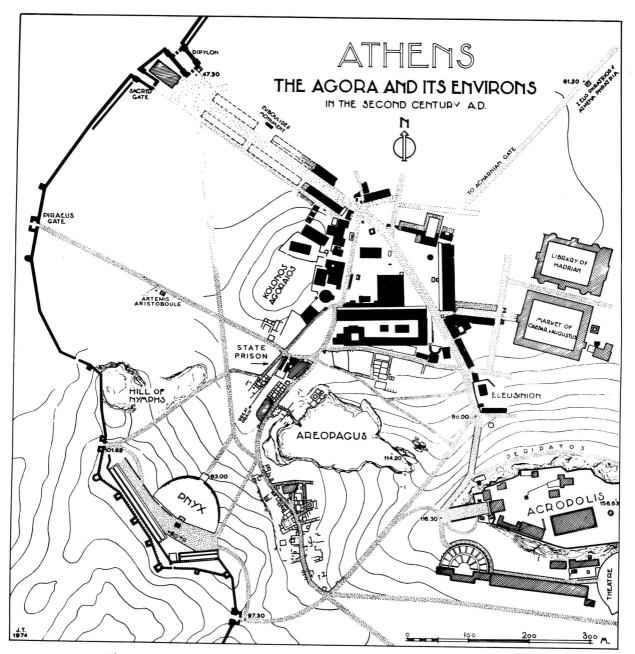

152 *The Agora and northwest Athens in the 2nd century* AD. *The Library of Hadrian and the Market of Caesar and Augustus lie east (right) of the Agora, which is shown in heavy black.*

31 BC. With his victory Octavian (later Augustus) became master of Rome and her empire.

With this string of poor guesses, backing consecutive losers in Mithradates, Brutus and Cassius, and Antony, one might expect Athens to have fared poorly under Roman rule, and for the early part of the 1st century BC this seems to have been the case. By the middle of the century, however, the cultural and educational achievements of Athens, so admired by the Romans, led to her recovery. Together with the politicians and military leaders came Roman men of letters such as Cicero, Horace, and Ovid to study at the famed centre of education and philosophy. As early as the time of Julius Caesar, perhaps in *c.* 50 BC, Roman benefactors of the city are evident, fulfilling the role of the

153 The Agora in the 2nd century AD, at the period of its fullest development.

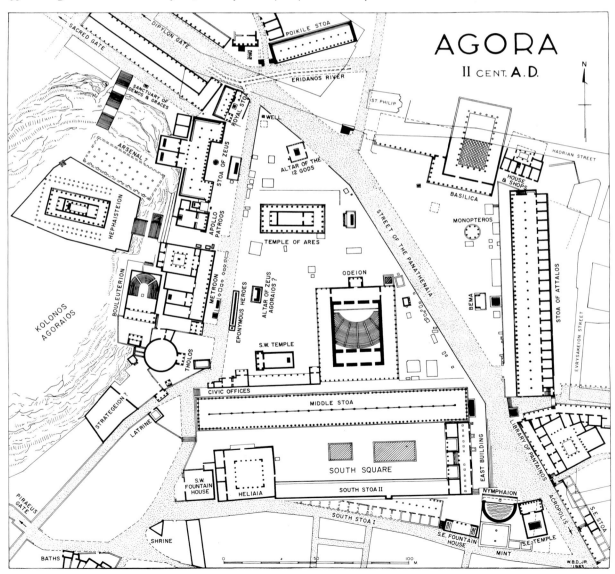

Hellenistic monarchs of the preceding centuries for exactly the same reason. As we shall see, many of the new buildings closely reflect Athens' role in that they are cultural and educational monuments, such as libraries, odeia, lecture halls, gymnasia, and schools.

152 An important development for the old Agora in Roman times was the construction of a new market-place some 150 m to the east. A large courtyard, open to the sky and surrounded on all four sides by colonnades, the building was begun with money provided by Julius Caesar, presumably in the 50s BC, and completed in the reign of Augustus sometime around 11–9 BC. Its construction had a profound effect on the old Agora, for it was now apparently no longer thought necessary to maintain the large open square and late in the 1st century BC it was largely covered by two buildings, the Odeion of Agrippa and the Temple of Ares.

The Odeion of Agrippa

153, 154 By far the most imposing structure of the Roman additions to the Agora was
140 the great Odeion (concert hall) known as the Agrippeion, after M. V. Agrippa, the victorious general at Actium and son-in-law of the emperor Augustus. It was built in the centre of the old square, fittingly enough not far from the early orchestra, along the north side of the Middle Stoa. The date of construction should coincide with Agrippa's visit to the city between 16 and 14 BC, and it was completed most likely before his death in 12 BC. The Odeion boasted a huge span of 25 m with no internal supports over the auditorium, which seated about a thousand people. The semicircular orchestra was paved with thin marble slabs, and the face of the low raised stage was adorned with sculpture. The outside was decorated with large Corinthian columns and pilasters. Entered at ground level from the north or at an upper level from the Middle Stoa terrace to the south, the new Odeion stood several storeys high, completely dominating the other buildings of the Agora. The original function, as the name implies, was to serve as a concert hall. There is often a functional and architectural distinction to be made between theatres and odeia. A theatre was for dramatic performances of plays, both comedies and tragedies, whereas an odeion usually housed concerts or musical performances. Architecturally, a theatre was open to the sky, while an odeion was a roofed building. The function of the Odeion of Agrippa changed somewhat, as we shall see, when the roof collapsed in the mid-2nd century AD.

The Temple of Ares and other itinerant temples

The second building erected near the centre of the old open square in the late 1st century BC was actually an old-timer. It was a handsome marble temple of
153, 155 the Doric order, dating to the 5th century BC and close in both date and style to the Hephaisteion. It was dismantled piece by piece and re-erected in the Agora on a set of newly-laid foundations, just north of the Odeion. Masons' marks carved on all the blocks of the superstructure as the building was disassembled

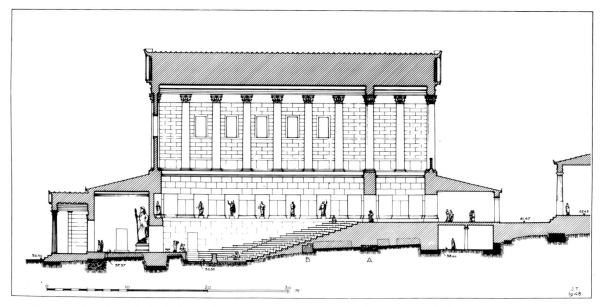

154 *Cross-section through the Odeion of Agrippa, 1st century* BC. *Looking east, with the Middle Stoa on the right.*

guided the workers when the temple was reassembled. From Pausanias' account of this part of the Agora, the temple should probably be that of Ares, which the traveller saw after the Eponymous Heroes and before he mentions the Odeion. If this identification is correct, then we may also have a hint as to where the temple originally stood, for we learn from inscriptions of the 4th century BC that there was a cult of Ares at the deme of Acharnai in the foothills of Mount Parnes, several miles to the north of Athens.

The Temple of Ares is just one element in an unusual building programme during the reign of Augustus, and perhaps somewhat later, which involved the reuse of several excellent examples of Classical architecture in the Agora.

155 *The Temple of Ares. Built in the 5th century* BC *and set up elsewhere in Attika originally, it was dismantled piece by piece and reerected in the Agora in the early Roman period. It is similar in size and design to the Hephaisteion.*

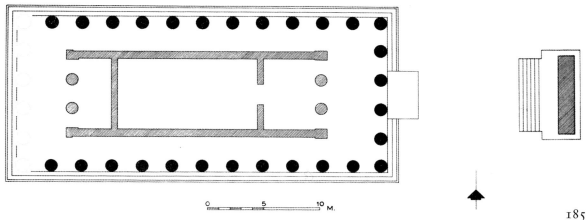

Often the original location of these buildings can be determined, and it is clear that they were brought in from all over Attica. The countryside was apparently depopulated in this period and the old shrines sadly neglected. The practical and useful solution was to dismantle the old structures and reuse them in whole or in part in new buildings in the Agora. The Temple of Ares is but one instance of a fairly widespread practice. Other examples have been recognized by means of masons' marks of the Roman period on marble architectural fragments of the 5th and 4th centuries BC, and by matching pieces in the Agora with others left on the original site when only part of the old building was moved.

Parts of two buildings from Sounion found their way into the Agora at this time. The marble gutter off the roof of the Temple of Poseidon was taken and reused on the Ares temple, and eight columns from the Temple of Athena at Sounion were used in the façade of a small temple which was built over the ruins of the Mint, which went out of use when Athens stopped minting coins in *148* the late 1st century BC. Known simply as the Southeast Temple, it faced north, looking right down the Panathenaic Way.

Another series of columns came from an enigmatic building at Thorikos, on the east coast of Attica. Six Doric columns of the characteristic local marble were brought in and reused, probably in the so-called Southwest Temple, a small prostyle building which faced west, lying just east of the Tholos. The original building at Thorikos was unfinished, and the columns were fluted only in their Roman reuse. The Doric architrave and frieze came from other buildings of varying dimensions and were recut to fit the temple.

A third series of Classical architecture has not yet been assigned to any foundations. It consists of several Ionic columns of the highest quality and finest workmanship. Two series of columns of different heights are represented. The capital of one still retains traces of the original paint with *XI* which the upper parts of all Greek colonnades were decorated. The original location of the building these columns came from is not known.

The foundations of another prostyle temple of the same period may be part of this same programme. It lies north of the altar of Aphrodite, facing south, its position analogous to that of the Southeast Temple, which it faces, looking right up the Panathenaic Way. No fragments of the superstructure of this temple have been recognized.

Yet another religious monument apparently moved into the Agora at this time was a handsome altar of white marble, set up just northeast of the *156* Eponymous Heroes. Its platform measures *c.* 9 m by 5.5 m, and the orthostats were decorated with a series of elaborately carved mouldings: a guilloche, a Lesbian leaf, and a bead and reel. The style and workmanship suggest a date in the 4th century BC while the characteristic masons' marks of the Roman period indicate that its present position is a secondary one.

All these architectural elements have common features which seem to suggest that they were part of a deliberate building programme. All of the

156 Marble altar possibly of Zeus Agoraios. Originally set up elsewhere in the 4th century BC, it was dismantled and reerected in the Agora in the early Roman period.

architecture is of first-rate workmanship of the 5th and 4th centuries BC, and all the foundations and masons' marks indicate that they were moved to the Agora during and soon after the reign of Augustus, a time when Rome was strongly influenced by the achievements of Classical Athens. The deities of these new temples may also be of interest, for it is just at this time that we get inscriptions in the Agora referring to numerous cults of the Imperial family. Starting with Alexander, Hellenistic kings and then Roman emperors were accorded divine worship as gods. In Athens thirteen altars dedicated to the deified Augustus have been found, and a small round temple on the Acropolis was dedicated to Rome and Augustus. Other members of his family such as C. Caesar, Livia, and Tiberius were also worshipped, often in conjunction with an established Olympian deity, and we should perhaps regard the itinerant temples as a way of providing suitable housing for the Imperial cults which at the same time rescued some magnificent Classical architecture from obscurity and neglect.

Following the reign of Augustus there was little building activity for almost a century, until the reign of Trajan ushered in the 2nd century AD and a period of renewed prosperity for Athens.

The Library of Pantainos

The earliest building of the Agora which dates to the 2nd century AD was actually built by a local man, Pantainos, the son of Flavius Menander. The building lies along the Panathenaic Way just south of the Stoa of Attalos, and it has a very unusual plan. The core of the building is made up of just two rooms, *157* the first a large central courtyard open to the sky and measuring 20 m by

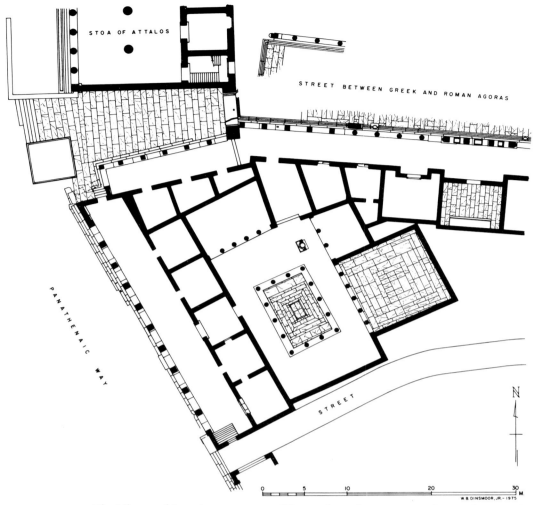

Within the image:

STOA OF ATTALOS

STREET BETWEEN GREEK AND ROMAN AGORAS

PANATHENAIC WAY

STREET

N

0 5 10 20 30 M

W.B. DINSMOOR, JR. - 1975

157 The Library of Pantainos, c. AD 100. Three colonnades are wrapped around a central courtyard and the library itself which opens off the court.

13.5 m. This court was originally paved with marble chips set in mortar. At some later date the courtyard had a small peristyle added to it, with the central part paved in marble slabs. Opening off the courtyard to the east was a large square room, also with a marble floor. Around these two rooms were wrapped three stoas set at irregular angles to one another. The western stoa ran along the east side of the Panathenaic Way, a short northern stoa faced the south end of the Stoa of Attalos, and a long eastern stoa ran for 70 m along the south side of the street which connected the Agora with the Roman market of Caesar and Augustus. Soon after the construction of the stoa the street itself was paved in marble at the expense of the people of Athens. All three stoas were of the Ionic order and behind the colonnades were rooms which have been identified as shops.

158
159

158 View looking east along the marble street connecting the Classical Agora and the Roman Agora, or Market of Caesar and Augustus (background), c. AD 100. Along the side of the street runs the north stoa of the Library of Pantainos.

159 (below) The north stoa of the Library of Pantainos, looking east towards the Gateway of the Market of Caesar and Augustus (Roman Agora). The edge of the marble street is visible just to the left of the colonnade. Compare ill. 158.

160 Dedicatory inscription of the Library of Pantainos, c. AD 100. The building, made up of three stoas, a peristyle courtyard, and a collection of books, was dedicated to Athena, the Athenians, and the emperor Trajan by Pantainos, priest of the Muses. Length 2.8 m.

160 The identification of this complex and much more besides can be determined from the dedicatory inscription on the lintel of a doorway that led from the western stoa into the courtyard behind. It reads:

To Athena Polias and to the Emperor Caesar Augustus Nerva Trajan Germanicus and to the city of the Athenians, the priest of the wisdom-loving [philosophical] Muses, Titus Flavius Pantainos, the son of Flavius Menander the head of the school, gave the outer stoas, the peristyle, the library with the books, and all the furnishings within them, from his own resources, together with his children Flavius Menander and Flavia Secundilla.[153]

Here we have an inscription that epitomizes Roman Athens: a man who describes himself as the priest of the philosophical muses, the son of the head of a philosophical school, making the gift of an educational institution, a *161* library. The library rules, little changed today, are preserved in another inscription found in the building: 'No book is to be taken out since we have sworn an oath. The library is to be open from the first hour until the sixth.'[154] The date of Pantainos' work can be narrowed down thanks to the dedication to Trajan, who carries here the epithet Germanicus. By the end of his reign Trajan, having fought the Dacians (AD 102) and the Parthians (AD 115), was known as Trajan Germanicus Dacicus Parthicus. The date of the building is therefore between the emperor's accession in AD 98 and his Dacian campaign in AD 102, and Pantainos' library is among the most precisely dated structures in the Agora. Trajan seems actually to have been worshipped in the building. Found in its ruins were parts of his statue, dating after AD 102, with a captured Dacian crouching at his feet, along with the base for a second statue dedicated by his priest Herodes Atticus Marathonios. The precise wording used to

161 *Rules for the Library of Pantainos: 'No book is to be taken out because we have sworn an oath. [The Library] is to be open from the first hour until the sixth.' Width 32 cm.*

describe those elements given by Pantainos and the fact that the inscription runs up onto the decorative mouldings of the lintel block both suggest that Pantainos is making additions to a pre-existing building. This is further suggested by the remains themselves for, as we have seen, the peristyle is an addition to the courtyard, replacing the earlier marble-chip floor. If, as seems reasonable, these additions are being made to his father's establishment, then we may have here not only the 'library of Pantainos' but also one of the famed philosophical schools of Athens.

After Trajan the emperor Hadrian came to the throne in AD 117. More than any other Roman emperor he was a Philhellene and especially fond of Athens, visiting the city three times during his reign. He made the city a centre of his worship, finishing the great temple of Olympian Zeus and then sharing the sanctuary with him. Pausanias lists among his benefactions to Athens a shrine of Panhellenian Zeus and Hera, a Pantheon, a library, and a gymnasium. The Athenians were grateful for these and other gifts: Hadrian was made an Eponymous Hero, and some ninety-four altars dedicated to the deified   74
emperor have been found in the city. The great arch which bears his name still stands near the Olympieion, honouring the emperor for his many donations to the city. Along the west side of the Agora a large torso of an armed Hadrian   162

191

162 Torso of a large marble statue of Hadrian (AD 117–138). The cuirass has a scene of Athena supported by the wolf of Rome.

was found. The cuirass was decorated with imagery appropriate to the Roman sense of Athenian primacy in cultural matters: Athena stands, flanked by two Nikai (Victories), on the Wolf of Rome with Romulus and Remus below. Archaeological evidence suggests further that two more buildings, in the Agora and not listed by Pausanias, were also built in Hadrian's reign.

The basilica

Along the east half of the north side of the square a great basilica was built, *139* dated according to the stratigraphy and architectural elements to the reign of Hadrian. The word basilica is an architectural term referring to a large three-aisled hall, used by the Romans for markets, administration, lawcourts, and the like, the way the Greeks used stoas. When early Christians began building large churches they copied this same three-aisled plan from the Roman civic examples, and the term now has a strongly religious connotation which should be avoided with these early examples. Only the southern part of the Agora basilica has been uncovered; most still lies under a street and modern houses. Nonetheless, enough has been revealed to indicate that it was a large building, *189* elegantly decorated with marble revetment and sculptured piers. While the Athenians seem to have been permitted to keep many of their local governmental institutions intact, relations with other cities and the crucial relations with Rome were under the administration of officials appointed by Rome. The basilica may be seen as a physical reflection of the intrusion of Roman administration into the affairs of the old Agora. Similar basilicas ring the forum of Roman Corinth, and we may suppose that administrative matters such as arbitrations and other legal proceedings were settled in these new buildings.

The Nymphaion

The other major addition to the Agora of the 2nd century was a Nymphaion built just west of the Panathenaic Way, near the southeast corner of the square *148, 163* and partially overlying the ruins of the Mint. A Nymphaion was a large, elaborate fountainhouse, taking its name originally from the Nymphs, who are often associated with springs, rivers, lakes, and other sources of water. The Agora example is in the form of a large hemicycle facing north and looking down the Panathenaic Way. Like so many Agora buildings, it is in a state of terrible disrepair and its original appearance can only be conjectured. On the basis of examples at Olympia and elsewhere, however, we can probably assume that the walls had niches in which statues of the imperial family were set and that the lower area was made up of basins, pools, and fountains. The water apparently came from the great aqueduct whose course can be traced for several miles north of Athens to the Kephalari springs on the lower slopes of Mt Penteli. The dedicatory inscription of this aqueduct records that it was begun under Hadrian but finished only in AD 140 during the reign of his successor, Antoninus Pius.

163 The Nymphaion at the southeast corner of the Agora, mid-2nd century AD, in a restored view. Most of the actual building lies under the Church of the Holy Apostles. A nymphaion was a large, elaborate fountain, often adorned with sculpture representing the imperial family of Rome.

The rebuilding of the Odeion of Agrippa

Also to the middle years of the 2nd century AD should be dated the rebuilding of the Odeion of Agrippa. After more than a century and a half the huge span over the auditorium was too great and the roof collapsed. The Odeion was extensively remodelled in its second phase, and even its function seems to have changed. A handsome series of sculptured figures of Giants (with snake tails) and Tritons (with fish tails) was added to the north façade; their torsos are virtually copies of some of the male figures in the pediments of the Parthenon. The auditorium was greatly restricted in size by the addition of a cross-wall which cut the seating capacity roughly in half, to about five hundred. This was possible because in the years around AD 160 a millionaire citizen by the name of Herodes Atticus built the Athenians a new Odeion on the south slopes of the

164 (opposite) A Giant from the façade of the second phase of the Odeion of Agrippa, c. AD 150–175, reused in the 5th-century gymnasium.

Acropolis. The old Odeion of Agrippa was now used largely as a lecture hall by philosophers and sophists if we may judge from two passages in Philostratos referring to events in about AD 177. One of these descriptions reads as follows: 'They assembled in the theatre in the Kerameikos (Agora) which is called Agrippeion; and as the day went on and Herodes tarried the Athenians became restive, thinking that the lecture was being cancelled. They thought the whole thing was a trick. So it became necessary for Alexander to come forward to give his discourse before Herodes arrived.'[155]

The remodelling should be dated on archaeological grounds to between AD 150 and 175. Stamped roof tiles used to date the building more precisely carry names which refer either to magistrates or simply to the contractor responsible for the manufacture of the tiles.

During and after these improvements and additions to the city in the 2nd century AD, the Agora continued to flourish as the focal point of the active intellectual life of the city, which is described in detail by Philostratos and others. Dozens of philosophers, sophists, rhetoricians, grammarians, and the like crowded Athens during these years, assuring the city's place as a seat of learning. Several philosophers held formal academic positions actually endowed by the emperors of Rome: 'When Marcus (Aurelius) had come to Athens and had been initiated into the Mysteries, he not only bestowed honours upon the Athenians, but also, for the benefit of the whole world, he established teachers at Athens in every branch of knowledge, granting these teachers an annual salary.'[156]

Athens' other great claim to the world's attention was her glorious past. That the Athenians continued to derive pleasure from their famed ancestors is clear from a large inscribed statue base set up on the steps of the east stoa of the Library of Pantainos. Only part of the base is preserved; originally it held a group of three statues, probably husband, wife, and child. The woman's name is missing but her genealogy is preserved. She is of noble descent, with grandfathers who served as Kerykes and Dadouchs, the chief priests of the Eleusinian mysteries. The text continues, listing her as 'the daughter of Kasianos Apollonios and Klaudia Menandra, sister of Kasianos Philippos, and twenty-first in descent from Perikles'.[157] The claim might not be so wild as it first appears. Her brother, Kasianos Philippos, is known from other sources to have been active early in the 3rd century, in the years around AD 230. If one multiplies out twenty-one generations of thirty years each, that brings one back to the 5th century BC and the time of Perikles. The old genealogies would have been kept in good order for a very practical reason: money. This is clear from Plutarch, who studied in Athens in the 1st century AD with a descendant of Themistokles who was still living on the proceeds of honours paid to his ancestor more than five hundred years before: 'For the descendants of Themistokles there were certain grants maintained in Magnesia down to my time, and the revenues of these were enjoyed by a Themistokles of Athens, who was my companion and friend in the school of the philosopher Ammonios.'[158]

The Herulian sack of Athens in AD 267

The 2nd and 3rd centuries AD represent the last great period of prosperity, when the Agora reached its fullest development, before a decline which began in the second half of the 3rd century. Though the city as a whole continued to prosper off and on, the old civic centre of the Agora never fully recovered from the attack of the Heruli.

According to Syncellos, 'The Heruli with 500 ships . . . sailed to the Pontos, took Byzantium and Chrysopolis . . . and reaching Attica they attacked Athens, Corinth, Sparta and Argos and overran all Achaia until the Athenians, ambushing them in rough terrain, destroyed most of them.'[159] The Heruli, otherwise little known in history, made their mark with their thorough destruction of Athens in AD 267. Evidence of this devastation was encountered all over the excavated area of the Agora, in the form of burnt fragments, collapsed walls, piles of broken roof tiles, and other debris. In the excavation notebooks what came to be recognized as the Odeion is regularly referred to simply as the 'burnt building' from the evidence of its destruction at the hands of the invaders. Under Herennius Dexippos the Athenians managed to drive off the Herulians, but not before the character of the Agora was changed forever. Some structures such as the Tholos and Royal Stoa survived, along with the institutions they housed, but most of the buildings, especially the Odeion and the great Hellenistic stoas, were totally ruined.

The post-Herulian wall

It took the Athenians some time to recover. One of their first projects was to refortify the city. In doing so they chose not to repair the old Themistoklean wall of the 5th century BC, a huge circuit which could be adequately defended when Athens was the most powerful independent polis of Greece, but not when she was a small provincial university town of the Roman Empire. Instead, the Athenians fortified a much smaller area, including just north of the Acropolis. The wall began with a new gate at the entrance to the citadel, *166* flanked with towers, and then ran down the east side of the Panathenaic Way to the Agora. Once in the Agora, one face of this wall rested on the line of the colonnade of the ruined west stoa of the Library of Pantainos. It then incorporated the back part of the Stoa of Attalos, also in ruins, before turning east towards the library of Hadrian. What this meant was that the old Agora, for centuries the centre of the city in all respects, was now not even within the fortified limits of the late Roman city.

The wall itself where it skirts the Agora bears eloquent testimony to the *165* Herulian destruction. Virtually every block in it was taken from some Agora building destroyed by the invaders. Pieces of the Temple of Area, the Library of

Pantainos, and the Southwest Temple have all been recognized, along with inscriptions, statue bases, sculpture, and numerous blocks from several other buildings. The wall was built with two faces of squared reused blocks, with the area between filled with rubble. Two coins from the rubble core prove that the wall was not built before the reign of Probus (AD 280–282), some fifteen years after the Herulians were driven off.

The 4th century AD: Alaric and the Visigoths

The 4th century was a period of relative decline and large-scale abandonment of the Agora. Much of the area seems to have been given over to industrial activity. Higher up on the hill to the south several large and luxurious villas were built in the 4th century, indicating that the city was far from dead; only the old Agora was neglected and Athenian energies must have been directed to other areas of the city within the walls, unexcavated at the present time.

In AD 395 Alaric and his Visigoths appeared outside the walls of Athens, having crossed the Roman frontier far to the north as early as 376. Our principal sources are in disagreement as to what happened next.[160] Some tell us that Alaric took and destroyed Athens, another that Athena and Achilles appeared fully-armed on the walls of the Acropolis and scared him away. In either case he then went on to spectacular success in his chosen career, destroying Corinth in AD 396 and Rome in 410. From the archaeological

165 East face of the post-Herulian fortification wall where it runs south of the Stoa of Attalos, c. AD 280 (cf. ill. 166). The wall here is built almost entirely of reused pieces taken from buildings in the Agora destroyed by the Herulians in AD 267.

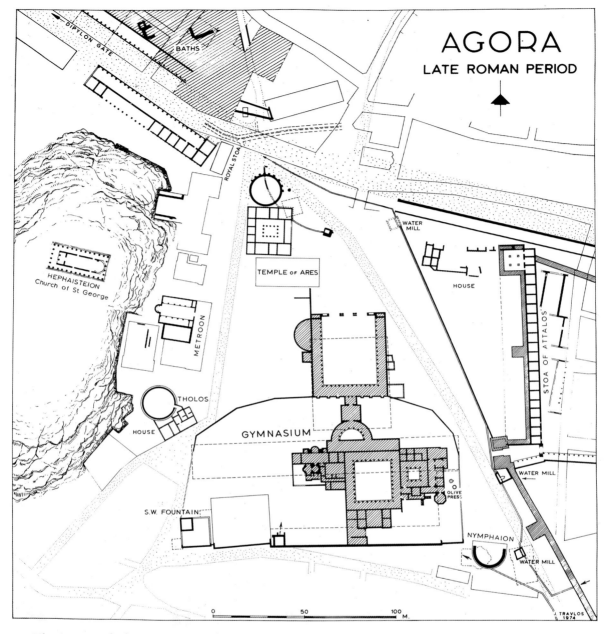

DIPLON GATE

BATHS

ROYAL STOA

HEPHAISTEION
Church of St George

TEMPLE of ARES

WATER MILL

HOUSE

STOA OF ATTALOS

METROON

THOLOS

HOUSE

GYMNASIUM

OLIVE PRESS

S.W. FOUNTAIN

NYMPHAION

WATER MILL

WATER MILL

0   50   100
M.

J. TRAVLOS
1974

166 The Agora in the late Roman period, c. AD 400–700.

evidence it is clear that Alaric did considerable harm in the area of the old
Agora. In particular there is evidence of damage to those buildings along the
west side which had survived the Herulians. But as these lie outside the
innermost fortification walls of the period, we have no way of determining yet
which source to believe regarding the fate of the city as a whole. The answer
lies buried under modern buildings to the east.

The 5th-century gymnasium

166
167
Following the departure of Alaric, there was something of a renaissance in Athens which extended to the old Agora. The better part of the entire square was taken up with a huge gymnasium complex which can be dated to the years after AD 400. It extended from the old entrance of the Odeion southward to the back wall of the ruins of South Stoa II. Four of the Giants and Tritons from the second phase of the Odeion were rescued and set up on high pedestals to adorn the new entrance. Behind were peristyle courtyards, numerous rooms, and bathing facilities. Space for exercise was limited, and we should probably think of the gymnasium as a school or university complex. The Greeks had always regarded their gymnasia as places to train and exercise the mind as well as the body, and several of the great philosophical schools such as the Lyceum and Academy were in fact directly associated with gymnasia. In modern Greek today the word for school is *gymnasion*. On the site where lectures were given in the 2nd century AD (p. 196), we find the same activity 250 years later in a striking but not uncommon example of continuity of function over long periods of time and despite intervening destructions.

The complex east of the Stoa of Attalos

168
169
Extensive rebuilding was also carried out in the area of the old Library of Pantainos in the early years of the 5th century AD. In particular the eastern stoa was rebuilt, this time with the addition of a second storey for the eastern two-thirds of its length. The stoa now served as a façade for a large new complex built on two levels. The rooms at ground level behind the colonnade were also refurbished, to serve as a basement suite for the principal rooms on the floor above, which had a small peristyle court, an apsidal room (audience chamber?), and provisions for bathing. The function of this large building is

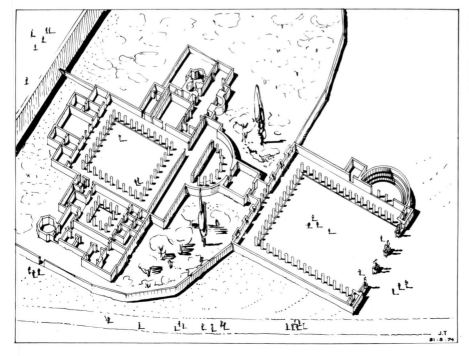

167 A cut-away perspective of the late Roman gymnasium, c. AD 400–420, seen from the northeast. The building was used not so much for athletic exercise as for lectures, philosophical discourses, and general academic instruction.

168 Reconstruction of the stoa in the complex east of the Stoa of Attalos, c. AD 420. The second storey is a new addition, cf. ill. 158. At left is the Gate of Athena, the entrance to the Roman Agora.

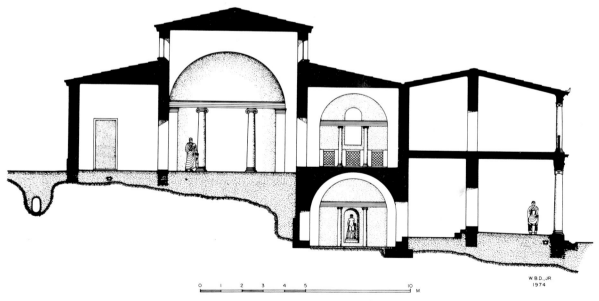

169 Cross-section of the late Roman complex east of the Stoa of Attalos, c. AD 420. Built on two levels and incorporating the north stoa of the Library of Pantainos, the complex may have served as some sort of official headquarters or residence. Destroyed by the Slavs in AD 582/3, it was restored and reused briefly in the 7th century (cf. ills. 168 and 188).

170 Plan of the Omega House on the slopes of the Areopagos. Built in the 4th century AD and destroyed in AD 582/3, it apparently served as a philosophical school until taken over by Christians in the 6th century AD. A collection of ten sculptures was found abandoned in the courtyards or thrown down three wells. A particularly elegant suite of rooms lay in the southeast corner (lower right, cf. ills. 180–82).

unknown, but its plan and later history suggest that it was a public building, perhaps an official residence of some sort.

The philosophical schools and the Omega House

Throughout these centuries the philosophical schools of Athens continued to thrive. Eunapius, writing in the 4th century AD, described the rich and occasionally acrimonious intellectual life of the city as various philosophers and their students contended with each other. Here still, after centuries, was the life-blood of Athens; long after she had relinquished all other claims to primacy in the ancient world, the descendants of the Academy and the Lyceum and the teachings of the Classical philosophers flourished. The schools were pagan establishments, with honours paid especially to Hermes and Herakles. In the end, their very popularity proved to be their downfall, for their success inspired resentment among the Christian rulers of the Empire, now established at Constantinople. In AD 529, the emperor Justinian forbade the teaching of philosophy at Athens, thereby wiping out by imperial decree a tradition of education dating back without interruption over a thousand years. The law was the death knell of the city, depriving Athens of her last claim to significance.

A good candidate for one of these late schools was found in 1970 up on the slopes of the Areopagos, just south of the Agora square. It is a large rich private house measuring 25 by 35 m, with sixteen rooms grouped around two courtyards. Lacking any ancient name it is often referred to as the Omega House, taking its name from the excavation section in which it lies. The large central courtyard was adorned with a peristyle of twelve marble columns of

170–72

171, 172 Cut-away and restored perspectives of the Omega House, viewed from the northwest.

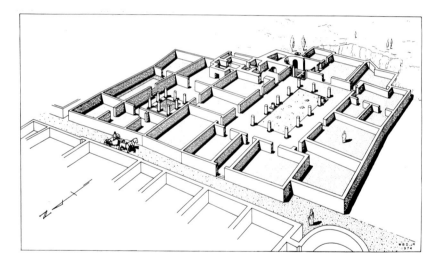

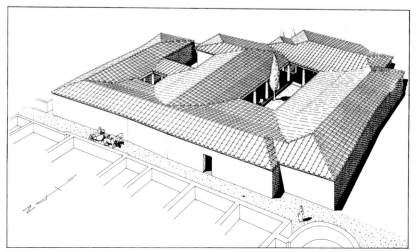

The Omega House: sculpture

173 *A marble head of the goddess Victory (Nike), found in the courtyard well of the Omega House, 2nd century* AD. *Height 42 cm.*

174 *(below, left) A portrait head of the 2nd century* AD *found in the courtyard well. Height 33.5 cm.*

175 *(below) A head of the sun-god (?Helios) from the courtyard well. Height 52 cm.*

176 A relief of Artemis, dressed as a huntress with dog and holding a torch, found in a courtyard well of the Omega House. The face has been deliberately mutilated, presumably by Christians. Height 26 cm.

177 (right) A small statue of Athena, reused as a step-block in the last phase of the Omega House.

178 (below) Relief of the Cave of Pan, originally dedicated by Neoptolemos in c. 330 BC, and reused in the Omega House. Note again how all the faces have been carefully mutilated. Height 65 cm.

The Omega House: architecture

179 An aerial view from 50 m of the southeast corner of the Omega House, showing the rich suite of rooms with mosaic floor (ill. 182) and horseshoe-shaped swimming pool (ill. 180). Part of the courtyard with its marble well-head can be seen at the upper left; the later bathing complex is at the upper right.

180–182 (opposite) The Omega House. Above: Southeast suite of rooms. The swimming-pool is visible in the foreground, as is the channel which supplied it with water. Below, left: View of the southeast suite, with the mosaic floor and marble revetment in situ. Below, right: The mosaic floor. The central scene, surrounded by a guilloche pattern, has been removed and replaced by marble slabs. Presumably it originally held some pagan mythological representation deemed unacceptable by the Christians who occupied the house just before its destruction in AD 582/3.

177
178
173–76
the Ionic order; in the line of both east and west colonnades wells were found, the one in the southwest corner still covered with a handsome marble well-head. Abundant sculpture was found here: a headless statue of Athena and a relief of the Cave of Pan in the courtyard, and three marble heads and a relief of Artemis as huntress in the wells. A particularly elegant suite lay off the southeast corner of the courtyard. Walking down the east aisle of the peristyle, one descended four marble steps flanked by Ionic columns into two lower

179–182
rooms. Here one came first to a mosaic floor with a central panel of marble slabs. In the east half of the same room was a horseshoe-shaped pool with steps leading down into it, the pool small but clearly functional, for the interior is painted turquoise with the edges of the steps highlighted with red paint. The walls of the room were revetted with thin marble slabs, many of which remain in place on the west wall. Nine different coloured marbles were used for their decorative effect. Whenever looking at most brick or concrete walls of the Roman period one should try to imagine such revetment, which almost always falls off or is stripped away when the building is destroyed. Given the usual state of preservation, we normally deal with the bare bones of Roman architecture which would have originally been hidden behind a handsome veneer of marble of the sort we can appreciate here. East of this sumptuous room with its marble walls, mosaic floor, and pool, there was a second room with a brick vault and arched niches where one could sit and stay cool on a hot summer's day.

179
A second interesting group of rooms lies just to the northeast where there is a small bathing complex consisting of a frigidarium (cold room) with two small plunge pools, a tepidarium (warm room), and a caldarium (hot room), also with a pool. The last two rooms have the typical hypocaust heating system of a raised floor with hot air circulating under the floor, drawn in by vertical flues set into the thickness of the wall. The bath is a later addition, dated by the stratigraphy to the first half of the 6th century AD. The north wall of the caldarium pool was built right over the mouth of a well that was sealed with a marble slab. Four more pieces of sculpture were found in this well, three

183, 184
heads and a small statue of Herakles. Of interest is the fact that the heads were deliberately discarded in the first half of the 6th century, before the house went out of use.

With all this information in hand we are in a position to discuss the use of this house. First of all, one might assume that a house of this size and apparent wealth might have belonged to one of the philosophers or sophists of Athens. They were usually not poor men; they charged fees for their teaching, some held endowed chairs, and in many ways they represented the aristocracy of the late Roman city. Philostratos described the situation as early as the 2nd century AD: 'Proclus laid down the following rules for attendance at his school of declamation. One hundred drachmae paid down gave one the right to attend his lectures at all times. Moreover, he had a library at his own house which was open to his pupils and supplemented the teaching in his lectures.'[161]

183 *Bust of the emperor Antoninus Pius (AD 138–161), found in a well of the Omega House. Height 75 cm.*

184 *(right) Portrayal of a Roman matron found in a well of the Omega House. Height 79.5 cm.*

Eunapios, writing of Athens some two hundred years later, painted a similar picture of the way in which the private houses became actual schools:

The author himself saw Julian's house at Athens; poor and humble as it was, nevertheless from it breathed the fragrance of Hermes and the Muses, so closely did it resemble a holy temple. This house he had bequeathed to Prohaeresius. There, too, were erected statues of the pupils whom he had most admired; and he had a theatre of polished marble made after the model of a public theatre, but smaller and of a size suitable to a house. For in those days, so bitter was the feud at Athens between the citizens and the young students, as though the city after those ancient wars of hers was festering within her walls the peril of discord, that not one of the sophists ventured to go down into the city and discourse in public, but they confined their utterances to their private lecture theatres and there discoursed to their students. Thus they ran no risk of their lives, but there competed for applause and fame for eloquence.[162]

Several aspects of the excavation of the Omega House suggest that it served as just such a school. First there is the sculpture, discarded in wells or reused as building material in the final phase of the house. By the early 6th century AD, the owner had clearly amassed a handsome collection of sculpture of all periods dating from the 4th century BC to the 3rd century AD, all of which

185 A 'sigma' table found in the destruction fill of the Omega House. Such tables, with their cut-out depressions, were used for dining in early Christian ritual and are often found in churches. Its presence presumably indicates Christian activity in the house just before its destruction.

perhaps became readily available after the visits of the Herulians (AD 267) and Alaric's Visigoths (AD 395). In all, the collection as recovered consisted of two statues (Athena and Herakles), two reliefs (Cave of Pan and Artemis) and six portrait heads. As noted, most of it was deliberately discarded down three wells in the first half of the 6th century AD, before the house itself went out of use. That is, just at the time when the pagan schools were being closed down on orders from the Christian emperor Justinian (AD 529). Secondly, there is the mutilation of some of the sculpture, particularly the two pieces not thrown down the wells. The statue of Athena, for instance, was beheaded before being used face down as a step-block in the last phase of the house. Even more telling is the Cave of Pan relief. This handsome piece shows a scene in a cave which is best interpreted as Hermes handing over the infant Dionysos to the safe keeping of the Nymphs. Zeus looks on from above and Pan himself can be seen at the lower right, lounging on his wineskin. An inscription across the bottom carries the name of the dedicator: Neoptolemos the son of Antikles of Melite. This wealthy man was active in the 330s BC and was honoured for his other

173–78
183, 184

177

178

religious benefactions, as we learn from Plutarch: 'He [Lykourgos] also made a proposal to crown Neoptolemos the son of Antikles and to set up a likeness of him, because he offered to gild the altar of Apollo in the agora in accordance with the oracle of the god.'[163] The relief therefore dates to the third quarter of the 4th century BC and may well have originally been dedicated at the Cave of Pan on the north slopes of the Acropolis, not far above the house. Of especial interest for our purposes is the fact that the carving is still fresh and the figures still clear, but all the heads have been carefully and deliberately defaced. It does not take much imagination to see here the hands of a zealous Christian at work. Athena and the Artemis relief seem also to have been subjected to similar treatment; for the heads, drowning in the wells was apparently considered sufficient. A third noteworthy anomaly is the mosaic floor. Surrounding diamond patterns of red, blue, white, and black tesserae lead up to a handsome guilloche border framing the central panel. But the panel itself is made of plain marble slabs, arranged in a cross, which seem to have been inserted later. Surely for the original design we should imagine some offensive pagan scene such as Dionysos on a panther or Ganymede and the eagle, torn up and replaced with these innocuous slabs by the Christians who also mutilated and discarded the sculpture.

176, 177

181, 182

That this interpretation is correct is further suggested by finds from the final levels of occupation of the house until its destruction in 582/3; lamps with crosses indicate Christian activity, as does the discovery of a 'sigma' table, used for ritual dining in early Christian society. A thin slab of highly polished marble with eleven places cut out for the diners, the whole table with its curved end is in the form of the Greek letter sigma in its late, lunate form.

186

Thus we have in the Omega House something we might never have expected to find: archaeological evidence for the shift in Athens from paganism to Christianity. The philosophers who carried on the traditions of learning in the Classical city could only be silenced by imperial decree, and the Omega House, lying just below where Paul addressed the Areopagites,[164] carries the scars of what must have been a very difficult transition in this most pagan of Greek cities.

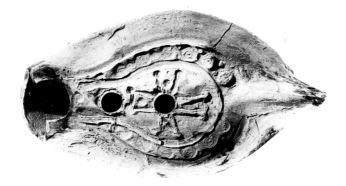

186 A terracotta oil lamp of the 6th century AD, decorated with a cross. One of several found in the Omega House. Length 10.5 cm.

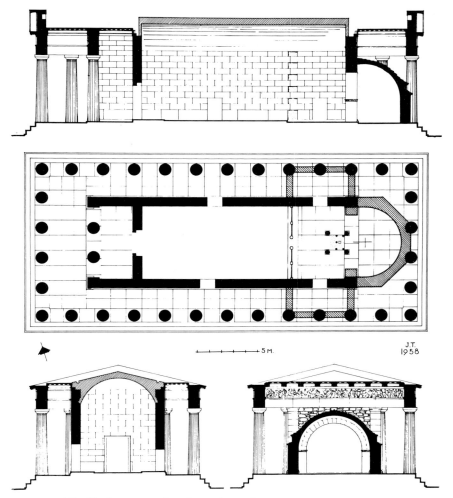

187 The Hephaisteion, the Classical temple, as converted into a Christian church of St George, apparently in the 7th century AD. *The entrance was shifted to the west end and a vaulted apse was added at the east.*

The Slavic invasion

While the closing of the philosophical schools meant essentially the end of the ancient city of Athens, the physical collapse did not occur until AD 582/3 when the Slavs arrived from the north and destroyed the city once again. John of Ephesos describes the invasion, or indeed migration, of the Slavs at this time:

In the third year after the death of the emperor Justin and the accession of the victorious Tiberius, the accursed people of the Slavs set out, overran all Hellas and the provinces of Thessalonica and all Thrace, took many towns and castles, laid waste, burned, pillaged and seized the country, and dwelt there in full liberty and without fear, as if it belonged to them. Those things lasted four years, and until the present, because the emperor was occupied by the Persian war.... That is why they flooded the country and quickly spread throughout it.... Until now, that is, up to the year 895 [AD 583/4] they live there and are peacefully settled in the Roman provinces.[165]

From the evidence of the destruction debris, particularly in a late Roman water mill along the Panathenaic Way, it is clear that the initial arrival of the Slavs in Athens was anything but peaceful. Those buildings surviving or rebuilt after the Herulians and Alaric were demolished in this last great sack of Athens in antiquity: the Omega House, the late Roman gymnasium, and the Painted Stoa all went out of use at this time, and for the most part we have only scant evidence of squatters in the ruins of the old Agora from the 7th century until the town extended this far out again in the 10th century AD.

The conversion of the Hephaisteion

Among the few works to be dated to the 7th century, apparently, was the conversion of the Hephaisteion from temple to church. This involved the reorientation of the building and the addition of an apse. A temple faced east and was entered from the east. The early churches had their altars at the east *187* and were approached from the west. A door was therefore cut in the back (west) wall of the cella. An apse was added at the east by removing the two columns of the pronaos and replacing them with an arch.

188 Basement suite of rooms of the complex east of the Stoa of Attalos. The post-holes in the central room apparently represent an attempt to shore up the vaulted ceiling during repairs made for a brief reoccupation of the building in the 7th century AD (cf. ills. 168, 169).

The treatment of the sculptures at the time of this conversion gives some insight into the early Christian mind. Being pagan in origin, a sculpture had to be mutilated if it was to remain on the new church. Taking the metope of Theseus and the Minotaur as one example of a common practice at that time, one notes that Theseus has lost his head but the Minotaur has not; to the Christians of this early period pagans were evidently worse than monsters.

Closer to the centre of town, the public(?) building incorporating the east stoa of the library of Pantainos shows some slight signs of life in the 7th century as well. A new dirt floor was laid in the basement rooms, post-holes probably indicate an attempt to shore up the vaulted ceiling, and new walls were built, all just after the middle of the 7th century AD and then all abandoned soon thereafter. A possible explanation of these repairs followed by almost immediate abandonment may perhaps be found in one of the few events known about Athens in this period, a visit to the city by the emperor Constans II, who spent the winter here in AD 662/3. His army and court must have required suitable quarters, and the old public residence may well have been refurbished for this last imperial visit following which Athens began long centuries of decline.

63, 62

188
169

Epilogue

Thus the world of the Agora came to an end. Used as a cemetery reflecting the wealth of the Bronze Age and the bleakness of the Dark Ages, the Agora from Archaic times shared the history of Athens. Bearing the scars of the Persian destruction of 480 BC, it was rebuilt to serve as the focal point of the triumphs of the democratic achievements of the 5th and 4th centuries BC. In decline and under Macedonian domination after Alexander, her great traditions of learning caused the square to be adorned with handsome buildings from the 2nd century BC until the end of the Roman Empire. Damaged by the attacks of the Heruli, Alaric, and the Slavs, the Agora ceased to be of significance only when Athens herself finally sank into obscurity at the end of antiquity.

Finally abandoned in the 7th century, the area of the Agora seems to have been totally deserted throughout the 8th and 9th centuries AD, if we may judge from the archaeological evidence. Only in the 10th century AD do we find signs of occupation once again, this time in the form of small private houses. By the end of the century there was apparently a large enough population to justify the construction of the little church of the Holy Apostles, which dates to the years around AD 1000. From that time on the area was a populous residential district until the start of excavations, despite extensive damage in 1205 and again in 1826.

Since 1931 the dozens of ancient buildings and thousands of inscriptions which tell the story of Athens and her Agora have gradually come to light. Battered ruins have been carefully studied and have revealed themselves as the setting of much of Greek history. The great square, the civic buildings, and the surrounding shops were the daily haunts of all those responsible for the remarkable flourishing of Classical Athens. And for centuries afterwards people came from all over the world to study at the renowned centre of learning and culture. Now the same is true once again, as close to a quarter of a million visitors come to the archaeological site each year, to stand in the ruins of the senate house, an ancient lawcourt, or the humble cobbler's shop where Sokrates once taught. Others come to see buildings which are more complete, the Hephaisteion, the best preserved ancient Greek temple, or the reconstructed Stoa of Attalos, or the church of the Holy Apostles. Finally, many come simply to rest from the bustle of present-day Athens and its nearby modern market area, finding peace in the landscaped park, with its large collection of native Greek trees, flowers, and herbs, and a small but vociferous population of birds.

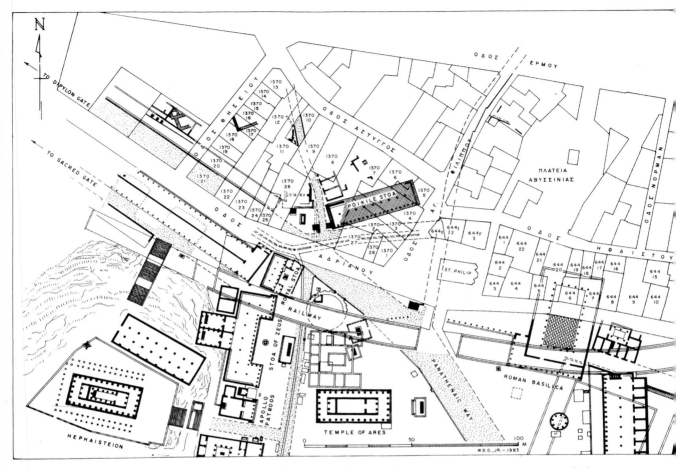

189 The area north of the Agora showing the new excavations (1980–1982) with the Painted Stoa (Poikile). Shown on this plan are the modern property lines of houses overlying the stoa, which still waits to be fully excavated.

189　　Further work still waits to be done. In the immediate future the rest of the Painted Stoa and the sanctuary of Aphrodite Ourania remain to be explored to the northwest, and that area should then be joined to the main archaeological zone by closing and excavating the intervening modern street. Occasionally proposals are made to extend farther the area of excavation, linking it to the east with the Roman Agora and to the west with the ancient cemetery and city walls at the Kerameikos. These last are long-term projects which will take decades to accomplish. In the meantime the slow scholarly work of studying what has already come to light goes on, adding piece by piece to our knowledge of the Agora, the heart of ancient Athens.

Chronological table
Ancient passages cited or translated
Bibliography
List of illustrations
Index

Chronological table

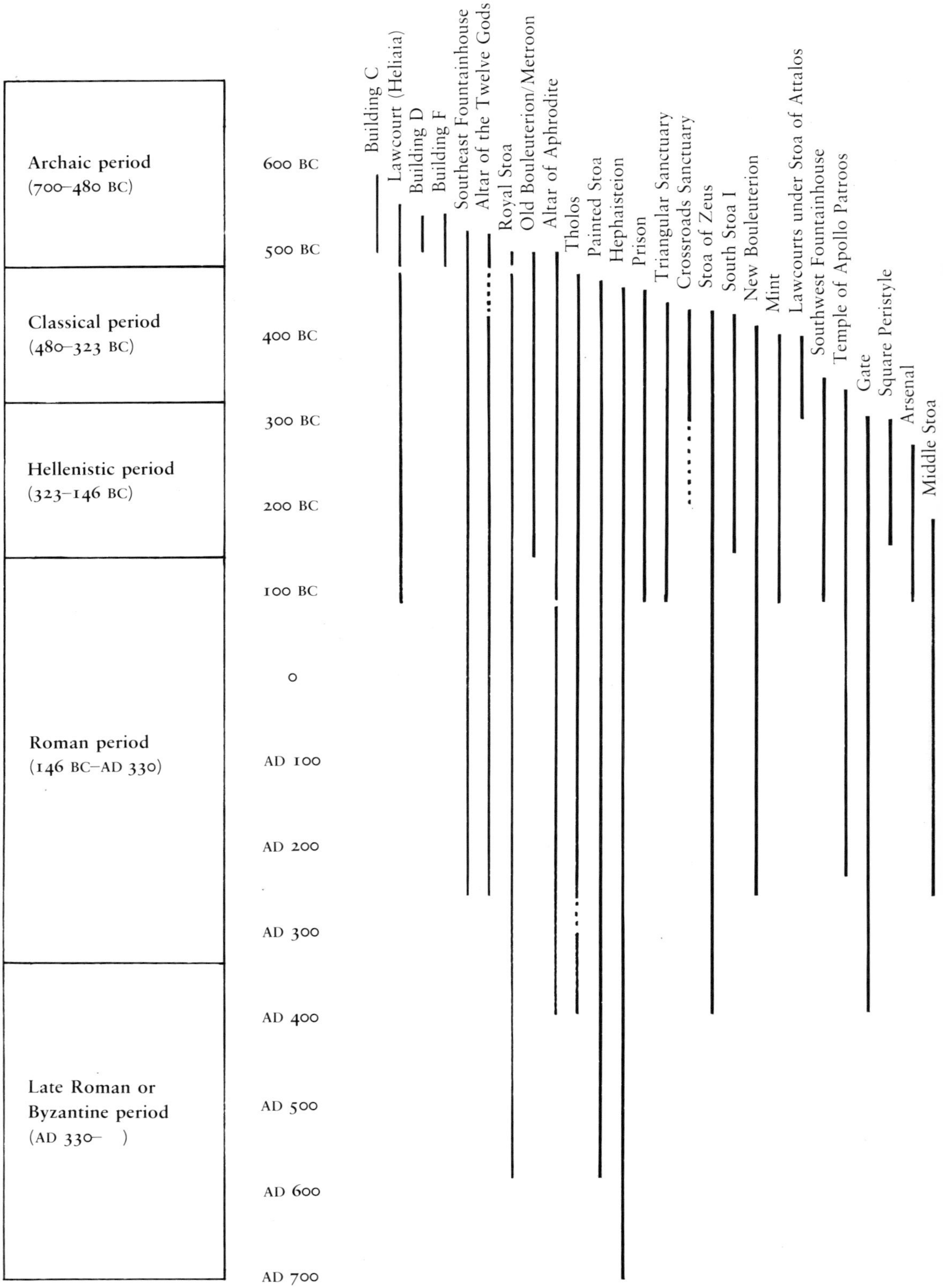

Archaic period (700–480 BC)	600 BC
	500 BC
Classical period (480–323 BC)	400 BC
	300 BC
Hellenistic period (323–146 BC)	200 BC
	100 BC
	0
Roman period (146 BC–AD 330)	AD 100
	AD 200
	AD 300
	AD 400
Late Roman or Byzantine period (AD 330–)	AD 500
	AD 600
	AD 700

Building C
Lawcourt (Heliaia)
Building D
Building F
Southeast Fountainhouse
Altar of the Twelve Gods
Royal Stoa
Old Bouleuterion/Metroon
Altar of Aphrodite
Tholos
Painted Stoa
Hephaisteion
Prison
Triangular Sanctuary
Crossroads Sanctuary
Stoa of Zeus
South Stoa I
New Bouleuterion
Mint
Lawcourts under Stoa of Attalos
Southwest Fountainhouse
Temple of Apollo Patroos
Gate
Square Peristyle
Arsenal
Middle Stoa

	EVENTS	PEOPLE
600 BC		Solon
		Peisistratids
500 BC	490–479 Persian Wars 480 Persian Sack of Athens	Kleisthenes Miltiades Themistokles Kimon
400 BC	431–404 Peloponnesian War	Perikles Sokrates Konon
	338 Battle of Chaironeia 323 Death of Alexander	Demosthenes Lykourgos
300 BC		
		Macedonian rule
200 BC		
100 BC	86 BC Sack of Athens by Sulla	
0	Reign of Augustus	
AD 100	Reign of Hadrian	
AD 200		
AD 300	267 Herulian Sack	Roman rule
AD 400	395 Alaric	
AD 500		
AD 600	582/3 Slavic invasion	
AD 700		

Stoa of Attalos
East Building
South Stoa II
New Metroon
Odeion of Agrippa
Temple of Ares
Southwest Temple
Library of Pantainos
Southeast Temple
Nymphaion
Basilica
Post-Herulian Fortification Wall
Omega House
Gymnasium
Complex east of the Library of Pantainos

Ancient passages cited or translated

1 Pindar, Fr. 75
2 Aristotle, *Athenaion Politeia* 4
3 Thucydides II.15.3
4 *Iliad* II, 546–56, *Odyssey* VII, 81
5 Thucydides II.15.2
6 Plutarch, *Theseus* 24
7 Aristotle, *Ath.Pol.* 7.3
8 Aristotle *Ath.Pol.* 3.1
9 *Iliad* XI.706–761 and XXIII 638–642
10 Pollux VIII.28
11 Harpokration (*ho katothen nomos*)
12 Aristotle *Ath.Pol.* 7.1
13 Aristotle, *Ath.Pol.* 14.3 and 16.2
14 Herodotos VI.108.4
15 Thucydides VI.54
16 Agora Inscription, I 4120
17 Herodotos II.7
18 *IG* II², 2640
19 Pausanias I.14.1
20 Thucydides II.15.4–5
21 Aristophanes, *Lysistrata*, lines 327 ff.
22 Scholia to Aelius Aristeides, 13.189.4–5
23 Athenaeus 4.167 ff.
24 Pollux VII.125
25 *IG* II², 2317
26 Photius (*ikria*)
27 Hesychios (*par'aigeirou thea*)
28 Souda (*Pratinos*)
29 Thucydides VI.57–59
30 Aristotle, *Ath.Pol.* 18.3
31 Demosthenes 54.7–8
32 Agora Inscription, I 5510
33 Aeschines III.176
34 Demosthenes 24.60
35 *IG* II², 1180
36 Pausanias I.3.1–2
37 Agora Inscription, I 7168
38 Agora Inscription, I 7185
39 Pausanias I.14.7
40 Herodotus VI.102–118
41 Aristotle, *Ath.Pol.* 22.3–6
42 Plutarch, *Aristeides* VII.2
43 Herodotus IX.13
44 Thucydides I.89.3
45 Pausanias I.8.5
46 Agora Inscription, I 3872
47 Plutarch, *Themistokles* 31.1
48 Dio.Sic. XI.29.2 and Lykourgos, *vs Leokrates* 81
49 Plutarch, *Perikles* 12
50 Plutarch, *Kimon* 13.8
51 Pausanias I.17.2–7
52 Pausanias I.28.3
53 Pausanias I.28.4
54 Pausanias I.15.1–4
55 Synesios, *Epist.* 135
56 Pausanias I.15.5
57 Thucydides IV.38.5
58 Agora Inventory, B 262
59 Scholion, Aristophanes *Frogs*, lines 369 ff.
60 Demosthenes 45.17 and *IG* II², 1641
61 Diogenes Laertius VII.1.5
62 Thucydides VI.27.1
63 Harpokration (*Hermai*)
64 Thucydides VI.27.1 (cf. Plutarch, *Vit.XOrat.* 834d)
65 Aeschines III. 183 (cf. also Scholion, Demosthenes 20.112)
66 Aristotle, *Ath.Pol.* 18.3
67 *BCH* 91, 1967, pp. 92–95
68 Harpokration (*Kolonetas*)
69 Valerius Maximus VII, 11, ext. 3
70 Plato, *Apology* 32 c–d
71 Xenophon, *Hell.* II.3.50–56
72 Diogenes Laertius VII.5
73 Xenophon, *Hell.* II.4.10–35
74 Aeschines III.187, plus Agora Inscriptions: I 16, I 16b, I 17, I 18, and I 93
75 *IG* II², 10
76 Agora Inscription, I 7169
77 *IG* II², 1579 and Agora Inscriptions: I 627, I 1092, I 1681, I 1894, I 6225, I 7202
78 Pausanias I.3.5
79 *IG* I², 27
80 Schol. Aeschines III.187
81 Pausanias I.3.5
82 Pliny, *Nat.Hist.* 36.17
83 Arrian, *Periplous* 9
84 Deinarchos, *vs Demosthenes* 86
85 Harpokration (*tholos*)
86 Demosthenes 20.94 and 24.23
87 Agora Inscription, I 4266
88 Lysias IX
89 Aristotle, *Ath.Pol.* 57
90 Pollux VIII.86
91 Plutarch, *Solon* 25.2
92 Aristotle, *Ath.Pol.* VII.1–2
93 Andokides, (*DeMyst.*) I.82
94 *IG* I², 115, lines 4–8
95 Andokides, (*DeMyst.*) I.84
96 Aristophanes, *Ekklesiazousai* lines 684–685
97 Plato, *Theatetos* 210 D
98 Pausanias I.3.3–4
99 Pausanias I.26.2

100 Pausanias X.21.5–6
101 Plutarch, *Solon* 18.2
102 Pausanias I.28.8
103 Aristotle, *Ath.Pol.* 57
104 Athenaeus 14.640 b–c
105 Aristotle, *Ath.Pol.* 67.2
106 Isokrates 18.51
107 Lysias 23
108 Isokrates 15.320
109 Agora Inventory, P 28470
110 Plato, *Laws* 937B
111 Thucydides V.18.6–7
112 Andokides, (*DeMyst.*) I.48
113 Plutarch, *Phocion* 36
114 Plutarch, *Nikias* 5.1
115 Plutarch, *Nikias* 15.2
116 Aristotle, *Ath.Pol.* 53
117 Pausanias VI.24.2
118 Athenaeus 9.402 ff.
119 Xenophon, *Hipparchikos* II.5
120 Pausanias I.15.1
121 Theophrastos *Characters* V.7 and Plato, *Apology* 17C
122 Aristotle, *Ath.Pol.* 51.2
123 *IG* II², 1013, lines 37–43
124 *IG* II², 1013, lines 18–29
125 *IG* II², 1013, line 30
126 Scholion, Aristophanes *Wasps*, line 1007
127 Harpokration (*poletai*)
128 Agora Inscription, I 5509, lines 40–44
129 Agora Inscription, I 7180
130 Lysias 24.20
131 Agora Inventory, IL 997
132 Xenophon, *Memorabilia* IV.2.1

133 Diogenes Laertius II.13.122
134 Plutarch, *Moralia* 776 B
135 Xenophon, *Cyropaedia* 8.2.5
136 Agora Inscription, I 7396
137 Herakleides, *FGH* II.254
138 Demosthenes 23.207 and *Olynth.* 3.25
139 Demosthenes 18.169
140 Harpokration (*gerra*)
141 Plutarch, *Demosthenes* 30.5–31.1
142 Agora Inscription, I 6524
143 Demosthenes, *vs Phormio* 37
144 Pausanias I.3.4
145 Harpokration (*Apollon Patroos*)
146 Dio.Sic. 20.46.2
147 Pausanias I.15.1
148 *Ath.Mitt.* 66, 1941, p. 221
149 Agora Inscription: I 7294, lines 11–32
150 Livy 44.4–8
151 Agora Inscription, I 6135
152 Dio.Cass. 47.20.4
153 Agora Inscription, I 848
154 Agora Inscription, I 2729
155 Philostratos, *Vit.Soph.* II.5.4
156 Dio Cass. 72.31.3
157 Agora Inscription, I 7483
158 Plutarch, *Themistokles* 32.5
159 Syncellos, p. 382
160 Zosimus V.5; Claudian *in Rufin.* II.191; Philostorgias XVI.2
161 Philostratos, *Vit.Soph.* 604
162 Eunapios, *Lives* 483
163 Plutarch, *Vit.XOrat.* 843 ff.
164 *Acts*, 17.
165 John of Ephesos VI.25

Bibliography

The basic work on the Agora remains *The Agora of Athens*, *The Athenian Agora Volume XIV*, Princeton 1972, by H. A. Thompson and R. E. Wycherley. Also useful is the site guide, *The Athenian Agora*, Athens 1976 (revised version in preparation) and R. E. Wycherley's *Literary and Epigraphical Testimonia*, *The Athenian Agora Volume III*, Princeton 1957. The full bibliography on the site is vast, and includes over 440 books, picture books, and articles. Included here are those articles and books which have appeared since the last edition of the guide, in order to bring the bibliography up to date for scholars and students. For the non-specialist the main interest will perhaps be the tremendous range of topics on which the excavations continue to shed new light.

ARMSTRONG, J. E. and J. McK. CAMP II, 'Notes on a Water Clock in the Athenian Agora', *Hesperia* 46, 1977, pp. 147 ff.

BOEGEHOLD, A. L. 'A Lid with Dipinto', *Hesperia*, Suppl. 19, 1982, pp. 1 ff.

CAMP, J. McK. II, 'A Spear Butt from the Lesbians', *Hesperia* 47, 1978, pp. 192 ff.

—— 'A Drought in the Late Eighth Century BC', *Hesperia* 48, 1979, pp. 397 ff.

—— *Gods and Heroes in the Athenian Agora*, Princeton 1980.

—— 'Drought and Famine in the 4th Century BC', *Hesperia*, Suppl. 20, 1982, pp. 9 ff.

—— and W. B. DINSMOOR, Jr., *Ancient Athenian Building Methods*, Princeton 1984.

CLAY, D. 'A Gymnasium Inventory from the Athenian Agora', *Hesperia* 46, 1977, pp. 259 ff.

—— 'Epicurus in the Archives of Athens', *Hesperia*, Suppl. 19, 1982, pp. 17 ff.

CLINTON, K. 'A Law in the City Eleusinion concerning the Mysteries', *Hesperia* 49, 1980, pp. 258 ff.

—— 'The Nature of the Late Fifth-Century Revision of the Athenian Law Code', *Hesperia*, Suppl. 19, 1982, pp. 27 ff.

DINSMOOR, W. B., Jr. 'The Roof of the Hephaisteion', *AJA* 80, 1976, pp. 223 ff.

—— 'Anchoring Two Floating Temples', *Hesperia* 51, 1982, pp. 410 ff.

EDMONSON, C. N. 'Onesippos' Herm', *Hesperia*, Suppl. 19, 1982, pp. 48 ff.

EDWARDS, C. M. 'Aphrodite on a Ladder', *Hesperia* 53, 1984, pp. 59ff.

FOLLET, S. *Athènes au IIe et au IIIe siècles*, Paris, 1976.

FOSTER, G. 'The Bones from the Altar West of the Painted Stoa', *Hesperia* 53, 1984, pp. 73 ff.

FRANCIS E. D. and M. VICKERS, 'Leagros Kalos', *Proceedings of the Cambridge Historical Society*, 1981, pp. 97 ff.

FRANTZ, A. 'A Public Building of Late Antiquity in Athens', *Hesperia* 48, 1979.

GEAGAN, D. J. 'Greek Inscriptions from the Athenian Agora', *Hesperia* 52, 1983, pp. 155 ff.

GRACE V. 'The Middle Stoa dated by Amphora Stamps', *Hesperia* 54, 1985, pp. 1 ff.

HARRISON, E. B. 'Alkamenes' Sculpture for the Hephaisteion', *AJA* 81, 1977, pp. 137 ff, 265 ff, 411 ff.

—— 'A Classical Maiden from the Athenian Agora', *Hesperia*, Suppl. 20, 1982, pp. 40 ff.

—— 'Two Pheidian Heads: Nike and Amazon', in *The Eye of Greece*, ed. Kurtz and Sparkes, 1982, pp. 53 ff.

—— 'A Pheidian Head of Aphrodite Ourania', *Hesperia* 53, 1984, pp. 379 ff.

IMMERWAHR, S. A. 'The Earliest Athenian Grave', *Hesperia*, Suppl. 20, 1982, pp. 54 ff.

KLEINER, F. 'The Agora Excavations and Athenian Bronze Coinage 200–86 BC', *Hesperia* 45, 1976, pp. 1 ff.

—— *Medieval and Modern Coins in the Athenian Agora*, Princeton, 1978.

KOUMANOUDES, S. 'Theseus sekos', *Arch.Eph.* 1976, *Meletia*, pp. 194 ff. (in Greek).

—— 'Perhaps > usually > certainly', *HOROS* II, 1984, pp. 71 ff.

KROLL, J. 'An Archive of the Athenian Cavalry', *Hesperia* 46, 1977, pp. 83 ff.

—— 'Some Athenian Armor Tokens', *Hesperia* 46, 1977, pp. 141 ff.

—— and F. MITCHEL, 'Clay Tokens Stamped with the Names of Athenian Military Commanders,' *Hesperia* 49, 1980, pp. 86 ff.

—— 'More Athenian Bronze Allotment Plates', *Studies Presented to Sterling Dow*, GRBS Supplement 10, pp. 165 ff.

KUHN, G. 'Das Neue Bouleuterion von Athen', *Archäologische Anzeiger* 99, 1984, pp. 17 ff.

LALONDE, G. V. 'A Boiotian Decree in Athens', *Hesperia* 46, 1977, pp. 268 ff.

—— 'A Hero Shrine in the Athenian Agora', *Hesperia* 49, 1980, pp. 98 ff.

LAMBERTON, R. and S. ROTROFF, *Birds in the Athenian Agora*, Princeton 1985.

LANG M. *Socrates in the Agora*, Princeton 1978.

—— 'Writing and Spelling on Ostraka', *Hesperia*, Suppl. 19, 1982, pp. 75 ff.

MATTUSCH, C. C. 'Bronze- and Ironworking in the Area of the Athenian Agora', *Hesperia* 46, 1977, pp. 340 ff.

—— *Bronze workers in the Athenian Agora*, Princeton 1982.

MERRITT, L. S. 'Some Ionic Architectural Fragments from the Athenian Agora', *Hesperia*, Suppl. 20, 1982, pp. 82 ff.

OLIVER, J. 'Flavius Pantaenus, Priest of the Philosophical Muses', *H.Th.R.* 72, 1979, pp. 157 ff.

—— 'Marcus Aurelius and the Philosophical Schools at Athens', *AJP* 102, 1981, pp. 213 ff.

OWENS, E. J. 'The Enneakrounos Fountain-house', *JHS* 102, 1982, pp. 222 ff.

PALAGIA, O. 'A Colossal Statue of a Personification from the Agora of Athens', *Hesperia* 51, 1982, pp. 410 ff.

PANTELIDOU, M. *Ai Proistorikai Athinai* (in Greek), Athens 1975.

POLLITT, J. J. 'Kernoi from the Athenian Agora', *Hesperia* 48, 1979, pp. 205 ff.

POUNDER, R. L. 'Honors for Antioch of the Chrysaoreans', *Hesperia* 47, 1978, pp. 49.

—— 'A Hellenistic Arsenal in Athens', *Hesperia* 52, 1983, pp. 233 ff.

RAUBITSCHEK, A. E. 'The Dedication of Aristokrates', *Hesperia*, Suppl. 19, 1982, pp. 30 ff.

RHODES, P. J. *Commentary on the Aristotelian Athenaion Politeia*, Oxford 1981.

ROTROFF, S. I. 'An Anonymous Hero in the Athenian Agora', *Hesperia* 47, 1978, pp. 196 ff.

—— *Hellenistic Pottery, Athenian and Imported Moldmade Bowls; The Athenian Agora Volume XXII*, Princeton 1982.

—— 'Three Cistern Systems on the Kolonos Agoraios', *Hesperia* 52, 1983, pp. 257 ff.

—— 'Spool Saltcellars in the Athenian Agora', *Hesperia* 53, 1984, pp. 343 ff.

ROUX, G. 'Aristophane, Xénophon, le pseudo-Démosthène el l'architecture du bouleuterion d'Athènes', *BCH* 100, 1976, pp. 475 ff.

SHEAR, T. L., Jr. 'Tyrants and Buildings in Archaic Athens', *Athens Comes of Age*, Princeton 1978, pp. 1 ff.

—— *Kallias of Sphettos and the Revolt of Athens in 286 BC*, *Hesperia*, Suppl. 17, Princeton 1978.

—— 'Athens: From City-State to Provincial Town', *Hesperia* 50, 1981, pp. 356 ff.

—— 'The Athenian Agora: Excavations of 1980–1982', *Hesperia* 53, 1984, pp. 1 ff.

SOKOLOWSKI, F. 'The Athenian Law Concerning Silver Currency (375/4 BC)', *BCH* 100, 1976, pp. 511 ff.

STROUD, R. 'State Documents in Archaic Athens', *Athens Comes of Age*, Princeton 1978, pp. 20 ff.

—— *The Axones and Kurbeis of Drakon and Solon*, University of California Press, Classical Studies 19, 1978.

THOMPSON H. A. 'Some Hero Shrines in Early Athens', *Athens Comes of Age*, Princeton 1978, pp. 96 ff.

—— *The Athenian Agora, A Short Guide*, Princeton 1980.

—— 'The Libraries of Ancient Athens', *The St. John's Review*, Winter 1981, pp. 166 ff.

—— 'The Pynx in Models', *Hesperia*, Suppl. 19, 1982, pp. 133 ff.

TRACY, S. V. 'Greek Inscriptions from the Athenian Agora', *Hesperia* 45, 1976, pp. 283 ff.

—— 'Greek Inscriptions from the Athenian Agora', *Hesperia* 48, 1979, pp. 174 ff.

—— 'Greek Inscriptions from the Athenian Agora', *Hesperia* 51, 1982, pp. 57 ff.

—— 'Greek Inscriptions from the Athenian Agora', *Hesperia* 53, 1984, pp. 369 ff.

TRAILL, J. S. 'Greek Inscriptions from the Athenian Agora', *Hesperia* 47, 1978, pp. 269 ff.

—— 'Prytany and Ephebic Inscriptions from the Athenian Agora', *Hesperia* 51, 1982, pp. 197 ff.

VASIC, R. 'Some Observations on Euphranor's Cavalry Battle', *AJA* 83, 1979, pp. 345 ff.

WALBANK, M. B. 'Greek Inscriptions from the Athenian Agora', *Hesperia* 49, 1980, pp. 251 ff.

—— 'The Confiscation and Sale by the Poletai in 402/1 BC of the Property of the Thirty Tyrants', *Hesperia* 51, 1982, pp. 74 ff.

—— 'Greek Inscriptions from the Athenian Agora', *Hesperia* 51, 1982, pp. 41 ff.

WALKER, A. 'Worn and Corroded Coins: Their Importance for the Archaeologist', *Jour. of Field Archaeol.* 3, 1976, pp. 329 ff.

WILLIAMS, E. R. 'Ancient Clay Impressions from Greek Metalwork', *Hesperia* 45, 1976, pp. 41 ff.

—— 'Figurine Vases from the Athenian Agora', *Hesperia* 47, 1978, pp. 356 ff.

WYATT, W. F. Jr. and C. N. EDMONSON, 'The Ceiling of the Hephaisteion', *AJA* 88, 1984, pp. 135 ff.

WYCHERLEY, R. E. *The Stones of Athens*, Princeton 1978.

List of illustrations

All colour plates are by Craig Mauzy, with the exception of Plate I, which is by Will and Ellie Myers, who were also responsible, together with Julian Whittlesey, for the balloon photography. The remaining black-and-white photographs from the Agora Excavations were taken by successive staff photographers: Alison Frantz, James Heyle, Eugene Vanderpool, Jr., R. K. Vincent, Jr., and Craig Mauzy.

Colour plates

AFTER PAGE 48

I The Agora excavations from a balloon in 1975.
II The Agora square from the west.
III The Agora excavations from the Areopagos hill, looking north.

AFTER PAGE 66

IV The Hephaisteion ('Theseion').
V An ivory cosmetics box (*pyxis*).
VI Gold jewelry from the Agora excavations.

AFTER PAGE 132

VII Kneeling boy terracotta vase.
VIII Red-figure cup with youth.

AFTER PAGE 150

IX Bronze head of the goddess Nike.
X Watercolour of the restored upper parts of the Middle Stoa.
XI Ionic Capital.

Monochrome illustrations

Frontispiece: Surviving fragment of the victory monument.
1 Map of Athens and the southern Aegean.
2 The Agora in 1931.
3 The Agora in 1959.
4 Model of the Agora.
5 Reconstruction of the Agora, *c.* AD 150.
6 Map of Attica.
7 Plan of prehistoric wells and graves in the Agora.
8 Red-burnished Neolithic pots.
9 Middle Helladic cup.
10 Mycenaean chamber tomb from the Agora.
11 Plan of Iron Age wells and graves in the Agora.
12 Mycenaean pottery.
13 Protogeometric pottery.
14, 15 Geometric pottery.
16 Ceramic jewelry box, or *pyxis*.
17 Geometric cremation burial.
18 Geometric pottery jewelry box.
19 Watercolour of Geometric wine pitcher.
20 Amphora of 7th century BC.
21 Plan of the Archaic Agora.
22 The earliest civic buildings along the west of the Agora.
23 The Altar of the Twelve Gods in a reconstruction drawing.
24 The Altar of the Twelve Gods: view of the extant southwest corner.
25 Plan of the Southeast Fountainhouse.
26 Terracotta pipeline from the Southeast Fountainhouse.
27 Plan of Building F and the Old Bouleuterion.
28 The Panathenaic Way, view from the north.
29 South side of the Agora in a partially restored perspective.
30 Boundary stones of the Agora.
31 The Old Bouleuterion.
32 Restored elevation of the Royal Stoa.
33 Remains of the Royal Stoa viewed from the south.
34 Foundations of exterior colonnade of the Royal Stoa.
35 Inscribed base for a herm dedicated by the King Archon Onesippos.
36 Plan of the Royal Stoa: actual state.
37 The Altar of Aphrodite Ourania, as found.
38 The Altar of Aphrodite Ourania in a restoration drawing.
39 Ostraka with the names of Aristeides, Themistokles, Kimon, and Perikles.
40 Plan of the northwest corner of the Agora in 300 BC.
41 Balloon view of the northwest corner of the Agora.
42 Steps along the west end of the Painted Stoa.
43 Restored cross-section of the Painted Stoa.
44 Perspective view of the Painted Stoa.
45, 46 Bronze shield taken from the Spartans at Pylos.
47 Alley behind the Painted Stoa, with terracotta pipe.

48 A herm from the western steps of the Painted Stoa.
49 A herm found in the crossroads enclosure.
50 A herm found behind the Royal Stoa.
51 The Tholos.
52 Tiles from the roof of the Tholos.
53 Model of the Tholos.
54 North wall of the triangular sanctuary.
55 Reconstruction of the northwest corner of the Agora, c. 400 BC.
56 Interior of the crossroads enclosure.
57 Balloon view of the northwest corner of the Agora.
58 The sacred well and crossroads enclosure.
59 Plan of the Hephaisteion, 5th century BC.
60 The Hephaisteion from the southwest.
61 Aerial view of the Hephaisteion.
62 Frieze at west end of the Hephaisteion.
63 Metope at southeast corner of the Hephaisteion.
64 Planting pits on south side of the Hephaisteion.
65 Four sides of a bronze spear-butt, 5th century BC.
66 Plan of the Classical Agora.
67 Plan of the New Bouleuterion.
68 Aerial view of the west side of the Agora.
69 Marble copy of the statue of the Mother of the Gods.
70 Fragments of public dining ware marked with the ligature demosion.
71 Restoration drawing of the west side of the Agora, c. 400 BC.
72 Restored plan and elevation of the Monument of the Eponymous Heroes.
73 Restored perspective of the Monument of the Eponymous Heroes.
74 Monument of the Eponymous Heroes viewed from the south.
75 The lithos, or oath-stone, from in front of the Royal Stoa.
76 Restoration drawing of the Royal Stoa.
77 Fragment of the inscribed law-code of Athens.
78 Monumental statue of Themis.
79 Restoration drawing of the Stoa of Zeus Eleutherios.
80 Five bronze ballots.
81 'Ballot box' found at the northeast corner of the Agora.
82 Reconstruction drawing of an allotment machine.
83 Fragment of an actual allotment machine.
84 Bronze juror's identification ticket (pinakion).
85 Working model of the 5th-century water-clock found in the Agora.
86 Lid of a cooking pot with an inscription listing documents sealed inside.
87 Restored plan of what may have been the state prison.
88 General view of the possible state prison.
89 Medicine bottles from a cistern in the possible state prison.
90 Small marble statuette, possibly of Sokrates, from the possible state prison.
91 Plan of the southwest corner of the Agora.
92 Terracotta token of Xenokles, 4th century BC.
93 Terracotta tokens of Pheidon, 4th century BC.
94 Lead strip from the cavalry archive, 4th century BC.
95 Bronze tokens showing armour distributed to the cavalry.
96 Reconstruction drawing of the victory monument.
97 Surviving fragment of the victory monument.
98 Wall in South Stoa I.
99 Plan of the south side of the Agora, c. 400 BC.
100 Aerial view of the east end of South Stoa I.
101 Reconstruction drawing by Piet de Jong of a dining room in South Stoa I.
102 A set of official bronze weights.
103 A bronze measure.
104 A set of official dry and wet measures.
105 An official container.
106 A marble tile standard.
107 Restored plan of the Mint.
108 Aerial view of the southwest corner of the Mint.
109 Athenian silver tetradrachms, 5th and 2nd centuries BC.
110 Black-figured cup fragment showing a man and spectator at a board game.
111 Typical undecorated black-glazed table ware.
112 Unglazed cooking pots.
113 Hemispherical mould-made bowl and its mould.
114 Terracotta hedgehog.
115 Reconstruction drawing of a bronze-casting pit.
116 Terracotta mould for lower half of a bronze statue of Apollo.
117 Plan of two private houses, 5th and 4th centuries BC.
118 Lead curse tablet.
119 Ancient clay impression with Odysseus mourning Ajax.
120 Plan of the area just outside the southwest corner of the Agora.
121 Bone stylus with name of sculptor Mikion.
122 Amphora handle from Rhodes stamped with head of Helios.
123 Amphoras in the storerooms of the Stoa of Attalos.
124 Remains of the house of Simon the cobbler.
125 Material from the house of Simon the cobbler.

126 Dedication showing a cobbler's shop.
127 Plan of three private houses on the Areopagos.
128 Anti-tyranny decree of 337/6 BC.
129 Plan of the Agora, *c.* 300 BC.
130 Excavated remains of the Agora water-clock.
131 Reconstruction drawing of the water-clock.
132 Plan of the temple of Apollo Patroos.
133 Colossal marble statue, perhaps by the sculptor Euphranor.
134 Reconstruction drawing of the early temple of Apollo Patroos.
135 Plan and cross-section of gate piers near the Painted Stoa.
136 Foundations of the gate beside the Painted Stoa.
137 Reconstruction drawing of the gate beside the Painted Stoa.
138 Sword and leg from a bronze equestrian statue of Demetrios Poliorcetes.
139 Plan of the Agora, *c.* 150 BC.
140 The Stoa of Attalos soon after its reconstruction in 1956.
141 Reconstruction drawing of the north end of the Stoa of Attalos.
142 Plan of the Stoa of Attalos.
143 Interior column capital from the Stoa of Attalos.
144 View of ground floor of reconstructed Stoa of Attalos.
145 Cut-away model of the Stoa of Attalos.
146 Cut-away drawing of the South Square, 2nd century BC.
147 View of the excavated South Square.
148 Plan of southeast corner of the Agora, *c.* AD 150.
149 Cross-section of south side of the Agora.
150 Cut-away drawing of the Hellenistic Metroon.
151 Plan of Hellenistic civic buildings on west side of the Agora.
152 Plan of northwest Athens and the Agora, 2nd century AD.
153 Plan of the Agora, 2nd century AD.
154 Cross-section through the Odeion of Agrippa.
155 Plan of the Temple of Ares.
156 Marble altar, possibly of Zeus Agoraios.
157 Plan of the Library of Pantainos.
158 Reconstruction drawing looking east along street connecting the Classical and Roman Agoras.
159 North stoa of the Library of Pantainos.
160 Dedicatory inscriptioo of the Library of Pantainos.
161 Rules for the Library of Pantainos.
162 Torso of statue of Hadrian.
163 Restoration drawing of the Nymphaion.
164 Giant from façade of the Odeion of Agrippa.
165 East face of the post-Herulian fortification wall.
166 Plan of the late Roman Agora.
167 Cut-away perspective of the late Roman gymnasium.
168 Reconstruction drawing of the stoa in the complex east of the Stoa of Attalos.
169 Cross-section of the late Roman complex east of the Stoa of Attalos.
170 Plan of the Omega House.
171 Cut-away drawing of the Omega House.
172 Restored perspective of the Omega House.
173 Head of goddess Nike, from the Omega House.
174 Portrait head, from the Omega House.
175 Head of sun-god, from the Omega House.
176 Relief of Artemis, from the Omega House.
177 Small statue of Athena, from the Omega House.
178 Relief of the Cave of Pan, reused in the Omega House.
179 Aerial view of the Omega House.
180, 181 Southeast suite of rooms in the Omega House.
182 Mosaic floor in the Omega House.
183 Bust of Antoninus Pius, from the Omega House.
184 Bust of Roman matron, from the Omega House.
185 A 'sigma' table, from the Omega House.
186 Terracotta oil lamp, from the Omega House.
187 Plan, elevation and cross-section of the Hephaisteion as converted into a church.
188 Basement rooms of the complex east of the Stoa of Attalos.
189 Plan of area north of the Agora, with the new excavations.

Index

Numerals in *italics* refer to illustration numbers

abaton 79, *55–58*
Academy 63, 66, 71, 72, 87, *47*
Acharnai 63, 185
Acropolis 14, 19, 22, 23, 25, 36, 37, 38, 40, 43, 45, 59, 60, 61, 62, 63, 66, 77, 78, 87, 88, 91, 116, 187, 211, *2, 3, 4*
Aeschines 51, 62, 77, 108, 220
Agorakritos 93
Agrippa, donor of Odeion 184, *154, 164*
Aiantis, tribe 97
Aigeis, tribe 97
Aeschylus 15, 61
akroteria 53
Alaric 198, 200, *50*
Alexander the Great 60, 156, 162, 187, 215
Alkamenes 86
Alkibiades 58, 87, 88
Alkmaionidae 48
allotment 108, 109, 111–12, *82, 83*
altars 14, 38, 40, 42, 45, 46, 57, 78, 154, 186, 187, 191, 211, *23, 24, 37, 38, 40, 41, 55, 156*
Amazons 69
amphorae 105, 143–45, *122, 123*
Andokides 104, 116, 220
anthippasia 122
Antigonos 163
Antiochis, tribe 112
Antiochos, of Syria 168
Aphrodite 57, 78, *37, 38, 40, 41, 55*
apobates 46
Apollo 38, 90, 97, 100, 140, 159–61, 211, *115, 116*
Apollo Patroos 100, 106, 159–61, *132–34*
aqueducts 42, 72–73, 156–57, 193, *47*
arbitration 72, 112–13, *86*
archives 14, 91–99, 162, *94*
archons 18, 100, 116, 117
Areopagos 104, 155–56, 201
Ares (temple) 184–86, 197, *155*
Argos 20, 35
Aristeides 39
Aristogeiton 38, 47, 48, 79, 163, 181
Aristophanes 44, 61, 97, 101, 104, 220–21
Aristotle 31, 38, 40, 47, 48, 62, 79, 100, 108, 112, 125, 161, 220–21
armour 120, 167, *95*
arsenal 167, *139, 151*
Artemis 82, 208, *176*
Asklepios 116
Athena 36, 37, 45, 62, 71, 82, 86, 131, 135, 186, 190, 198, 208, *109, 177*
Attalos I 168
Attalos II 172

Attica 19, 22, 26, 27, 34, 48, 57, 63, 77, 79, 97, 130, 161, 167, 186, 197, *6*
Augustus 183–87
axones 38

ballots 109, *80, 81*
bankers 122
barbershop 135
basileus 100–104
basilica 193
baths 208
benches 94, 95, 125
Boule 52, 90, 91, 94–97, 131, 132
Bouleuterion 14, 38, 39, 52, 53, 60, 90, 107, 131, 156, 166, *31, 67, 71*
boundary stones 17, 38, 48–52, 78, 79, 138, 145, 175, *29, 30, 54, 124*
bronze 19, 71, 86, 111, 118, 129, 130, 139–41, 161, 164, 168, *45, 46, 65*
bronzeworkers 84, *115–17*
Brutus 181, 183
Bryaxis 120
Building C 39, *22*
Building D 39, 52, *22*
Building F 44–45, 52, 60, 95, *22*
burials 20, 24, 26, 28, 29, 31–34, 141, *7, 10, 11, 14, 15, 17*

Canaanite jar 27
Caesar, C., adopted son of Augustus 187
Caesar, Julius 181, 183
Cassander 163–64
Cassius 181, 183
catapult balls 181
cavalry 45, 118–22, *93–97*
cemeteries 24, 26–30, 38, 45, 215
centaurs 86, 119, *62*
Chaironeia 153–54
Chios 105, *143*
Christians 193, 211, *62, 63, 182, 185, 187*
churches 84, 130, 193, 213–14, 215, *62, 63, 108, 187*
cisterns 72, 130, 139, 149, 156–57
clamps 42, 66, 164
cobblers 145–47, *124–26*
coins 128–35, 198, *109*
commercial activity 14, 122ff., 177, *102–106*
Constans II 214
Corinth 22, 32, 35, 43, 136, 143, 150, 181, 193, 198
Corinthian order 184
coroplasts 138–39
council (Boule) 52, 90, 91, 94–97, 131, 132

Council House (Bouleuterion) 14, 38, 39, 52, 53, 60, 90, 107, 131, 156, 166, *31*, *67*, *71*
cremation 29, 31, *14*, *15*, *17*
crossroads shrines 78–82, *40*, *41*, *49*, *54–58*, *120*
curse tablets 141, *118*
Cynics 72

Delphi 58, 97, 99
deme 48, 111, *6*
Demeter 88
Demetrios Poliorcetes 162–65, 168, *138*
democracy 15, 62, 77, 105, 154–56, 163, *128*
Demos 77, 90, 105, 154–56, 166, 172, *128*
demosion 95, 102, 103, 105, 109, *70*, *104*
Demosthenes 15, 51, 62, 72, 108, 112, 122, 149, 153, 220–21
dining rooms 94–95, 123–25, 149, *70*, *101*
Dionysios, cobbler 147, *126*
Dionysos 40, 46, 101, 156
Dipylon 45, 120, 138, *152*
Dorians 20, 27
Doric order 36, 53, 62, 66, 84, 106, 172, 175, 177, *60*
drains 130
Drako 22, 31, 38, 102, *104*
dromos (Panathenaic Way) 43, 45–46, 53, 57, 62, 66, 74, 79, 118, 128, 164, 186, 188, 197, 213, *21*, *28*

earrings 31, *VI*
East Building 177–79, *146*, *148*
Ekklesia 99, 156
Eleusinion 88
Eleusis and Eleusinian Mysteries 22, 34, 63, 72, 88, 100, 126, 196
emery 181
Enneakrounos 42, 43
ephebes 118
epistatai 130
Eponymous Heroes 97–100, 118, 162, 163–64, 167, 191, *68*, *72*, *73*, *74*
Erechtheion 62, 107
Eridanos 38
Euboulos 156
Eumenes, king of Pergamon 163
Euphranor 106, 159, *133*
Euripides 61
Eurysakeion 82

fortifications 20, 23, 25, 63, 66, 150, 172, 197–98, 199, *165*, *166*
fountains and fountainhouses 25, 38, 42, 43, 44, 66, 156–57, 177, 193

gardens 87
gates 164–65, 197, *135–37*
Gauls 90, 106

generals (*strategoi*) 116–18, 153, *see also* Strategeion
Geometric period 29, *13–17*
giants 194, *164*
gold 27, 31, 62, 79, 82, 104, 163, 164–65, 179
goldsmiths 88
graves 20, 24, 26, 28, 29, 31–34, 141, *7*, *10*, *11*, *14*, *15*, *17*
gymnasia 68, 184, 200, 213, *167*

Hadrian 191, 193, *74*, *162*, *182*
Harmodios 38, 47, 48, 60, 79, 163, *181*
Hekate 78
Heliaia (lawcourt) 47, 60, 108, *29*, *99*
Hephaisteion 14, 57, 63, 78, 82–87, *139*, *184*, *213–14*, *2*, *3*, *4*, *60*, *61*, *62*, *63*, *64*, *71*, *187*
Hera 191
Herakles 71, 84, 201
Hermes 74, 164, 201, 209
herms 63, 74–77, 88, 100–101, 116, 118, *35*, *48*, *49*, *50*
Herodes Atticus 190, 194–96
Herodotus 42, 58, 59, 61
Heroes 14
Heruli 172, 197, 199
Hipparcheion 118–22
Hipparchos 35, 38, 40, 42, 47, 79
Hipparchs 46, 118–22, 93
Hippias 35, 40, 42, 47, 48, 58
Homer 25
horoi (boundary stones) 17, 38, 48–52, 78, 79, 138, 145, 175, *29*, *30*, *54*, *124*
horses 20, 32, 118–22, *frontispiece*, *17*, *18*, *96*, *97*
houses 33, 38, 40, 42, 44, 60, 88, 141, 142, 145, 148–50, 166, 201, 209, *117*, *127*, *170–72*
Hymettos 22, 34
Hypereides 108

ikria 46, *28*
ikriopoioi 46
Iliad 25, 32, *19*
Ilissos river 43, 46
Imperial cults 187, 190
inscriptions 17, 18, 88, 100, 104, 117, 118, 131–35, 154–56, 166, 190, 220–21, *30*, *35*, *45*, *46*, *54*, *65*, *77*, *128*, *160*, *161*
Ionic order 62, 172, 179, 188
iron 29, 84
ironworkers 84
Isokrates 62, 108, 112, 222
ivory 20, 27, 31, 62, 179, *V*

Justinian 201, 210

Kalamis 161
Kallias, Peace of 77
Kallias of Sphettos 166

Kallippos 90
Kallirrhoe 43
Kallistephanos 147
kara limestone 42
Kephalos 53
Kerameikos 34, 45, 58, 73, 138, 196
Kimon 66–77, 87, 39
Kleisthenes 15, 35, 38, 48, 52, 58, 62, 95, 97
klepsydra 19, 24, 25, 66, 112, 157–59, 85, 130, 131
kleroteria 111–12, 82, 83
kneeling boy 138, VII
Knidos 143, 150
Kolonos Agoraios 38, 39, 82, 100, 167
Konon 150
Kritios 60
kurbeis 38, 102
kybele (Mother of Gods) 38, 93, 131, 179, 69
Kydias 106
Kylon 22

Lakedaimonians (Spartans) 35, 48, 61, 72, 87, 88, 96, 116, 130, 150, 197, 45, 46
lamps 18, 130, 211, 186
landscaping 66, 73, 87, 60, 64
late Roman wall (post-Herulian wall) 197–98, 165, 166
Laureion 22, 130, 150, 156
law codes 104, 77
lawcourts 14, 38, 46, 60, 100, 105, 107–13, 167, 29, 81, 99
laws 104
Leagros 40, 23, 24
Lemnos 119, 93
Lenaia 100
Leochares 161
Leokorion 47, 79
Leontis, tribe 97, 99, 122
Leos 47, 79
Lesbos 87, 143, 65, 123
lesche 72
libraries 184, 187–91, 197, 200–202, 157–61
lithos 101–102, 75
Livia 187
loom weights 79, 149
Lyceum 71
Lykourgos 108, 156
Lysias 108, 135, 220–21
Lysimachos 163

Macedon 150, 153–56
Marathon 19, 22, 35, 36, 57–58, 59, 69, 71
marbleworkers 142, 181
market buildings 122, 172, 184
mason's marks 184–86
measures 93, 96, 125–28, 103–105
Megara 22, 43
Meletos 105

Mende 143, 123
Menon 142, 166, 120
metalworkers 84, 139–41, 181
metopes 175, 214, 63
metronomoi 125–26
Metroon 14, 91–94, 179, 68, 71, 150, 151
Middle Stoa 175–79, 146, 147, X
Mikion 142, 166, 120, 121
Mikon 62, 69
mill 213
Miltiades 58, 66
Minotaur 27, 214
Mint 63, 123, 128–35, 177, 99, 107, 108
Minyan ware 25, 9
Mithradates of Pontus 181, 183
models 4, 53
Molione 32, 19
mortar 149, 188
mosaics 149, 177, 188, 208, 182
Mother of Gods 38, 93, 131, 179, 69
moulds 139–40
Muses 190, 209
Mycenae 20, 22
Mysteries 100, 116, 196

Naxos 35, 57
Neoptolemos 210–11
New Bouleuterion 63, 90–94, 67, 68, 71
Nike 62, 193, 173, IX
Nikias 58, 87, 117
Nomothetai 131
notices, public 99
Nymphaion 130, 193, 148, 163
Nymphs 79, 210, 178

oaths 101
Odeia 63, 157, 184, 194–96, 197, 154, 164
Odyssey 25, 32
oinoe 69
Old Bouleuterion 52–53, 63, 90–94, 31, 71
olive oil 88
Olympia 58
Olynthos 153
Orchestra 46
ostracism 57–58, 87, 39
ostraka 57–58, 39

paint, on architecture 177, 186, 52, X, XI
Painted Stoa 57, 63, 66–72, 77, 87, 90, 96, 107, 108, 163, 213, 40–46, 55, 57, 189
paintings 15, 36, 58, 62, 69, 71, 90, 105–107, 136, 167
palace 45, 95
pan 208, 210–11, 178
Panainos 69
Panathenaic amphorae 88
Panathenaic festival 27, 36, 47, 88, 122, 156

Panathenaic Way 43, 45–46, 53, 57, 62, 66, 74, 79, 118, 128, 164, 186, 188, 197, 213, *21, 28*

Pantainos, donor of library 187–91, 198, 200–202, *148, 157–59, 160–61*

Paredroi 100, 104

Parian marble 57

Paros 35, 57

Parthenon 45, 62, 84, 87, 194

Paul, St 211

Pausanias 16, 43, 53, 57, 66, 69, 71, 72, 82, 86, 90, 94, 96, 105, 108, 122, 138, 159, 164, 179, 191, 193, 220–21

Peace of Nikias 87

pedimental sculpture 194

Peiraieus 22, 90, 116, 122, 125, 126, 111–32, 148, 150, 157, 166

Peisianax 69

Peisistratos 22, 35, 36, 38–40, 42–45, 47, 95, 167

Peloponnese 20, 27

Peloponnesian War 61, 63, 72, 75, 87, 88, 96, 104, 118, 122, 150, 161, *45, 46, 65*

Penteli and pentelic marble 22, 57, 84, 105, 142, 193

Pergamon 169, 172, *143*

Perikles 15, 58, 62, 63, 77, 82, 117, 196, *39*

Peripolarch 118, *92*

Perirrhanteria *51*

peristyle courts 108–109, 148–49, 167, 184, 187–91, 200

Persians and Persian wars 35–38, 44, 48, 53, 58, 59–60, 61, 62, 63, 66, 69, 74, 77, 78, 82, 93, 95, 100, 130, 138, 150, 161, 215

Pheidias 15, 57, 62, 93

Philip II of Macedon 61, 153

Philip V 167–68

philosophy, philosophers 14, 15, 66, 71, 72, 168, 190–91, 196, 200, 202–11

phylarchs (cavalry officers) 118–19

Phyle 90

pinakia 111, 130, *84*

Pindar 14

pipelines 26, 47

plague 161

Plataia and Plataians 35, 40, 58, 60, 61, 63, 66, 69, 77, *106*

Plato 18, 62, 107, 113, 220–21

Pleistarchos 164

Plutarch 26, 38, 63, 101, 107, 145, 196, 220–21

Pnyx 91, 156

Poikile Stoa 66–72, 75, 90, 108, 40–46, 55, 57, *189*

Polemarch 116

Poletai and Poleterion 130–31, 132, *91*

Pollux 38

Polygnotos 62, 69, 71, 72

polygonal masonry 42

Poros 79, 100

Poseidon 186

post-Herulian wall 197–98, *166, 167*

post-holes 46, 214, *28, 188*

potters 135–38, 181, *VIII*

pottery 17, 18, 19, 20, 22, 24, 25, 27, 29, 30, 31, 32, 42, 44, 46, 53, 57, 66, 77, 82, 87, 88, 95, 105, 106, 112, 126, 135–38, 143–45, *8, 9, 12, 13, 18, 19, 20, 56, 70, 89, 110, 111, 112, 113, VIII*

Praxiteles 15, *2*

prison 105, 113–16, *87, 88*

Propylaia 62, 87, 107

Prytaneion 48, 95, 107, 154

Prytaneis 94–97, 153

Ptolemies of Egypt 163, 166, 167

Pylos 71, 72, 87, 116, *45, 46*

Pythion 42

Pyxis *32*

railway 120

reliefs 122, 146, 156, 210, *96, 97, 126, 128, 176, 178*

re-used material 53, 84, 197–98, *34, 165*

Rhodes 143, *122*

Rome 14, 167, 181–84, 187, 198

roof tiles 23, 53, 77, 128, 149, *52, 106*

Royal Stoa (Basileios) 14, 38, 53–54, 57, 60, 63, 75, 77, 84, 100–105, 108, 120, 122, 197, *31–34, 36, 40, 41, 55, 57, 71*

Salamis 35, 59, 61, 89, 130

sculptors 55, 90, 93, 120, 139–42, 159–61, 181, *120, 121, 133*

sculpture 84, 122, 139–42, 208–11, *48, 49, 50, 62, 63, 69, 78, 96, 97, 133, 164, 173–78, 183, 184*

Senate (Boule) 52, 90, 91, 94–97, 131, 132, *6*

shields 71–72, 106, *45, 46*

shops 14, 122, 135, 138, 143, 172

Sicilian expedition 75

silver 20, 22, 27, 96, 130–35

Simon the cobbler 145–47, *124, 125*

Skias (Tholos) 94–97

slaves 88, 131, 132, 135

Slavs 212–13

Sokrates 15, 62, 89, 105, 107, 108, 116, 145–47, *90*

Solon 15, 31, 32, 35, 38, 39, 101, 102, 104, 107, 108, 153

Sophokles 61, 118

Sounion 22, 52, 186

South Square 175–79, *139, 146, 147*

South Stoa I 14, 63, 122–30, *98–101*

South Stoa II 123, *146*

Southeast Fountainhouse 42–44, 59, 73, 128, *25, 26, 99*

Southeast temple 186, *148*

Southwest Fountainhouse 156–57, *177*

Southwest temple 186, 198

Sparta and the Spartans 35, 48, 61, 72, 87, 88, 96, 116, 130, 150, 197

Sphakteria 71, 72

springs 19
square peristyle 167
stairs and ramps 36
statues 17, 86, 87, 90, 93, 104, 105, 154, 159–61,
    163–65, 167, 168, 191–93, *69*, *78*, *90*, *116*, *133*,
    138, *162*
stelai 17, 104, 132, 154–56, 166, *128*
stoas 14, 63, 66, 105–107, 108, 172–77, 197, *145*
Stoa of Attalos 172–75, 181, *4*, *139*, *140–45*, *II*
Stoa of the Herms 77
Stoa of Zeus 78, 105–107, *79*
Stoics 72
Strategeion 116–18, *91*
strategoi (generals) 116–18, 153
streets 25, 39, 45–46, 73, 188, *22*, *47*, *158*
Sulla 106, 181
swords 27, 31–32, 164, *138*
symbolon 112
Synedria 100, *71*

tables 122, 131, 177–79
terracotta 50, 53, 138–39, *VII*
Thasos 145, *123*
theatres and theatrical events 15, 46, 100–101,
    156, 184
Thebes 35, 42, 59, 61, 150
Themis 105, *78*
Themistokles 58, 59, 60, 130, 196, *39*
Theramenes 89
'Theseion' 82, *see also* Hephaisteion
Theseus 25, 27, 66, 71, 84, 105, 214
Thesmothetai 107, 132
Thesmotheteion 107
Thirty (Tyrants) 89, 90, 96
Tholos 63, 77, 89, 94–97, 105, 117, 126, 128, 166,
    197, *51*, *52*, *53*, *68*
Thorikos 26, 34, 63, 186
Thucydides 15, 25, 26, 42, 43, 47, 48, 59, 62, 75,
    87, 220–21

tickets (jurors') 111
tile standards 128, *106*
tokens (armour) 120, *95*
tokens (jurors') 112
Trajan 187–91
transplanted temples 184–87
trees 66
triangular shrine 78, *120*
tribes 48, 97, *6*
Twelve Gods, Altar of the 38, 40–42, 45, 46, 78,
    105, 154, *23*, *24*
Tyrannicides 38, 47, 60, 164–65, 181
Tyrants 58, 89, 96
Tyranny 22, 58, 154–56, *39*, *128*

Victory (Nike) 62, 193, *173*, *IX*
Visigoths 198

walls 20, 23, 25, 150, 181, *165*
water basins 130
water channels 26, *75*
water-clocks 108, 111, 112, 157–59, 177, *85*
water pipes 42, 73, *26*, *47*
weights 93, 96, 125–28, 130, *102*
wells 24, 25, 33, 34, 40, 60, 79, 119–20, 130, 138,
    139, 141, 149, 156–57, 165, 208–11, *7*, *11*, *58*
wine jars 105, 143–45, *123*
wine trade 128, 143–35, *122*, *123*
wood 90, 99, 108
workshops 139–42

Xenophon 90, 107, 145–46, 220–21

Zeno 72
Zeus, Stoa of 38, 40, 42, 63, 78, 90, 105–107, 191,
    71, *79*